D0707723

O Mother Sun!

A NEW VIEW OF THE COSMIC FEMININE

BY PATRICIA MONAGHAN

THE CROSSING PRESS
FREEDOM, CA 95019

To Janet, Susan, Miriam,
who take joy in the light

Copyright ©1994 by Patricia Monaghan
Cover design by Sheryl Karas
Interior design by Victoria May
Printed in the U.S.A.

Library of Congress Cataloging-in-Publication Data

Monaghan, Patricia.
  O Mother Sun!: a new view of the cosmic feminine/ by Patricia Monaghan.
    p.   cm.
  Includes bibliographical references.
  ISBN 0-89594-722-6 (pbk.)
  1. Goddess religion. 2. Shamanism. 3. Women—Religious life. 4. Medicine,
magic, mystic, and spagiric. 5. Mythology. I. Title.
BL473.5.M67 1994
291.2'114—dc20
                                                      94-20557
                                                      CIP

ACKNOWLEDGMENTS

In following the obscure (and obscured) traces of the sun goddess through three continents and a dozen years, I have the generous help of many people. Primary among them have been Janet McCrickard in England, whose early enthusiasm for this subject as well as her eagerness to share her own research make her a shining exemplar of scholarly cooperation; and Susan Gitlin-Emer and Miriam Robbins Dexter in California, who through their own work have helped bring the sun goddess back to consciousness and who have cheered on my work as well.

The work of Marija Gimbutas has sustained and inspired me, as it has so many researchers in this field; similarly I have found inspiration in the groundbreaking work of Miranda Green, Joanna Hubbs, Mary Kelly, Carmen Blacker, Laurel Kendall, Maire McNeill, and Ernst Krause, who've braved scholarly disregard for the solar feminine to make available important sun goddess material.

Sustaining such a project over many years has meant that I've benefitted in many ways from the far-flung spiritual and intellectual community of which I am a part. My thanks to those whose insights and enthusiasm for this subject have helped see it to completion, including Margaret Arndt-Caddigan, Isaac Bonewits, Z Budapest, Helen Farias, Margaret Blanchard, Fontaine Belford, Barbara Bruno, Ginger Costello, Kay Doyle, Liz Davidson, Ryn Etter, Starr Goode, Lucy Goodison, Tom Hannon, Susan Hawthorne, Helane Hulburt, Karen Jackson, Allen Kim, Jade, Deborah Lipp, Lynnie Levy, Tarika Lea, Mary Jo Neitz, Carol Poston, Park Soon-Ham, Judith Roche, Jim Roginski, Lindsay Throm, Deb Trent, Lisa Tantillo, Clare Tuffy, Teri Vierick, Barbara Wallant, B.J. Webb, Eleanor Wilner, as well as the members of ACE, the women of Limina, the women of the Re-Formed Congregation of the Goddess, the women of No Limits for Women Artists, the folks at *Green Egg*, and the editoral staff of *Woman of Power*.

And with enduring gratitude, my thanks to Natalie Kusz and Bob Shea.

TABLE OF CONTENTS

Introduction

THE APOLLO CONSPIRACY

Night and day. Death and life. Black and white. Yin, yang. Moon, sun. Evil, good.

These, we are told, are opposites. Opposites, like body and mind, like the flesh and the spirit. And—in all these pairs—the first is feminine, the second masculine. So we are told.

Women are said to be connected to the dark, to the moon goddess; to anything that broods and grows in darkness; to dreams, fantasies, emotions, illusions. Our sphere is a fragile one: the mortal body, that resilient source of joy that ultimately dooms us to die. Women are "the flesh," aligned always with "world" and "devil." Women are the passive power of sex, a power we share with bitches and mares and cows.

Women are not as men are, radiant beings connected to the intellect, to reason and to thought. While we stew in our fleshy juices, "the masculine" shines forth in heavenly splendor. If femininity is the moon, masculinity is the sun. In incarnate form—as human men—this force is responsible for everything that distinguishes us from mere animality. It is art, it is culture, it is language and philosophy.

Implausible as it seems, this is the message our culture conveys.[1] The alleged inferiority of women is mythically based in our presumed connection to that realm of world, flesh and devil, while men's alleged superiority is based on their supposed freedom from such connection. The solar hero is hailed as the savior of the race; the moon-woman is a lunatic, a witch, a sexual temptress, a danger.

Of course, it can be argued that space and time are not the abodes of inequity. It can be argued that, as progenitors of the race, women have true creative power. It can be argued that the spirit is embodied in the flesh, not merely visiting for a spell before moving to its true heavenly domain. It can be so argued, but the reasoning of our culture denies it. Over and over, we are told that this is a world of opposites, and that woman stands on the wrong side.

The past two decades have seen many effective attacks on this flawed world view, but even feminist philosophers often unwittingly accept one part of the fallacy: that women everywhere are mythically connected with darkness, the earth, the moon.[2] And so, to honor our femininity, we dance by the light of the goddess moon. We celebrate our menses and our connection with the land. Taking back the night, we reclaim its beauties.

And thus we argue from the same wrong-hearted stance as our opponents. Salutary as these actions are, they do not attack the foundation myth: the duality of man and woman, yin and yang, light and dark. To do that, we must shift ground in this philosophic dispute, disengage from the false dichotomies that our culture offers, and claim the light as well as the darkness, the sky as well as the earth, as part of Goddess. "God" does not live in heaven while "the goddess" lies prone beneath him on the earth. To limit Her sphere is to ignore cosmic goddesses of past cultures whose sky-mantle swept each day over their children. It is to falsify the vision of cultures for whom the sun was radiant mother, the stars her innumerable children. It is to deny ourselves the pleasure of walking through this world, not with feet on Our Mother and heads aimed at Our Distant Father, but utterly surrounded by, enveloped by, Her.

One part of this reclamation must be the acknowledgement of the sun goddess. Textbook after textbook, reference work after reference work, tell us the sun is always male, the moon always female. They are brother and sister, we are told; sometimes they are husband and wife. This is true. But we are also told that the brother, the husband, is always the sun; the sister, the wife, always the moon. This is a lie.

How did we get here? That is a tale more than two thousand years old, one that begins with Apollo.

Let us dispense with his claims to solar antiquity immediately—he became a sun god very late in his career. He was not the sun-god to Homer; in fact, he descended "like the night" in the Iliad, certainly an odd image for the sun. The first reference that seems to connect Apollo to the sun comes in 500 B.C.E, in Aeschylus—but even that reference, the poet's use of the word *Phoebus* ("bright" or "shining"), is suspect, for Phoebe was originally a goddess's name, reputedly that of the ruler of the moon. Apollo was not new to the pantheon; he had been around for quite a few centuries, but his identification with the sun was a new twist. A complex of religious, intellectual and political factors drove his followers to promote him into a new status.

Apollo arrived in Greece with the Indo-Europeans; their homeland was in eastern or northern Europe, possibly on the steppes east of the Caspian Sea, possibly on the shores of the Baltic. They overran Europe and moved into India, invading in several waves; about 2000 B.C.E. they arrived in Greece, driving herds before them and dragging gods behind. Encountering goddesses, they "married" them to compatible male divinities. The goddesses, current theory holds, were assigned night, earth, home, while the gods got everything else—everything above the earth and everything outside the home.

Unfortunately, this simplified version is inaccurate. Hyperion, the earliest Greek sun god, never ruled alone. At the beginning, standing next to him in the solar chariot, there was Theia, "the bright one," an ancient sun goddess and mother of the later solar divinity Helios. Thus, at its origins, Greek culture recognized a feminine sun. It was the Greek world's growing bias against women, that led to the demotion of the sun goddess and her replacement by a male god of the luminary.

Apollo began his career as ruler of rodents: as Apollo Smintheus, he was worshiped at Hamaxitna in a temple distinguished by the half-tame mice under the altar and a statue of the god with mice at his feet. In many cultures, the mouse is connected to darkness, or the moon waxes when nibbled by mice. (Our joke about the moon being made of cheese is perhaps a latent Apollonian mouse-image.) Mice, especially white mice, are an omen of death in many lands; elsewhere, mice rule hell. The mouse in folklore opposes the cat, a sun figure. These are inauspicious, not to say suspicious, beginnings for a sun god, especially one who bears the name Phoebus. Was Phoebe originally a moon goddess, as current theory holds, and Apollo's name a reminder of his true lunar nature as her twin? Or was the "shining" label applied to him when he was needed to ascend like the patriarchy rather than, as in Homer, to descend like the night?

Apollo's solar divinity came so late that not a single monument shows him as the sun—not one. Two Rhodian coins portray Apollo tossing his hair in a solar aura, but that's all. As Richard Lewis Farnell emphasizes, there was absolutely "no consciousness of the solar character of Apollo" in Greece before Aeschylus.

Apollo began to be associated with then–sun god Helios on coins from Asia Minor in the sixth century B.C.E., but there was no cult of Apollo; he was not worshiped. Aeschylus's hint at the affinity between Apollo and the sun was offhanded, a sophisticated allusion. At about the same time, the Iambic poet Skythinos offered the opinion that Apollo's lyre was visible in the sun, and Timotheus the lyric poet said that Helios was an archer, a transparent attempt to connect archer-Apollo with the sun. By the time of Euripedes, the third century B.C.E., Apollo was frequently compared to the sun by poets, though the common people still didn't believe that he ruled the daystar.

This move to promote Apollo came in large part from the Orphics, a spiritual movement that distinguished a lower stage of being—entirely material and earthly—from a higher, immaterial, solar region. As a person developed, they believed, the earthly self gave way to the solar. Slowly, the earth/flesh was purified, leaving a being utterly spirit and sun. This solar realm included no goddesses but was crowded with gods: Vulcan, Priapus, Pluto, Zeus and Apollo. Macrobius tacked on Janus, Saturn, Dionysus, Pan, Hercules, Osiris, and Adonis. Few gods were overlooked. The sun became a male realm.[3]

In Rome, a similar development occurred.[4] It is unclear to most scholars engaging in *cherche le dieu,* why there was no Roman sun god until the founding of the temple of Sol Invictus—not even a name for the fellow, but merely a title, *all-conquering sun*—in 274 B.C.E; no one has looked for a sun goddess. Apollo, invited from Greece in 320 B.C, came as a god of healing, not light. But, as in Greece, the identification of Apollo with the sun slowly took hold; in 250 B.C.E., Callimachus wrote a poem, considered revolutionary by contemporaries, actually calling Apollo the sun god.

With the influx of religious cults from Asia during imperial times, variations on the solar theme appeared. A young African named Eglabius, caesar for a time, announced himself the incarnation of the god Eglabius, also known by the title of Sol Invictus. The emperor, who fancied lavish clothing and hordes of ritual attendants, didn't reign long, but his sun cult took root in the Roman Legion.

It was the Roman soldiery that determined the course of Sol Invictus's career—not because they worshiped Eglabius, but because they worshiped Mithras. The religion of this lion-wrestling god from Persia, which arrived in Rome about the same time as Christianity, was fantastically popular with the Legionnaires. They brought their religion wherever they invaded, throughout Europe.

That Europe is a Christian continent today, rather than a Mithraic one, testifies to the shrewdness of ancient church fathers who adopted Mithraic ritual and symbols wholesale into their new religion. Christianity preserved a strong masculine solar orientation far beyond the dreams of the soldiers who marched under the banner of the all-conquering sun. Born on winter solstice, day of the sun's return, and constantly referred to with solar imagery, Christ was the triumphant bearer of centuries of accumulated male solarity.

By the fall of Rome, the male sun was unquestioned in the Empire.

During the Middle Ages, astrology and alchemy reinforced dualistic beliefs; sun and moon were opposed, signs and planets divided by gender. Then came the Renaissance and an infatuation with classical learning from the Greco-Roman period. Renaissance paintings showed the solar Apollo crowned; learning stressed the need to subjugate the emotions, to became enlightened. The solar masculine's apotheosis was reached in France, when Louis I reigned in the guise of a "sun king." In America, at the same time, gynocratic native societies, descendents of the solar Ancestress, met with genocidal invaders who exterminated entire mythologies together with their believers.[5]

Enlightenment scholars of comparative religion leaped on the male-sun bandwagon. In 1774, Jacob Bryant was the first to articulate a comprehensive theory that all religions were based on a solar masculine, served by a patriarchal priest-king who was the direct descendent of the sun god; all known pagan beliefs were degenerated versions of Judaic solar monotheism. Charles Dupuis, almost exactly a hundred years later, argued the same thing—that the sun is the central object of worship throughout the world—and he included Christianity, with its solstice-born savior.

This momentum was slowed but not stopped during the nineteenth century, when folklorists began to gather tales from the illiterate European peasants who had not yet gotten news of the male sun. On farms in Lithuania where Saule was still greeted each morning, among the nomadic Saami, in the desperate poverty of western Ireland, the sun goddess began to reemerge. At the same time also emerged solar mythology, a school of thought that tried to find connections among the stories and rituals that were being published. Leading the movement was Max Mueller, who saw patterns in myths from many sources—patterns that challenged the old view. He was himself a fervent Apollonian, believing in "the brilliant majesty of Him whom they call 'the Life, the breath, the brilliant Lord and Father.' " Mueller discovered and published information—especially about Vedic dawn goddesses—that controverted his own fiercely held world view. His intellectual honesty earned him the spite of a rival named Andrew Lang, who waged a decades-long attack on Mueller personally as well as on the "excesses of solar mythology."[6]

That catchphrase has kept serious work from being done in the last century on the subject of sun worship. With few exceptions, anthropologists with access to information on sun goddesses have avoided the subject, or shown what Miranda Green calls a "perverse desire to interpret symbols which strongly resemble the sun as anything other than solar."

Meanwhile, texts have been issued, year after year, announcing the sun to be male. In an attempt to avoid "the excesses of solar mythology," anthropology, comparative religion and folklore have been responsible for the reinforcement of outdated lies.

Some of today's anthropologists and linguists have avoided discussing the sexes of the heavenly bodies by dismissing them as simply accidents of grammatical gender. The ancient Germans, they argue, denoted the sun by nouns of feminine gender, then had to make up myths starring female suns; this begs the question, at best, and certainly does not sufficiently consider alternative explantions for assignment of sex to luminaries. Some scholars have recently come to the realization that all is not as simple as earlier mythographers would paint it. Claude Lévi-Strauss, for instance, notices that the sun-moon opposition, "whose binary nature seems too evident to the Western observer, could be expressed in other cultures in extraordinarily complex and, to our eyes, unexpected ways"—yet then goes on to select for discussion only myths that uphold current dichotomous thinking, showing the feminine sun as "simply a rather special form of the moon" or playing "only a minor role in the traditional mythology" of the people in question. Only a rare few, like Lucy Goodison and Janet McCrickard, have challenged the view, still astonishingly firmly held, that the division between superior male sun and inferior female moon is natural and worldwide.[7]

In the mid–twentieth century, Apollonian philosophy got a boost from Jungian psychology. Starting from the idea that there are universal, unchanging archetypes of masculine and feminine, followers of Carl Jung extended that perceived dichotomy to equate the masculine with reason and the daylight world, the feminine with the moon and the night world.[8] Although information was available which showed that the solar female was still a living part of many cultures, this was not incorporated into Jungian world view then; nor is it now. Not only are books written using this false, possibly harmful, duality, but women and men are psychoanalyzed according to it.

For two thousand years Apollo has held sway over our psyches. Our culture divides the sky and the earth at some invisible point about our necklines; our heads, our minds are in the sky, while our groins are part of the earth. Thinking is a sky-function, a spiritual occurrence; feeling and yearning are emotions, tied to the earth and therefore base. This dualism sneaks into social interactions as racism, too: the sun is imagined as a white male, blackness is associated with lunar femininity. It is time we abandoned this damaging, this damning, world vision.

We can begin by rediscovering the sun goddess. She is not an Apollo in skirts. She does not divorce the solar intellect from the inspirational world of the moon; rather, she joins them in the figure of the dancing shaman who entrances herself to visit worlds beyond. The sun is, in myths connected to these rituals, a goddess of magical mirrors, whose realm we visit in Part One. She does not claim the life of the mind as more important than the household tasks that maintain life; instead, the sun is a spinner, the creation of light and life her everyday work, as we see in Part Two. She is not forever young; she is a woman who ages, then restores herself to youth. Rather than promising a life beyond that of the body, which ages and dies, she transforms death into a new sunlit summer of life. The difficult and often violent stories that surround this mythic figure are examined in Part Three.

Learning these myths, we break the hypnotic hold of the Apollonian lie and learn to claim our sunny selves as well as our lunacies. We see the realm of the day as woman's, as much as the night can belong to men. Simply reversing roles will be a start. We praise what is most radiant in women: the intellect that sheds light on the obscure, the bright smile that cheers each day, the sense of adventure that illuminates life. And we acknowledge the typically lunar in men: the moodiness, the sudden surges of passion, the mystery.

But even in doing so we will remain within Apollo's domain. The message of the sun goddess is even more profound: we must not separate or dichotomize the world any more. Night and day, death and life, black and white—these are not opposites, any more than are the sun and the moon, or men and women. Her myths and rituals help us restore wholeness to our lives.

Part One

THE MIRROR IN THE CAVE

In the beginning, woman really was the sun.
She was a true person.
Now woman is the moon.
She depends on others for her life
and reflects the light of others.
She is sickly as a wan, blue-white moon.
We, the completely hidden sun,
must now restore ourselves.
We must reveal the hidden sun—
our concealed genius.

—"The Hidden Sun"
by Hiratsuka Raicho

Chapter One ✵

JAPAN:

THE FIRST MIRROR BRINGS HER BACK

Amaterasu was enraged.

First her stormy brother Susano-o had set loose piebald horses in her divine rice paddies. Then he had stuck banners painted with sneering incantations into the ravaged soil. But she had remained patient. Even when he used the space beneath her new throne for a toilet and smeared his product on the palace doors, Amaterasu was forgiving. "Surely what looks like excrement," she said calmly, "is just my brother's drunken vomit."

But then Susano-o destroyed the peace of the heavenly weaving hall, pulling off the roof-tiles to fling down a flayed colt upon the weaving maidens. The fright killed Amaterasu's young sister Wakahirume who, falling from her loom, fatally punctured her vagina with her shuttle.

Finally, Amaterasu grew enraged.

"I will no more see you face to face," the sun announced to the *kami*, the divine beings. With that she pulled closed the door of the Sky-Rock Cave, shutting out her light from the heavenly Land-of-the-High-Sky and the earthly Land-of-Reed-Plains. It grew dark—darker than night, for the moon and stars never rose. All the *kami* were grieved, we learn from the Japanese *Kojiki*, the Record of Ancient Matters, "and their noise was like the buzzing of flies in the fifth moon, and ten thousand woeful calamities befell."

By candlelight the *kami* gathered, eighty myriad of them—perhaps as many as eight million—before the Sky-Rock Cave. What could they do to make the sun return? They would make an image of her! They gathered copper-bearing rocks from the bed of the Sky-River so that Ishikore-dome—the Stone-Coagulating Old Woman—could create the world's first mirror. Her first attempt was a failure, inadequate to capture Amaterasu's beauty. So was the second. But the third mirror was so splendid it made the assembled *kami* gasp.

Then the *kami* strung together five hundred splendid curved jewels into a necklace; they sewed a soft blue and white brocade cloak; they made a new hat, a new shield, shiny new weapons for the sun. They built a new palace, even more lovely than the Sky-Rock Cave. And the *kami* who created this new world were those who would become ancestors of Japan's most famous families.

When all was completed and assembled, the *kami* worked divination on stags' bones and birch bark. They hung all the presents they had made for Amaterasu on an uprooted *sakaki* tree, which they placed before the closed door of the Sky-Rock Cave. All was now ready for the ritual to welcome back the sun. One of the *kami* cried out prayerfully, "The mirror I have is bright and beauteous, like you. Will you not open the door and look at it?"

There was no answer.

All were silent for a time. Then Uzume, the fierce shaman, pushed up her sleeves above her elbows and tied them with cords of moss. She fashioned a hat of leaves and a dancing fan from bamboo grass; she fastened bells around her wrists; she wreathed a spear with grasses; she kindled bonfires. Then she overturned a tub in front of the Sky-Rock Cave and leaped on it, stamping out a dance as she whistled through a flute, and the eighty myriad *kami* kept time on wooden clappers.

She sang a simple song: "*Hi, hu, mi, yo, i, mu, na, ya, ko, to,*" or "one, two, three, four, five, six, seven, eight, nine, ten, a hundred, a thousand, a myriad." As she sang, she began to remove her garments, exposing in the dim firelight first her breasts, then her genitals, in a striptease that was both comic and at the same time deeply serious, for to reveal the source of life in the absence of the Ancestral Mother was a reminder of the world's profound distress.

Raucous laughter from the eighty myriad *kami* shook the sky. Great Sky-Shiner Amaterasu heard the uproar and peered out. She was astonished by what she saw. "I thought," she said, "that since I had withdrawn and shut myself in the Sky-Rock Cave, there would be continued darkness. How is it that Uzume makes merry and the *kami* all laugh?"

Uzume the Sky Frightener had a ready answer, a taunting one. "We rejoice that a sun has been found more lovely than you." At that cue, two *kami* held up the mirror. Through the crack in the doorway, Amaterasu stared at the brilliant apparition. Little by little she edged forward. When she was entirely out of the cave, the sky flooded with light.

"*Aware! Ana omoshiroshi! Ana tanoshi! Ana sayake oke!*" cried the *kami*. How light it grows! How wonderful to see each other's faces! How wonderful to dance with hands outstretched! How wonderful is this refreshing sunlight!

They begged the sun goddess never again to hide her face for so long. They tied the door of the Sky-Rock Cave open with a sun rope, knotted at the bottom to represent Amaterasu's shadow. Some interpreters say that this disappearance of the Great Mistress of the Day brought on the first winter, some that she retreats into her cave whenever there is an eclipse. In any case, the magic mirror, Japanese scripture tell us, brought the sun back to her welcoming world and continues to do so today.[1]

The retreat and return of the sun goddess is the primary myth of Japanese Shinto, the only surviving major religion centered on a goddess; the mirror used to lure Amaterasu from her cave is its primary symbol. Although Japan is the only place where sun-goddess mythology and ritual have survived relatively unchanged into our century, Shinto is far from unusual in its ways of symbolizing the feminine sun. We will concentrate in this first section on the shining metal mirror and its connection to solar shamanism, but there are other images in Japanese myth that are common to sun-goddess cultures: her invention of weaving, her radiant necklace, her dance of power, her argument with her brother. These, however, play minor roles in Shinto iconography; the mirror is preeminent, the primary symbol of the sun.

The mirror, in fact, in virtually every area where it is found as a religious artifact, represents the sun goddess. Wherever a ritual mirror is found—among the Hittites, in Egypt, in Britain and Ireland, in Korea and Siberia, in tribal India—a sun goddess is also found, usually connected with shamanism and healing.[2] The mirror created by the smith goddess to lure Amaterasu from her cave is thus a prototype of those we'll find around the world. With this sun mirror, we find a complex of other solar images—eyes, cats, healing thermal waters, caves and ritual female self-exposure.

At the center of this web of imagery is the solar mirror. Amaterasu's primeval mirror, created in the *kami-yo*, the time before time, still exists. Together with the ten-span sun spear and the curved necklace of *yasaka* jewels crafted by the ancestral spirits, it rests at Japan's Great Shrine of Ise-Jingu, in Mie Prefecture. There are other Shinto mirrors—some ninety-six thousand of them, one in each of the simple shrines behind the *torii* gates and leafy gardens. Such shrine mirrors were traditionally mounted on wooden altars and decked with fresh flowers; home altars, too, often bore mirrors to remind Shinto worshipers of their ancestral mother. Mirrors, even household mirrors, still have a special place in Japanese culture. In ancient times, they were buried in graves along with other precious objects. From those times, too, date the many legends that emphasize the importance of the mirror. In one such story, a woman gave a mirror to a shrine to be melted into a bell, then later regretted it; her mirror, connected to her hard heart, refused to melt as had the other, more generously given mirrors. The mirror's continuing spiritual significance in Shinto is suggested by the Japanese proverb "When the mirror is dim, the soul is not pure."[3]

However significant other mirrors might be, however, only the mirror at Ise is that crafted by Ishikore-dome. When Amaterasu pushed open her cave's rock door, it struck the mirror and nicked it slightly. The nick is on the Ise mirror to this day. But there is no way to see that nick, nor the mirror itself, for the Ise mirror is forever protected from human sight as the most sacred Shinto treasure. You may only visit the shrine where it rests. For the non-Japanese, it can be a daunting trip: two hours from Tokyo to Nagoya on the Shinkansen bullet-train, another two hours up the Kinki Nippon Line to the small station at Uji-Yamada, then two miles up a road bordered with miniature stone pagodas to the shrine precinct. An easier route starts from Osaka and travels up the Kinki Nippon a mere two hours into Uji-Yamada. From either direction, the hours spent watching chartreuse rice paddies and craggy mountains flow by the window are amply rewarded by the simple grace of the Great Shrine.

Two glistening, twenty-foot *torii* mark the shrine entrance, one on either side of the curved Uji bridge of cypress and zelkhova wood over the Isuzu River—the very river from which the primeval smith goddess extracted the copper-bearing rocks in the *kami-yo*. Water is also present near the third *torii*, inside the shrine; there a sheltered spring offers a chance for purification. A bamboo pipe, from which water trickles, hoods a stone trough. Dozens of tiny buckets, hand-fashioned from bamboo and sporting two-foot-long handles, permit you to dip sacred water ceremoniously over each hand in turn. Parents carefully assist their children; infants have their hands sprinkled before the family proceeds to the riverbank. At a large gravel clearing overlooking a pool, ten-pound carp gather for feeding. If you've brought something—there is nowhere nearby for the empty-handed to purchase offerings—the fish ripple the calm water as they rise to feed.

From the river, gravel paths lead through the shrine precincts. The grounds are thickly forested and virtually wild, a delightful surprise to the eye acclimated to the tameness of contemporary Japan. But the Ise wilderness is kept within bounds by blue-kimonoed women raking leaves into neat piles with brooms of bound twigs. They especially devote their attention to removing litter from beneath the trees, for Ise-Jinju is more than its sacred buildings; it is a hallowed preserve where, according to Shinto belief, every rock and tree express the divine. In the 13,600 acres of the divine precinct, trees used for the shrine reconstruction may be cut, but only if they are out of sight of the main buildings; the rest are protected, and an active reforestation program continually plants saplings.

It is not surprising, then, to see an elderly woman standing in the center of a gravel path, looking tenderly at a particularly lovely hinoki cedar—a *sakaki*, or revered tree. She then joins the thousands of other visitors who follow the parkland paths to the shrine buildings. First comes the hall of sacred music and dance, the Kaguradon, now partially a media center where, if you understand Japanese, you can learn from a constantly playing videotape; if you cannot comprehend the words, you can at least enjoy images of the shrine at different seasons. A garden of combed sand inside the building offers a meditation spot and an opportunity to admire the careful finish work on this, as on all the wooden shrine buildings at Ise. Further along the path are shops built in the style for which Ise is famous, the style called *shinmei* —"divine brightness" or "deity gate." Here young Shinto priests sell souvenirs: models of the shrines, ceramic figurines and tea sets, brocade pouches tied with cord.

These last cost 1000 yen and are not so much souvenirs as containers for relics, wooden bits of earlier shrines. The two major sacred buildings of Ise—the Toyo-uke Daijingu, or outer shrine, and the inner Kwo Daijingu, or Naigu—are rebuilt every twenty years, the new buildings exactly replicating the old. Dedicated in October of 1974, after eight years of construction, the shrine buildings I saw in 1993 were torn down and packaged into relics in 1994. More than $30 million, donated by the Japanese government and by private individuals, funds the reconstruction. To complete it, two hundred thousand artisans—using ancient Japanese joinery techniques in which not a single nail cuts the wood, for nothing but unforged natural material may be used—are at work. Some thirteen thousand cypress trees and twelve thousand bamboo poles will be used to prepare for the next *shiki-nen-sengii*, the transfer of the *kami* to the new structure.

Moving the inner shrine in 1993 meant the temporary removal of Amaterasu's mirror from the outdated building. One autumn night, an imperial guard escorted the mirror to a small silk-encased wooden shrine, where it was consoled for the disturbance by further rituals. Later the mirror, banners and shrine furnishings were moved to the new building. Ancient courtly music, *gagaku*, was played while prayers were chanted:

> In accordance with ancient custom,
> The Great Shrine is built anew once in twenty years,
> The various articles of clothing of fifty-four types,
> And the sacred treasures of twenty-one types are provided,
> And exorcism, purification, and cleansing is performed.[4]

To the Western mind, it seems obvious that the new shrine will be a different one from the last; to the Shintoist, there is no difference. The new Naigu is the old one, just as the pieces of wood contained in the little brocade bags are mysteriously, mystically, pieces of the shrine standing today. This reflects an even greater mystery: that the *yato-no-kagami*, the mirror of Amaterasu, is the sun itself. It is not an image or portrait of the sun; it does not symbolize the sun. "Honor the mirror as me," Amaterasu told her followers thirteen hundred years ago, when they erected the first shrine at Ise; they understood this to mean that the mirror *is* the Goddess. There is no dualism in Shinto. But neither is it monotheistic; Shinto is pure monism, with no difference between divinity and the objects it inhabits.

They have the same understanding today, these Shintoists who daily crowd the relic shops to purchase calligraphed prayers to leave behind in the shrine precincts. "My child is handicapped and I become very tired," one reads. "I ask for a life less filled with sadness." Another: "I would like to find a nice home-loving girl to marry. I am fond of children and think I can be a good father. So I came here to pray."[5] The white-robed priests write in ideographs on *gohei*, strips of gauzy white paper, or on *ema*, wooden tablets. When you leave the inner shrine, the prayer remains to keep your petition in the sight of the sun goddess to whom it is addressed.

From the outer precincts, a colonnade of huge eight-hundred-year-old cyptomeria, skirted in bamboo, leads to the inner shrine. There, yet another massive *torii* indicates the increasing sacredness of the site; a final tiny stall holds priests reciting prayers and painting them in quick calligraphic strokes. There, too, is Ara-maturi-no-miya, the shrine of *ara-mitama*, the rough spirit of the goddess, which spurs us to creative action. This spirit is one of two aspects of *kami*; the other, *nigi-mitama* or gentle divine spirit, takes less energy to harness, but both are necessary for life to continue. Similarly, *kami* is most readily experienced in a landscape that is neither too regular nor too wild—a setting like Ise-Jingu.[6]

The house of the goddess is one of a conglomeration of buildings surrounding an inner courtyard. Even the visitor prepared with the knowledge that the Great Shrine consists only of huts thatched with miscanthus grass will be surprised by the starkness of the scene: It looks like a

Japanese farmstead of the last millennium from which all traces of human and animal life have vanished. A gate building, just inside the *torii*, is hung with a white silk curtain blocking the view into the shrine's interior. Reverent visitors make offerings of coins, then pause a moment in prayer. A particularly favored worshiper may be granted an instant's glimpse into the shrine, should a gust blow back the silken banner to reveal the tiny tabernacle of Amaterasu's mirror.

Nothing about the mirror is certain: not its shape, not its size, not the material from which it is made. Mythically and magically, it is connected to the number eight: It is described as eight feet across, as fitted with eight handles, as shaped like an eight-petaled flower, as graven with eight blossoms. But the number eight, Jean Herbert a Shinto scholar, cautions, symbolizes perfection; the solar mirror's name may then really mean "The Perfect Mirror," rather than "The Eight-Sided Mirror," as the name is usually translated. Whatever its shape, it rests inside a succession of brocade bags; a new one is added each time the outer begins to fray. Thus concealed, the mirror rests on a low silk-covered stand, hooded with a golden casket inside another golden casket, which is inside a barrel-shaped box. In front of the shrine, a little nine-inch plain round mirror, the *unsui*, stands on a wooden stand carved with clouds and water, fending off evil by magically reflecting its image.

Pilgrimage to Ise is the highlight of any Shinto believer's life; annually some six million make the journey. Favored times are September and April, when a dawn walk to see the Myoto-ga-Seki, the famous Wedded Rocks just off the coast, is rewarded by the sight of the sun rising between them, at which celebrants clap their hands in welcome. The smaller of these rocks represents Sky-Frightening Uzume, who brought Amaterasu from her cave. Other major pilgrimage times are mid-February and mid-June, and minor festivals in January and March draw thousands. Even in a mid-August downpour, hundreds of pilgrims flock to the shrine: grandmothers with identical umbrellas of purple and pink, their town name emblazoned in white; family groups of three, sometimes four generations; a motorcycle club uniformed in leather jumpsuits and matching red helmets. The outing is purely social for some, like the linguist who admitted that he visited Ise only to impress a girlfriend. For others, the shrine offers a chance to increase the depth of one's spiritual understanding, as it was to the father who brought his children to Ise to explain how the shrine exemplified the concept of *kami*. Pointing out a dynamic rock thrusting up against one of the shrine walls, he was able to show them how, according to Shinto, any object can be *kami*.

Although pictured in human form, the *kami* of the *Kojiki* are not gods and goddesses in a personalized Western sense. Rather, *kami* are hierophanies, breakings-through of spiritual power—what Carmen Blacker, in her study of Japanese shamanism so eloquently calls "an incomprehensible otherness which betokens power."[7] The word *kami* itself means "standing above" or "superior"; it is used to mean "top" in "top of the head," and sometimes "heavenly" in the Shinto sense that all earthly things partake of divine essence. The word is best expressed in English as "outstanding," a word that includes the sense of context missing in other possible translations.

Any object that embodies power—a dense grove of trees visible for miles, say, or an oddly angled waterfall—can be *kami*. Mountains such as Fuji-yama are *kami*. Especially beautiful moments of the year, like the blossoming of cherry trees, are outstanding, *kami*. Lakes, trees, animals, even people can be *kami,* for Shinto does not separate transcendence from embodiment: sacredness is *in* nature, not above it. Thus *mono no aware*, the sense that we are essentially connected with all nature, is the wellspring of Shinto. It was this sense that the father at Ise wished his children to feel. Kneeling in the slowing rain, he pointed upwards to the jagged rocks, holding his smallest boy by the shoulders and entoning, "*kami...kami.*"

To Amaterasu and the other personalized *kami*, such a Shinto believer does not offer prayer, if prayer is defined as worship, thanksgiving, repentance or petitions addressed to beings superior to the devotee. All beings partake of *kami*; prayer therefore is impossible. Rather, the Shintoist offers *norito*, praise-songs full of respect and gratitude and honor, more like a letter to a distant sister than the humble words of a vassal to a ruler. In the same way, there are no absolute codes or commandments in Shinto, for if we are all *kami*, the only maxim that can be truly offered is one often cited in Japan: "Follow the genuine impulses of your heart."

It seems to defy logic that Amaterasu is the supreme deity in a religion that denies hierarchies of the spirit. To understand how this came to be, we must consider the prehistoric background from which Shinto emerged. The islands of Japan were once connected to the continent of Asia; animals and early humans migrated to Japan some five thousand years ago. From the primitive groups emerged a Stone Age culture, the Jomon, whose Stonehenge-like stone circles clearly point to sun worship.[8] This aborginal culture left its traces in northern Hokkaido, among the Ainu, an ethnic group racially distinct from other Japanese. Driven before invaders until they occupied only the northernmost islands, on the perimeter of the empire, the Ainu maintained for generations their historic traditions and myths, including the belief in their sun goddess Chup-Kamui, "shining thing."

Among the few European writers who described Ainu ways soon after the opening of contact between the West and the Island Empire, the most prominent are anthropologist Neil Munro, adventurer Savage Landor, and missionary John Batchelor.[9] Munro noted the orientation of houses with a sacred window to the east, so the rising sun could visit the ancestral spirit of the hearth. The Ainu believed it improper, he said, to walk through sunbeams as they streamed across the floor; likewise it was improper not to greet the sun as a living woman. In the latter part of the last century, Savage Landor observed Ainu drinkers who included Chup-Kamui in their toasts with each round.

Chup-Kamui, legend said, was once the moon. But, shocked by the number of people who took advantage of darkness to have illicit outdoor sex, Chup-Kamui asked the male luminary to trade places with her. (The same story appears in Korea, where the goddess tells her brother, "I am afraid to go up in the sky alone, at night. Let's switch roles.") After taking over as ruler of the day, Chup-Kamui rose each morning from the mouth of a devil who had spent the night trying to eat her. A magical helper shoved crows and foxes into the devil's mouth while the sun escaped; thus crows and foxes were sacred to the Ainu.

The conservative missionary John Bachelor, who emphasized that the Ainu were similarly conservative in religious matters, noted that the sun goddess was second only to the world's creator in their cosmology. She was a genial, sustaining force, who used the solar orb as her vehicle. "Her brightness," he said, "shines through it." Without the goddess, light would vanish; for that reason, the Ainu feared eclipses. The reverend writer witnessed, in 1887, Ainu reaction to one of these celestial events:

> I blackened some glass, so as to enable an Ainu to see the eclipse when it took place. At the proper time, we bade him look up at the sun. Immediately the exclamation rang out, Chup rai, chup rai, "the luminary is dying, the sun is dying." Another person called out, Chup chikai anu, "the sun is fainting away," or "the luminary is dying." That is all that was said; silence ensued, and only now and then an exclamation of surprise or fear was to be heard.

In the diminishing light, the Ainu acted as though the sun goddess were a dying person who could be revived by water sprinkled on face or bosom. They dipped willow branches and cast droplets upwards while calling out Kamui-atem-ka, "Oh goddess, we revive you!" When this stratagem worked (as it always did), a party ensued, and much *sake* was drunk. Bachelor, the prudish missionary, described the scene: "A few cups of *sake* soon cause the talkers to speak what is not true or reliable, and they are not long before they begin to show signs of being in a somewhat maudlin state." As well they might be, having just saved the goddess who sustained their lives from a dreadful fate.

The Ainu lost most of their original territory to invaders who arrived in the islands in approximately the third century B.C.E., during the Yayoi period. These newcomers were more technologically sophisticated than the aboriginal residents, bringing with them metal objects—including mirrors. The earliest mirrors found in Japan were Chinese imports, with scenes from old Chinese myths engraved on their backs. Almost immediately the mirror was adapted into the indigenous sun religion. The favored earliest shape, the *Suzakagami* or bell mirror, had four to eight bells attached to its rim; these were made of iron or, more commonly, bronze polished with mercury. What the people found appealing was the shining surface; the religious scenes, copied by Japanese smiths, were soon abstracted into meaningless decorative patterns.

During this era, there were innumerable tribal divinities—the eighty myriad *kami* of the *Kojiki*. One began to take prominence: Amaterasu, Ancestral Mother of the Yamato family.[10] Centuries of political consolidation resulted in unification of the islands under a government controlled by this family; local rituals and deities were incorporated into a complex, decentralized religion over which the Yamato family ancestor ruled, just as the Yamatos ruled over the other tribes, each generation mirroring earlier ones.

The Yamato family, which insisted on its direct descent from the sun *kami*, may have saved this sun goddess from disappearing, under the guise of a male deity, into the pantheon of invading Buddhism—as she almost did, in the second period of Shinto history. In the first period, Shinto did not even have a name; today's word is the Chinese translation of a Japanese phrase, "way of the *kami*." Transmitted orally—the alphabet came with Buddhist contact—the rituals and liturgies and stories of early Shinto emphasized the feminine. Goddesses appeared singularly, in teams of two or three, in consort with gods, even as residents in shrines officially devoted to male divinities. Some scholars of Shinto argue the indigenous Japanese culture was a peaceable matriarchy, led by women shamans in the service of the sun-goddess.[11] Was the sun goddess, as Edward Kidder suggests, an emodiment of this shaman-queen?

This first period of Shinto history ended in 538 C.E., when a minor

Korean king sent Buddhist literature and a small gilded Buddha statue to the emperor of Japan. This exotic new religion was soon all the rage in the court. It was not long before the ruling family, in the person of Empress Suiko, declared Buddhism the state's official religion. The long-standing peace between light and dark, between Amaterasu and her brother Susano-o, gave way to what Post Wheeler calls a "tragic dualism" not previously part of Japanese thought.

But Shinto did not die; instead, the period of *shinbutsu-shugo*, "merging with Buddhism," began. Japan's two religions existed side by side. Though officially Buddhist, the court celebrated its festivals in Shinto fashion, with the *katari-he*, or "reciters of ancient words," telling the stories of Amaterasu and the other great *kami*. Shinto thus remained uncodified, unwritten, in its original form as stories, songs, rituals. But oral transmittal of religious material is risky in any newly literate culture. Shinto beliefs might have been lost, save for the efforts of a single woman.

A century and a half after Buddhism's arrival, Heido took it upon herself to memorize all the ancient tales in order to preserve them. She then kept them in memory for the next 32 years, until the Empress Gemmei, afraid of the destruction of Shinto knowledge when Heido died, assigned a scribe to her. The compilation of her words is known as the *Kojiki*. Gemmei suspected other stories, less sacred than those in Heido-no-Ame's repertoire, remained in the oral tradition. So she commissioned a great search for additional material, which resulted in the *Nihongi* or *Nihon Shoki*, the Annals or Chronicles of Japan, in 720 C.E.

It is tempting to imagine that this court woman and her empress were impelled to preserve the mythic heritage of Shinto because it afforded them so much more freedom than the invading religion, with its doctrine that no one could be saved unless incarnated in male form. Buddhist bias against the female extended into the heavens, but Shinto philosophy, conversely, looked for *kami* in any outstanding thing or person—woman or man. But Gemmyo and Heido left no record of their motivation. Whatever it was, it is well that the Shinto myths were recorded so soon after Buddhism's arrival in Japan, for during the next millennium, regular attempts were made to convert Shinto into a form of Buddhism and Shinto's sun goddess into a sun god. Had the material not been written, one of these attempts might have succeeded and Amaterasu might be counted among the sun gods.

One attempt to transsexualize the goddess came early. In 750 C.E., the syncretist monk Gyoki, a leader of Shinto's second period, when

Ryubo Shinto attempted to link the indigenous religion with Buddhism as "double-aspect" or "two-faced" Shinto, announced that he had received a divine revelation. The sun *kami* might appear female, he said, but in fact was really male, a Buddha-manifestation who should be called Vairochana the Illuminator. The people didn't buy it, just as they didn't accept the later argument that Amaterasu was really Marici-deva, his sex disguised by the Chinese woman's garments he was depicted wearing; this Tantric interloper, androgynous or at least cross-dressed in his home territories, was quickly spurned.

Another attempt to change Amaterasu's sex came during Shinto's third phase, the *Shinbutsu-bunri*, or period of separation from Buddhism, which began in the thirteenth century. With Buddhism established as the state religion, Shinto survived only marginally. Then Moto-ori Norinaga originated "pure Shinto" as a back-to-basics force for nationalism. One of his followers, Hirata Atsutana, ironically but enthusiastically announced the replacement of Amaterasu with Ameno-minaka-nushi, the Heavenly Central Lord, a Jehovah-like world creator who lived in the vicinity of the North Star. Even later, in the sixteenth century, the Shintoist Kurozumi Munetada called for ignoring the sun's gender and focusing on a now sexless luminary as an emblem of creative vitality; the chief way of expressing this awareness was praying to the rising sun and "inhaling" its divinity. (Even today attempts to change or ignore Amaterasu's sex continue: A recent book, significantly titled *The Looking Glass God*, insinuates that Shinto is based on a male solar figure by avoiding any mention of the goddess while discussing at length minor male *kami*.[12])

Again and again, Amaterasu retained her original sex. But another, more subtle, danger was at hand. The combination of growing nationalism and antiquarian interest in Shinto led to the Meiji Restoration of 1867; the emperor was put back on the throne and the religion of his ancestors back into the shrines. Suddenly, the millennia-old religion of the sun goddess became a mere imperial cult.

The danger was subtle because, on the surface, it seemed that Shinto was again becoming the central expression of Japanese spirituality. Ancient mirror rituals were restored, including the act of lying prostrate before a mirror in order to divine one's spiritual state; this was said to reflect the dying wishes of Amaterasu's father, who gave each of his kami-children a mirror that told the state of their souls. Restored, too, was the ancient New Year's rite of baking *kagami mochi*, flat mirror cakes made of the best rice and placed atop each other.

But by 1884, Shinto's religious aspects were denied in favor of its political significance to the Japanese nation which, marching under the *hi-no-maru*, or solar circle, called itself the Land of the Rising Sun. That year, the government declared that Shinto was not a religion (this would happen again in the twentieth century, ironically enough when the Japanese empire was crushed) but was, instead, an accurate historical account of the establishment of the Yamato dynasty. This led to a period, lasting through World War II, when membership in a Shinto shrine and attendance at its festivals were required to prove patriotism; severe repression of other worship resulted. This emphasis upon imperial importance meant the submersion of Amaterasu's solar worship and its spiritual meaning.

Then, in 1946, American imposition of the Shinto Directive upon a defeated Island Empire reversed the tide of centuries. The occupying Allies required Emperor Hirohito to renounce his claim to divine ancestry. Thus Shinto was severed from its attachment to the Yamato family. The sun goddess was no longer to be considered the Divine Ancestor of Japan's rulers.

The high tone of the Shinto Directive—which freed the Japanese "from direct or indirect compulsion to believe or profess to believe in a religion or cult officially designated by the state"—did not disguise its intention to destroy the philosophic and religious beliefs that had upheld the empire during the war. Shinto beliefs were forbidden to be mentioned in school textbooks, local officials were banned from participating in shrine activities, devout Shintoists could not display religious symbols in school or office. The message heard by Japanese believers was that the West wished to destroy Shinto; older women were especially insulted and outraged.

But Shinto survived again. Although the government Shrine Board was abolished, the shrines themselves remained, as well as Shinto priests with their knowledge of ritual. A decade of controversy followed: Was Shinto a philosophy, a religion, a set of antiquated superstitions with roots in Japan's prehistory? In the late 1950s, the Association of Shinto Shrines finally announced that the way of the *kami* was, indeed, a religion.

And so Shinto remains. Although no longer the state religion, it maintains ties to the Yamato family, whose members make ceremonial visits to Ise. The prime minister and cabinet, too, visit the Great Shrine each New Year, and after major elections and cabinet changes. And Hirohito's son Akihito, in 1990, underwent the ritual of *Daijo-sai*, in which he asked Amaterasu to take him into her womb and bear him anew as *Ninigi-no-mi-koto*, the rice-plant god. Thus the Japanese emperor continues to be *akitsu-kami*, *kami* made visible, in direct disregard of the treaty between the United States and Japan.[13]

For the average non-imperial worshiper, shrine visits may be combined with the practice of Christianity or Buddhism, for centuries of religious conflict have left a heritage of sectarian flexibility. Or Shinto rites can be used for purely secular reasons, as sociologist Larry Gooding found when he observed motorists who, upon passing their drivers' tests, adjourn to the local shrine to offer *norito* against traffic accidents.[14]

This is the world in which today's Ise pilgrims live, a world where the ancient religion of the sun goddess readily combines with patriarchal imports. It is this world they re-enter when, leaving the Ise shrine precincts, they find a warren of tea shops and kitsch stalls selling Mickey Mouse alarm clocks, bamboo paintings of the Shinkansen express, plastic wind-up robots. Rummaging in the stalls, they can also find Uzume dolls that portray the fierce shaman looking like a geisha, balsa-wood replicas of the outer shrine buildings, tiny copies of the *unsui*.

And there, too, they can find shaman's drums, painted either with the Chinese yin-yang symbol or the three-part circling swastika from Korea, the *tomoe*—for Shinto has never wandered far from its shamanic roots. Shamanism appears in Shinto myth, history and ritual. In the myth of the sun's return from her cave, Uzume dances a parody of shamanic ritual. Amaterasu herself, in another myth, dons the dress of a *miko*—a woman shaman, or "daughter of the goddess"—to combat her brother Susano-o. Both Amaterasu and Susano-o, this story relates, were children of Izanagi and Izanami—the Male Who Invites and the Female Who Invites, the original divine parents of all *kami*. Some versions say Amaterasu emerged from a mirror held in her father's hand, others that she was born from her father's eye when he bathed it after her mother's death, an echo of the connection between eye and sun and mirror we'll also find in Egypt and Ireland.

When all the *kami* had been born, Izanagi chose Amaterasu as most fit to rule the six quarters of the world: north, south, east, west, the world above, the world below. Taking his necklace of power, he shook and jingled it, then put it around his brilliant daughter's neck, investing her with the rulership of all creation.

Her first act was to provide food for humanity. She delegated her consort, the moon-*kami* Tsuki-yomi, to seek out the food-*kami* Ukemochi on earth, the Central-Land-of-Reed-Plains. When Tsuki-yomi requested food, Ukemochi vomited boiled rice, fish and other animals; she picked more food from her nose and excreted yet more from her anus (these were especially dainty morsels) the *Kojiki* tells us. Then she set forth a hundred tables of delicacies for the moon-*kami*. Disgusted by this mode of creation, Tsuki-yomi pulled out his sword and murdered her.

The moon returned to his sister-sun with his report. Amaterasu, appalled by his violence, sentenced him to eternal separation from her— thus the moon, even today, is never seen by the side of the sun. Yet all was not lost. When another heavenly delegation was sent to where Ukemochi lay, the *kami* found her body had decomposed into more food: Corn and horses and mulberry trees had exploded from her forehead; silkworms had crawled from her eyebrows; small beans had grown from her nose, large beans from her buttocks, rice from her belly, other grains from her vagina. Amaterasu popped the silkworms into her mouth and spun thread, thus inventing spinning; then, with the new thread, she invented weaving.

But more violence lay ahead. Susano-o began to wreak the havoc on Amaterasu's territories that led to her retreat from the world. When she had come forth again, a *kami* council sentenced Susano-o to a severe fine and a ceremony of purification that entailed extraction of his fingernails and toenails. He was then banished from heaven.

It was a time of continuous rainfall. Susano-o made a grass rain hat and cloak in which he went from door to door, begging lodging from the *kami*. All kept faith with Amaterasu and repulsed him. Unable to find a resting place in heaven, he impetuously decided to visit his sister. Hearing of his approach, she assumed he came intent upon more violence. But she stood her ground. "Though I am a woman," she asked herself, "why should I shrink?"

Amaterasu wound her hair up with jewels and tied her skirts into trousers. Piling more jewels onto her forearms and neck, she girded on three swords and slung quivers holding fifteen hundred arrows onto her back. Then she began to dance. Brandishing a bow and grasping tight the hilt of a sword, she kicked up the soil as if it were snow, all the time uttering incantations. She became a shaman, dancing her magic. And her brother, terrified by her appearance, departed the heavens forever.

Shinto is not now shamanic in its rituals; far less does it rely upon female religious celebrants. But vestiges of its early identity remain. Ancient masked dances like the *Kagura*—which enacts Amaterasu's emergence from the cave of heaven—are still performed by women. This remains the case even though, since the arrival of Buddhism, Shinto priests have been almost exclusively male; the sole exception is the emperor's sister Kazuko Takatsukasa, Sacred Priestess of Ise, the only woman in the Shinto hierarchy. Today it is usually the wife or daughter of the shrine priest who performs rites reserved for women, although in medieval times imperial princesses performed them. Even earlier, it is thought, the princesses were themselves Shinto's only priests, shamans who allowed the sun goddess to possess their bodies.

Whether the first *miko* was of the imperial lineage must remain conjectural, but we know that she existed and how she dressed from the *haniwa*, pottery figurines that show her in full panoply: jewels, flat hat, quiver and belled mirror. The latter, as in Manchuria and Siberia, was part of her regalia from the start; the same waistband mirror is donned by Korean shamans today as a lure for the sun's spirit.

A noted scholar of Japanese shamanism, Carmen Blacker, believes that the ancient *miko* united both political power and natural psychic ability. At first, she argues, any woman could become a *miko*, and the shaman most able to lead the people became queen. Later, queenship became restricted by family rather than by talent. Born into the imperial clan, Blacker contends, the ancient *miko* was nonetheless self-selected by visionary experiences; her mother did not necessarily need to have ruled. Whoever could unite lineage and political power with visionary skill would rule Japan as shaman-queen.

Himiko, in the third century C.E., was such a queen. Legend says that this "great child of the sun" never left her palace, living in seclusion with one thousand maidens and governing by messages received in trance from the *kami*. Himiko may have actually been not a single woman but the generic title of the shaman-queens who served the sun goddess by incarnating her. This particular Himiko was succeeded by an inept male ruler who was overthrown by the people and replaced by Iyo, a 13-year-old girl. Thus by the third century, Japan's period of rule by women incarnating the sun goddess was giving way to a period in which queens provided shamanic assistance to male rulers—their husbands or brothers.

From this era comes a famous story of imperial entrancement, a cautionary tale for any emperor prone to religious doubt. It is said that the empress Jingo was dancing to the emperor's zither music, while the prime minister Takeshiuchi-no-sukune stood by to interpret any divine messages she might speak. Though the room was completely dark, the empress danced in a sure-footed way, guided by the spirits. When finally she began to speak, the voice that issued from her mouth was not her own.

"Take the armies," the voice said, "and lead them to the west, and there seek treasures of silver and gold."

Now at this time the island empire knew little of its neighbors. And the emperor, besides, was skeptical of his wife's powers. "This is a lying *kami*," he said under his breath, neglecting even the expected ritual words of praise and thanksgiving for the message.

"Go straight in one direction!" shouted the offended spirit through the mouth of the empress, as it raised her arm in a gesture of cursing. Instantly the zither music stopped. A heavy sound was heard.

"Bring lights! Bring lights!" called the prime minister. When lights were brought they revealed the emperor, slumped over his instrument, stone dead.

It was clear the rite had to begin again, to rectify the insult done to the *kami*. This time the prime minister took up the musical instrument and played melodiously while the empress danced. Again the spirit from beyond took over her body and her voice, and again it spoke the same words.

The prime minister, shrewder than the king, asked the *kami* to explain. And so it did: Unknown even to herself, the empress was pregnant, by the will of Amaterasu herself. The child she would bear would cross the western seas and find a land to conquer. This indeed came to pass, when the queen's son subdued the nearby peninsula of Korea.

Throughout early Japanese history, women of the imperial Yamato clan continued to shamanize. A famous Yamato shaman was Totohi-moso-hime, aunt of emperor Sujin. When a great epidemic swept Japan, she brought it under control by revealing its mystical causes; later, she thwarted an uprising by magically obtaining its plans. It was said that she even married a *kami*, so close were her connections to the spirit world. Another imperial shaman was Yamato-hime-no-mikota, an emperor's daughter who was possessed by the sun goddess and who founded Ise shrine according to Amaterasu's instructions.

Shamanism was integral to Shinto, so much so that mediumistic trances outside the shrine precincts were disallowed in the Middle Ages. Beset on the one hand by the popular import Buddhism and on the other by a horde of unordained shamans, the shrine priests tried to establish, once and for all, that trance was legitimate only in the Shinto context. In decrees of 780 and 807 C.E., shamanic rituals outside the shrines were condemned as not only ineffective but dangerous. The rituals went on, however, and gained strength; by the nineteenth century, when non-shrine shamanism was the rule, a decree finally severed the religion from its base by declaring trance illegal at the shrines.

The ancient connection of shamanism and Shinto has not entirely died out, although women of non-imperial blood are today's beneficiaries of the solar presence. Sayo Kitamura, leader of today's Shinto-based *Odoru-shukyo*, or Dancing Religion, believes her body to be the living temple of the sun *kami*; followers of Nami Orimo's *Dai-hizen-kyo*, or Great Sun Teaching sect, believe that Amaterasu herself has descended into and speaks through their religious leader.

Althugh such beliefs are relatively rare in Shinto today, the tradition of female shamanism *outside* organized religion has never died out. While in neighboring Korea the women's shamanic culture actually flourishes, in Japan it simply continues to exist. Nonetheless, the connection between women and shamanism remains strong. Male shamans are so rare in Japan that the very word for shaman—*miko*—is feminine. There is no term for the male shaman, scorned as a poor substitute for the real thing. "Isn't there any competent woman in Azuma?" a twelfth century folksong derisively asks. "There are male shamans there!"

A generation ago, thousands of female shamans wandered the Japanese countryside, offering healing and ritual services where needed. Today's shamans are fewer; settled in villages rather than roving the land, they serve the needs of their immediate neighbors. Most are women who come to the craft through initiation rather than inheritance. Typical are the shamans of the Tohoku area of Honshu, most of them blind adoptees trained by older female practitioners. Through an arduous apprenticeship they learn to go into trance at will, to divine the future, to make contact with the deceased—the most important skills of the shaman. They also learn to make music to accompany the dancing rituals they and other female shamans perform.

In Okinawa and the other Ryukyu islands at the southern end of the Japanese archipelago, however, a rich shamanic culture continues to be based on women's power. Ryukyuan shamans—all women or cross-dressed men—practice both inherited and initiatory shamanism. Shamans of the first type are village priests—*noro,* or "living god-desses"—whose gifts are part of their family heritage; their brothers inherit secular offices. Because the men require access to oracular power that only the women possess, village leaders must constantly turn to their elder sisters for advice and aid. Such a sister is called *unarigami*, or "sis-ter-*kami*," and is said to be the brother's guardian goddess. So deep is the bond between siblings in this society that the phrase "happy as sister and brother" is used of unusually harmonious marriages.

Ryukyu men always wear something given to them by their sisters— a lock of hair, frequently, or a little handkerchief-like towel. This magi-cally attaches the siblings, so that the sister can exercise her power in case of danger to the brother. A Ryukyu legend says that a girl and her mother were weaving one day when the girl suddenly fell asleep. The mother, concerned, leaned over to waken her. As she did so, the girl shivered. "I just had the most awful dream," she related. "I dreamed my brother was drowning, and I was reaching out my hand to save him, and suddenly I woke up." When the news was brought of the boy's death by drowning, it was found to have occurred exactly when the girl was awakened; she would have saved him if her trance had not been interrupted.

Fifty years ago, the *noro* was kept in a state of prescribed ritual purity; the sacral regulations have been since relaxed, but she must still abstain from sexual intercourse before ceremonies and must reside in the shrine together with her instruments and regalia. She never enters trance when she performs her duties, but communicates with spiritual beings while in normal consciousness.

In the same island villages are women who follow the other tradition of shamanism. These *yuta* are called to the craft by the breakdown of normal consciousness called arctic hysteria: A severe personal crisis that includes hallucinations, lunacy, sickness, nightmares. Should the potential shaman deny her call, the experiences become more and more frightening until she is driven to accept the mantle. Then the hallucinations transform themselves into second sight, the nightmares into premonitory dreams, the hysterical deafness into clairaudience—each horror into a psychic skill to be used in the craft. Like her sister shamans, the *yuta* assumes power unwillingly, but thereafter serves her community as healer, medium, and specialist in exorcism.

Whereas the *noro* tradition derives from Polynesia, the *yuta*—and the early *miko* who were so much like her—derives her rites and practices from Siberia, by way of the long peninsula of Korea, which points towards Japan. According to the *yuta* belief system, shamans are properly women, able to intermediate between the feminine sun above and the sun's daughters below. Wherever the Siberian shamanic religion is found, a sun goddess can be traced. The likelihood that these divinities are related is suggested by the cognate words for shaman found in different localities: the Okinawan *yuta*, northeast Japanese *ichiko* or *itako*, Yakut *udoyan*, Buryat *udayan*, Mongol *udagan*, Tungus *idakon*—all of which are related to the Korean word *mudang*. And so it is to Korea we must now turn, following the trail of the shamanic mirror of the sun.

Chapter Two

KOREA, SIBERIA, CHINA:
GRAND-AUNT TIGER AND THE WATER MIRROR

Late one summer, the night after a typhoon, guests were climbing Seoul's South Mountain for a *kut,* a shamanic ritual. Rock stairs led a half-mile upwards through a thickly forested hillside. A small creek gurgled to the left, and stone landings allowed an occasional respite from the long climb. Halfway up the steep hill, the thrum of the shaman's drum could be heard—and felt as much as heard. A few tortuous final stairs led to a small clearing, in the center of which stood the tiny temple.

Built in traditional Korean fashion, it was of wood with heavy paper walls, which opened at intervals to form doors and windows. The roof seemed to pull back its skirts, curving upwards in the whimsical fashion that has been the hallmark of Korean architecture for almost a thousand years. Every available surface—roof, rafters, walls, lintels—was painted in geometrical designs.

Not only was the building a celebration of color and pattern, but the three altars—for three different *mudangs* were at work on this day—were like overwrought mosaics. In the center of each was a pig's head on a plate, fixing dead eyes on the elaborate ceiling. Stacked nearby in pyramids was a feast of fresh fruit; a huge melon, carved with a *tomoe* swastica, stood on its own platter.

Behind the central altar was another, topped by rows of fans and bamboo paintings that showed the spirits to whom the *mudang* had access. As they entered, each member of the Kim family stopped to bow and offer prayers and a token monetary gift to the images of power. Off to one side, an old woman—the *ch'angpu mudang,* or music shaman—drummed. Eyes half-closed, she sang to herself, occasionally altering the song, occasionally singing a bit louder, occasionally lapsing into silence.

A barefoot latecomer stepped over the high sill of the house. She took care not to tread on the neck of the house's resident spirit, who lived in that sill, for such an offense can halt a *kut* while special ceremonies rectify the insult. The newcomer pulled a tomato-red pillow of silk brocade from a pile near the wall and squatted on it, putting her arm around the *kut* sponsor, Kim Byong, the only one of the party wearing traditional Korean dress; purple chiffon silk flowed from tight shoulders in full gathers to the ground. She had begun to cry. Her eyes were fixed on the black-draped photograph that occupied the central place on the altar, just above the sanctified pig's head. A rosette of black satin stood out like a prize atop the picture, which showed a studious, chubby face beneath black horn-rimmed glasses. Her son had been only sixteen when he died.

The *mudang*, ignoring the family, entered and began to select her garments. Part of her talent was to know in advance in what order the spirits would possess her, so that she could assume the proper garments for them. All the necessary robes were put on at the start; the *mudang* stripped them off one at a time, as each spirit passed through her body and out of it. At all times, however, she wore a *myongdo*, a solar mirror, on her belt, for that magic ornament gave her access, through the sun goddess, to spirits in the world beyond. The mirror's reflections were themselves spirits and had the power to banish other spirits; the mirror thus served also as a purifying tool.

She had been asked, on this occasion, to perform the Descent into Hell, the most serious and dangerous of all shamanic rituals—dangerous both for the boy, whose soul could be taken away to torment if anything went wrong; and for the shaman, for so strong are the visitors from the realm of the dead that some *mudang* never return to normal consciousness. But Kim Byong had decided it needed to be done, for neither the Christian nor the Buddhist funeral had set her mind at peace about her son's welfare in his new spiritual state, although the magic forty-nine days had passed since the death.

As the *mudang* costumed herself, a clamor of music from the next room was accompanied by shrieks and the clatter of weapons; a shaman already in trance was dancing in the grip of possession. In yet another part of the temple, the third shaman leapt monotonously and vigorously in her mugam, her sacred dance, her hypnotized face appearing every few seconds above the heads of the Kim women.

The shaman's assistant, the *Duichon mudang*—garbed like the sponsor in purple traditional robes—came to sit with the family and to offer counseling to the bereaved. Her sisters were anxious about Kim Byong's emotional state, for the woman still sat crooning to herself and staring at her son's picture. For twenty minutes, they listened to quiet advice from the shaman's aide about how to help their younger sister bear her loss.

As they were talking, Kim Byong suddenly sprang to her feet. She threw herself on the floor in front of the photograph, screaming her son's name. No one made a move to console her. The sisters sat, weeping quietly, a chorus of shared grief. Kim's daughter, a woman in her twenties in Western clothes who had brought her own young son, clutched her child's shoulders as she sobbed. Kim Byong thrashed and moaned, screamed and wailed. Her emotional resources momentarily exhausted, she lay quietly for a few moments, then was guided back to her pillow-seat by the shaman's assistant.

This was hardly the time, a foreigner might feel, to bring up the price of the *kut*, but in the hard-bargaining world of Seoul it was just the right time. Kim, still wiping her eyes, took out a wad of money and a personal check. The assistant shaman demurred about the check—would it be good? It was all she had, Kim said. Others in the group, following Kim Byong's lead, made monetary offerings.

The assistant shaman looked dismayed, a little disdainful. Was this all they could afford? For the most difficult *kut* of all? Didn't they realize her mistress was about to risk her sanity to perform this ritual?

The shaman herself paid no attention to the haggling—which was, in fact, an elaborate game that constitutes part of the rite. A smaller sum is donated at first, then the *mudang* extracts more; this is supposed to trick the spirits into believing the sponsor has paid an immense extra sum for the event. When Kim Byong finally handed over another wad of money, it was just as carefully paper-clipped together as the first had been, demonstrating that the money had been pre-counted, the amount prearranged.

At last the assistant shaman murmured a few words to her *mudang*. They were ready for the ritual to begin. If the assistant was in her mid-thirties, the prime celebrant was twice that. A stern-looking woman, she was considerably older than either of the other *mudang* shamanizing on that day. In an anteroom on her left, a woman looking barely thirty, chubby and with Western-styled hair, was performing acrobatic feats. In another room to her right, a hard-faced, lean woman in her fifties continued to bounce on her toes, her face a mask of concentration. The distinguished older shaman chosen by the Kims moved more deliberately than either of the other shamans, but nonetheless energetically. She began to bounce, to dance in rhythm to the drumming. Face set, eyes staring straight ahead, she seemed almost to levitate with each drumbeat, so apparently effortless was her execution of the jumps that took her eighteen inches into the air. For three-quarters of an hour the *mudang* leapt to the drum's beat.

The Kim women sat rigidly for the first half-hour, then relaxed. No less attentive, they began passing cups of tea to relieve the lassitude of the 90-degree weather that had followed a week of typhoon rains. One sat with eyes closed, her head nodding in rhythm to the drumming. Another twisted her fingers together, untwisted them, twisted them together, untwisted them. The mother sat, scowling with pain, staring at the picture of her son.

Suddenly the shaman grabbed a pitchfork from the wall near the altar and began thrusting it about. No consciousness seemed to inhabit her eyes. At this point she was under the guidance of the first spirit—a "literary spirit" or gentle helper—who had urged her to cleanse the room of evil influences. She stabbed the pitchfork into each corner, seemingly oblivious to the people crouched there, but without injuring anyone. For nearly twenty minutes she continued to purify the room, bouncing high on her toes as she did so. Then she grabbed knives and cleared the evil influences that might, like threads, be clinging to Kim Byong. She paused momentarily, and went around the room asking for further donations, which were willingly given.

When the performance resumed, she tore off both hat and blue outer robe to reveal a lemon-yellow silk robe and a mirror-belt beneath. For hours now she would give her body over to the various ancestral spirits of the Kims. She spoke in their voices, urging one sister to stop being such a spendthrift, another to take better care of family obligations. Occasionally a newly arriving spirit would demand a certain garment, and the shaman's assistant would scurry to find it for the *mudang* to put on. By the time all the ancestors had had their say, it was mid-afternoon. The lunch break was near. Kim Byong was not only anxious and intensely sorrowful but proud, for her missing son had not appeared during the *kut*'s second section. Had he been nearby, with his family's other shades, he would certainly have spoken. That he did not showed she was right to sponsor this *kut* for him. He might be in dire trouble in the world beyond; the shaman would have to reach him there to resolve it. Sometimes, it is a special desire left unsatisfied that causes a spirit to be unwilling to rest; sometimes, it is merely that the natural course of life has been interrupted. Four victims of the 1983 Korean Air Lines tragedy were believed by their families to be restless in the grave because they had died unmarried. Two of these were female flight attendants on the downed plane; the other two, young male passengers. With the airline's aid the families found each other and arranged first for marriage ceremonies called *konnyong kut* for the "couples," who are not known to have met in the flesh.

Before departing the *mudang* 's body, the possessing ancestral spirits dined upon the sacred foods, the *chesa*, set out on the altar. To earthly eyes, the food looked untouched, but in fact it was blessed by the spirits' consumption. Sacramentally the Kim family partook of the foods eaten by their ancestors, then were pleased to see a traditional, spicy Korean meal appear from the temple kitchen.

Because of the length and intensity of the ritual, attendees slipped away now and again—to have a cigarette or a cola, to walk across the clearing and listen to the wailing cicadas rather than the shamanic drums, to descend into the city to run a few family errands. But Kim Byong had not left the *kut* for a moment. During the midday break she walked out with her sisters, away from the building, to rest on an out-cropping of rocks there.

When the *kut* resumed, the shaman's assistant performed the third act; a *kut* of this kind is so long that several shamans may share duties. The post-lunch dance was that of the martial spirits, which cause great commotion when they occupy a shaman. For this reason, the primary *mudang* had given it over to her apprentice in order to husband strength for the difficult last act. The young woman began with the usual dance, calmly bouncing two feet into the air for nearly twenty minutes before possession took hold. She grabbed a pair of knives and did a slow back-bend as she kept rhythm with her stamping feet. She writhed upright, leaping almost to the low roof of the building. Still leaping, shouting loudly, she thrust the knives about. Several martial spirits possessed her in turn, demanding physical feats that required not only strength and agility but impressive stamina. By the time this section of the *kut* ended, dusk was falling on Seoul. The assistant shaman sank down exhausted. The primary shaman had recovered sufficiently from her four-hour morning performance to again invoke the spirits for the final, and most important, part of the day's events. Kim Byong rose and bowed to the altar, tears in her eyes but not on her cheeks. The emotional extravagance of the day had worn out even the poignancy of a mother's grief. The shaman purified the air, the altar, the participants. For a moment, the atmosphere seemed calm after the pandemonium wrought by the martial spirits.

Then eerily, from behind the altar, something dark arose—a suit of men's clothing, a suit worn by the dead boy, borne on the arms of the assistant shaman. Kim Byong's eyes overflowed.

The *mudang* ceremoniously took the clothes and began to dance. At first it was as though she were dancing with the boy, holding his suit out from her body. But slowly the clothes swept closer to her; slowly the boy's spirit came into the *mudang*'s body. The Kim family watched with a sort of dreadful attentiveness. The drums kept up their insistent accompaniment. The shaman danced slowly, making boyish gestures, her gait changing.

Darkness fell. Neon flickered across the valley of Seoul. Kim Byong began to cry softly. The *mudang* turned to her with a look of surprise. "Mother?" she asked—in a changed voice, the voice of a man.

Kim gasped. Her sisters held her shoulders to keep her from leaping on the shaman. The *mudang* continued to dance slowly, speaking softly, manfully, to the weeping woman. His mother had grown too distant from the old rites, he told her. His soul had not rested until she sought out a *mudang* to perform this ritual. She must not lapse from belief again. And then the *Nokjuli*, the "talk of the soul," ended; the black clothing dropped slowly to the ground, revealing the *mudang* in a robe of white silk. She began to whirl, singing in the voice of an angel. The Kim women called out their goodbyes to the boy they had loved. Ringing a small bell and waving huge pompoms of white paper as she danced, the *mudang* embodied the spirits of the heavenly angels who bore the boy away—

And suddenly fell to the ground writhing. Her assistant threw a multicolored cloak over her, and she struggled into it as she twisted and was twisted by the new spirit that had entered her body. The most dangerous part of the *kut* had begun. Iljik Saja, the messenger of Hell, had taken over the shaman's body to steal the boy's soul for perpetual damnation— and the *mudang*'s soul, too, if he could get away with it. In a flash the shaman was on her feet, lunging for the altar with its sacred *chesa* and the white paper on which the deceased's soul was resting.

The shaman was screaming. The fury she embodied seemed unearthly. But one of the Kim sisters bravely interposed herself between the *mudang* and the altar. A fight ensued, and it was no easy victory for the sister, for the shaman had acquired superhuman strength in this new possession. Several sisters grabbed parts of the shaman's robe and tried to guide her to the lower altar, to the unclean foods. Thrashing and screaming, the possessed *mudang* finally was dragged to the pig's head—which she fell upon and devoured.

The danger that Iljik Saja would steal the boy's soul had been averted. Restored to herself, the *mudang* donned a mask and a green robe with striped sleeves and began to recite the story of Pali Kongju, the rejected seventh daughter of a king, who, although abandoned by her parents, made the trip to the other world for the magic water they needed for salvation. After the tempestuous possessions of the two previous sections of the *kut*, the legend of Pali Kongju calmed the watchers and prepared them for the anxious moment that closed the day.

Tenderly, the *mudang* lifted a cloth that covered a tiny mound of rice flour. This was the climactic moment: the family would soon know if their beloved son's soul had indeed been set to rest. The alternatives were terrible. If a snake pattern appeared in the rice, it meant that the family had miscalculated the time for the *kut*, which would then have to be restaged at a more auspicious time. Worse, no patterns at all would mean the soul was utterly lost, wandering in some empty, unreachable world of spirits.

In the silent room the anxiety was palpable. Then the *mudang* spoke. The rice flour, she said slowly, bore the marks of butterfly wings. The boy's soul was free.

Kim Byong wept again, this time with relief as well as with grief. Slowly the *kut* closed, and the women of the Kim family stumbled into the hot darkness, down the steep stone steps to the traffic noise that reminded them of the everyday duties they had left behind twelve hours earlier, when they mounted to Kooksadang, the spirit-shrine, for the Descent into Hell.[1]

On every auspicious day in the year, such rituals are enacted in Seoul and in smaller Korean communities where the sun goddess is served by female shamans who follow the old religion of *sinkyo*, which like Shinto is the aboriginal belief system of the area. *Sinkyo* is, in fact, the probable ancestor of Shinto; Japanese scripture suggests that Amaterasu, her mirror, and her dancing shamans originated in Korea, from which, in 27 B.C.E., the Japanese princess Ama-no-hikoko brought a sun-mirror.

Korean female shamans, called by the general term *mudang* ("dancer") or by the honorific *manshin* ("summoner of ten thousand spirits"), come from two traditions, which parallel those found in Japan. Southern-tradition shamans, *Tan'gol mudangs*—like the *noro* of Japan's Ryukyu Islands—derive their powers from hereditary access to certain spirits; the power can be passed on to a daughter or daughter-in-law. Many of the *tan'gol mudang's* activities revolve around the celebration of calendar feasts, for which she earns a small fee from her community; she can also, on occasion, perform rituals for individuals, although this is more generally the domain of the northern shaman. These latter, like the

Ryukyuan *yuta* and the Ainu *tsusu*, are self-selected by *shinbyong* or "spirit sickness" before being initiated by a practitioner. Located historically in the territory that is now North Korea, this tradition is the predominant one today in Seoul, to which many northern *mudang* fled to escape Communist suppression of their craft.

Persecution of shamans is nothing new to Korea. The country's strategic location between China and Japan led to invasion and occupation by both. When the Chinese arrived, bringing Confucianism and later Buddhism, they tried to eliminate the native religion. During the five centuries of the Chosen Dynasty, which began in 1392, officials attempted to replace shamanism with Confucianism as the state religion; the *mudang* was allowed to survive marginally a healer, because no provision had been made to school doctors. In 1409 C.E., all shamanic books were burned; in 1472, the shamans themselves were driven from Seoul. During this era, shamanism was considered the social equivalent of prostitution. Noble women who suffered the spirit sickness were killed—forced to drink poison by their families—or imprisoned (even walled into their rooms) and starved to death in their own homes. Though they could not themselves shamanize, well-born women patronized the craft; even queens relied on *mudangs* for rituals and advice. Most famous was Queen Min of the Yi Dynasty; she elevated her personal *mudang* to the status of princess and attempted to organize all the shamans in Korea; unfortunately, she was assassinated and her reforms reversed. When Japan took control of Korea early in this century, colonial officials attempted forcibly to convert shamanic believers to Shinto. But the *mudang* survived. She went underground.

The end of colonial rulership did not, at first, bring much change. In the North, the dictator Kim Il-sung made it his mission to end all religious practices save a token Buddhism. Shamanism in Communist Korea ended with the flight of thousands of *mudangs* across the border to Seoul. Since the 1950s these *mudangs* and their initiates have formed the basis of South Korean shamanism.

The new democracy in Seoul did not welcome the refugee shamans with open arms. The republic's first president, Sgyman Rhee, was a Christian convert who discouraged practice of the native religion. Then Park Chung-Hee, during his eighteen-year regime, actively suppressed it, sending police to break up the *kuts*. But the Fifth Republic, dedicated under its 1980 constitution to preserving Korean cultural heritage, now permits public announcement of the *kuts*; dedicatory rituals led by *mudangs* have opened several new skyscrapers in Seoul. Yet, like Native

American tribal dances, these new public performances, while they indicate the end of the darkest days of persecution, do not mean the new government actively supports or approves of the old religion.[2]

In Korea, shamanism remains a secret women's religion, as it has been during most of its three-thousand-year-old history. In Korean legend, shamanism was originated by a woman. The story of "Princess Thrown-Away," Pali Kongju—told during the *kut*—is the most famous origin tale; another tells of a Holy Mother who had eight daughters, whom she taught to shamanize and who later spread the craft through the peninsula. Dating to the middle of the Silla Dynasty, approximately 1500 B.C.E., these stories show how early was the connection between shamanism and women.

This connection remains. A few men, called *paksu*, dress as women to shamanize; a few men attend the ceremonies; even fewer commission the *kuts*. Today's believers are almost all women, who support women clergy and attend virtually all-women rites. Their religion, despite loosening restrictions, remains secretive. The combination of long-term legal marginality and the yearning so many Koreans feel towards Western culture means that today's *kuts*, while open to all, are not easy to locate, especially for the Western visitor. Although it has been estimated that half of Korea's households have shamanic connections, a Korean host may deny knowing anything about the practice; a tourist center will, with assurance, tell you the craft has died out and direct you to Korea House to see folk dancing; helpful clerks at your hotel, who yesterday understood English perfectly, today can make no sense of your questions. Yet one of the most active shamanic sites, the Kooksadang Temple, is but a short subway ride from the center of Seoul. There in a crowded, old-fashioned neighborhood, any auspicious day will find a single *mudang*, or two of them, or even more, dancing themselves into entrancement.

The *kut* used to be performed at the home of the sponsor—for each ritual is essentially a lengthy danced petition, paid for by a client— but several factors have led to the decline of this tradition. Noise-abatement laws have been enacted in an attempt to quench the din of nearly twelve million people; hours of drumming could lead a neighbor to complain. And shamanism has become an embarrassment to enough Koreans, including husbands and neighbors who practice newer religions, that women often hesitate to acknowledge their connection to the craft. Finally, the curious or unbelieving can more easily be discouraged from attending rituals held in the private temples, whereas a neighborhood *kut* is by tradition open to any who enter.

A traditional *kut* can be offered for the intention of bearing a healthy child, in which case one of the Birth Grandmothers will be called into the room. Modern Koreans sometimes schedule *kuts* for help with college entrance examinations or job interviews, or for other non-traditional reasons. And, although the craft brings neither wealth nor high status with it, it still attracts new applicants. In the past decade an adolescent girl stunned the *mudang* community—which in Seoul alone includes one hundred thousand shamans—by dancing on the knives. The ritual is just as it sounds: A barefoot shaman walks, leaps and dances on the blades of sharp swords. If the shaman is completely possessed, she avoids injury; her feet are not even nicked. Knife-dancing is the severest test of a shaman's ability to attain and maintain trance. The twelve-year-old girl, dubbed "the littlest *mudang*," showed the prowess she had attained in six years of training and was prophecied a great future in the craft.[3]

When the *mudang* dances, she wears the mirror of the sun goddess on her belt, like her sister shamans in Japan and Siberia, and watches sun-patterns in a water-mirror. She divines using the mirror; she sees visions of the sun, dancing on the wall of her house, as part of the spirit sickness that precedes her initiation. Despite a millennium of Buddhist and Confucian repression, the solar attributes of Korean shamanism remain—and so does the myth of the sun goddess, which was told in Korea prehistory, when, H. G. Underwood claims, religion was "the worship of the heavens, (with) absolutely no mention of any other spirits or lesser divinities."[4]

The sun goddess's myth is told in the *yennai yaegi*, Korea's "old tales." The luminary, the tales say, was once the girl Hae-soon. She lived with her mother and sisters, Dael-soon and Byul-soon, in an isolated valley filled with tigers. The mother often warned the girls to beware of the giant cats.

One day the mother set off to market, across the hills to the next valley. Warning the girls again about tigers, she left them. After finishing her marketing, she bought buckwheat pancakes as a treat for her little ones.

She started home, and around the first bend she met a tiger.

"What's in that box?" the tiger asked the mother.

"Buckwheat pancakes," she said.

"Give me one, or I'll eat you up!" said the tiger. Naturally, the mother gave it one.

Around the next bend was another tiger—or so the mother thought. Actually, it was the same greedy beast, but tigers all look alike to their victims.

"What is in that box?" the tiger asked the mother.

"Buckwheat pancakes," she said.

"Well, then, give me one, or I'll eat you up!" said the tiger. Naturally, the mother gave it one.

And around the next bend was the tiger again, and around the next bend again, and around the next, until all the pancakes were gone. Then there the tiger was again, around the next bend. "What are you carrying?"

"It's a box, you nasty, greedy creature!" said the mother.

"Give it to me to eat, or I'll eat you up!" said the tiger. And so the mother handed it over.

She walked along, swinging her arms, eager to get home. Around the next bend was the tiger.

"What is that swinging by your side?" asked the tiger.

"Why, it's my arm!" exclaimed the mother.

"Give it to me or I'll eat you up!" said the tiger. So the mother had to cut off her arm and give it to the tiger.

Around the next bend was the tiger who wanted—you guessed it, the other arm. Bleeding and desperate, the mother continued towards home.

Around the next bend was—the tiger again. "What are those things under your skirt?" it asked.

In great fear, the mother said, "My legs, of course."

"Give me one, or I'll eat you up!"

"But if I give you one, I won't be able to get home!"

"You can hop, can't you?" And the tiger ate her leg.

The woman hopped to the next bend. There was the tiger again. "Give me your other leg, or I'll eat you up!"

"But then I'll never get home!" the woman squealed.

"You can roll, can't you?" And the tiger ate the mother's other leg.

She was starting to roll away home when the tiger lost patience and ate her all up. Then she—for it was a tigress—dressed up in the mother's clothes and went to eat up her children. But they had locked the door.

"Children, it's your mother!" the tiger called.

But the voice didn't sound right, so the girls didn't open the door. Hael-soon called out, "Your voice is different from mother's."

"Why, I've been in the market crying out to sell our vegetables," the tiger said slyly.

Dael-soon came to the door and looked out. Through the peekhole she could see a big red eye. It didn't look like their mother's.

"Why is your eye so red? My mother has beautiful eyes," the girl said.

"I got red pepper in my eyes at the market!" the tiger said with impatience. "Don't worry, just let me in!"

But Byul-soon also did not believe the caller. "Put your hand through the window if you are our mother," she said. The tiger put a big yellow-haired paw through the window, and the girls knew this was not their mother.

"Wait just a moment, Mommy," the girls called out, and sneaked out the back door and climbed a tree. As they clung to the branches they heard the tiger break into the house. But she did not find them. And so the girls thought that they were safe.

But the tiger came outside at last. There she saw the girls, reflected in the shining water of a well at the bottom of the tree. She was such a stupid tiger that she thought it was the children themselves, deep under the water.

"Poor little children," she said. "How will I ever get you out?" The tiger began to scoop up the water, trying to capture the reflections. This stupidity made the children laugh out loud, and the tiger looked up to see them hanging in the treetop.

"Oh, there you are, children! You mustn't do that. It's very dangerous. I must get you down," said the tiger. But she didn't know how to do it. "How did you get up there?" she asked the children.

"Oil," they answered. "You have to go back to the kitchen and get oil and smear it all over the trunk." The tiger did so. Then of course she couldn't climb up the tree because it was so slippery. So she went back to get a saw to carve steps into the wood.

The children were frightened. They began to pray. "Please, someone. If you don't wish us to die, send down a Heavenly Iron Chain. But if you wish us to die, send down a Rotten Straw Rope!" At once a heavenly chain appeared, and the children scampered to safety in the sky.

The tiger heard them and saw them escape. She was not worried. When she'd finished carving steps and had ascended the tree, she called out to the heavens, "Please send the Rotten Straw Rope if I am to live, and the Heavenly Chain if I am to die." The tiger thought that, in punishment for her evil deeds, the gods would send the opposite of what she requested.

But gods are cleverer than tigers; they answered her prayer just as she had prayed it.

It was dark. The tiger didn't know that she was climbing up on a rotten straw rope—until it broke and she fell to her death.

The girls lounged around heaven until they were told they must work. So they found jobs: Hae-sun became the sun, Dael-soon the moon, Byun-soon a star. Hae-sun was the most modest of the three. Her first day as the sun, she looked down and saw people looking up at her. Unable to bear scrutiny, she grew brighter and brighter, until no one could bear to look at her directly.

There are many variants of "The Tale of Grand-Aunt Tiger." In some, there are two children, in others three; in some, the children are all girls, in others, they are of both sexes. Consistently, however, it is the devoured mother's daughter—never the son—who becomes the sun. In one tale, her brother tells Hae-soon that the sun's nature is masculine, and therefore she has to become the moon. They begin to fight, and the brother puts out the sister's eyes. Then, full of remorse, he lets her become the sun. In a third version, the pricking out of the goddess's eyes occurrs because of sheer nastiness on her brother's part; their mother puts the brother into a cell to starve him and puts the girl in heaven as the sun.[5]

Grand-Aunt Tiger herself descended from these early goddesses who were connected to the sun. Though the tale has many variations, there are constants: the mother's murder, the great cat, the well, the tree. Behind an apparently whimsical story we can detect an archaic religious myth in which the cosmic mother is torn apart, or tears herself apart, to form the universe; her daughter-double becomes the sun, her head shining through the treetops to be mirrored in well water. Shamans, attempting to transcend mundane consciousness, evoked the tiger and her sun-daughter as universal powers. We will see variations of this myth in Egypt and Ireland, two other lands where the sun goddess appeared as a cat.

The tale of Grand-Aunt Tiger is widespread in China, Taiwan and southern Japan as well as in Korea—all places where we find traces of an aboriginal pan-Asian tiger-cult. Early Korean historians say their ancestors "worshiped the tiger spirit"; more recent historians, like H. Hulbert, claim the tiger as the original deity of the Korean people. At the same time, the fact that the earliest Koreans worshiped only the heavens and "no lesser divinities" suggests that this tiger spirit lived in the heavens as the sun herself. This tiger-sun was, like Amaterasu, an ancestral mother of the matrilineal ancient Koreans; when she did not herself give birth to humanity, she brought the man who, mating with the only woman in the world, created all people.[6] Connections between sun and tiger occur also in Maylasia, where the tiger spirit is invoked whenever the shaman wishes to enter trance. Throughout Southeast Asia, the Tiger Ancestor is the mythical initiator of all shamans; Mircea Eliade traces the image to the most archaic strata of myth.

Even in China we find the tiger and her shamans. There, despite what Sukie Colgrave calls an ancient matriarchy, Confucian and Buddhist influences meant that in official mythology the sun represents the cosmic male force, the yin. But folklore remnants, like Grand-Aunt Tiger—or the tale that the sun is a boat guided by the shaman Lo Tze Fang, who climbed a tree till she reached the sky—continue an early Chinese tradition of the female sun. And some tribespeople maintained their sun goddess in legend. The Ch'uan Miao, for instance, told the story of the woman Na Bo Nok'o, who sewed up the sky and then brought out "the sister sun." This sun goddess, the folktales say, "went through a cave before she got out," suggesting a connection with Amaterasu of the Sky-Rock Cave.

In predynastic China, the source of these tales, we find a tradition of female shamans called *wu*—a name related to the *mu* in *mudang*—who were persecuted out of existence by the Han dynasty Confucians. The wu's cat-sun-goddess was demoted into a demon: the Great Mother of the West, a tiger-toothed woman with a leopard's tail, said to live in a mountain cave. But the sweeter aspects of the sun goddess remained in people's memories. In 1934, folklorists in China, who recorded the tales and songs of schoolchildren, found that the sun was a girl who lived in a house with much gold. In Peking, a folksong linked the golden sun-girl with tree and well:

> My little golden sister rides a golden horse.
> Refusing to gallop, the golden horse is beaten with a golden whip.
> In the glass well there is a gold toad. On the tree there is a gold crow. When the door of the temple opens there sits golden Buddha; in the gold-plated hands there is a gold-plated girl baby.

The glass well of the third line is the sun's original water mirror, and the toad—as we shall see in Part Two—is elsewhere connected with the sun goddess.[7]

In "Grand-Aunt Tiger," we see water—the well—as a solar mirror. Before the invention of metallurgy and glass-making, water was the world's only reflective surface. Japanese tradition recalls this when it says that, in primordial times, before the forging of Amaterasu's mirror, the sun *kami* used "The Mirror of the Land" and "The Mirror of the Deep" to admire her beauty; that is, she saw her light reflected in pools and lakes on the land, and in the dark ocean as well.

The sun's image in water is, mythically, the sun herself, for a mirror is magically whatever it reflects. Or, even more magically, the mirror is the soul or essence of what it reflects. Sir James George Frazer told of a pool of water that was said to kill anyone who gazed into it; a spirit living there stole reflected souls. Guianians believed you could see your soul in a mirror, if that mirror was another's eye. Disturbing water into which someone is gazing, according to the same belief system, can shatter the soul.

Mirror magic crosses cultures. The Aztecs, to keep away intruders, put a pot of water near the door with a knife resting in it, on the theory that a robber, seeing his image punctured, would flee in terror. In Russia, Cheremiss women prayed to their mirror after grooming, "Take not from me my appearance or image." And the famous Greek romance of Narcissus reflects the belief that it is dangerous to gaze too long at the mirrored surface of a pool.[8]

When a culture moves from the Stone Age—the age of the water-mirror—to the Bronze Age, metal mirrors are among the first objects produced by the new smiths. Most archeologists assume these to be simply grooming aids. But a really sharp knife to carve meat, a sword for self-defense, a set of good light hunting arrows—any of these would be more important than a reflecting surface for hair styling and the application of colored muds. And a toilet mirror, if that's what the primeval smith intended, could more easily be a square sheet of metal than a round one. It is clear, as the story of Amaterasu indicates, that the first polished metal mirrors were fashioned to echo the shape and brilliance of the sun's disc; even today we refer to the "face" of a mirror, meaning its surface, just as we refer to the "face" of the personified sun. Mirrors were invented as ritual sun-traps to bring the sun goddess to earth, for if the image is the essence, the sunshine in the mirror is the goddess herself.

Once artificial mirrors were created, beliefs about water-mirrors were transferred to them; the mirror became a soul-trap. New superstitions grew up: A bride must never look into a mirror on her wedding day, lest she be stolen from the earth; mirrors must be turned to the wall in a sick-room, lest the hapless sufferer lose her soul; mirrors must be covered in a house of death, to keep ghosts from stealing the souls of the survivors. One magical belief has survived to the present: Breaking a mirror puts one's soul in jeopardy for seven years.

The mirror goddess found in East Asia appears in Asia's southern peninsula as well. A solar shamanism practiced in Mysore, India, probably descends from the same Asiatic source as the *mudang* religion. People of Mysore worship a deity named Bisal-Mariamna, "the Power of

Sunlight," whose symbol is a brass pot full of water, called *kunna-kannadi*, or "eye-mirror." Into the pot are put pepper leaves and coconut flowers, and a small metal mirror leans against it. The image of the sun-mother who fosters plant growth and thus, human life, though her light is here combined with the water mirror and its artificial descendant. One of seven sister goddesses, Bisal-Mariamna is worshiped in an unroofed shrine into which sunlight pours, and her mirror is used in this and neighboring cities as an auspicious part of any religious ceremony. As in other parts of Asia, the intention is to bring the sun-goddess into her worshipers' midst by mirror magic.

The Minyong, another Indian tribal group, told a lovely tale about the sun goddess. She was the daughter of earth and sky, and sister to the moon. She was born after her father, beaten in a fight, ran away to the highest heavens. The deserted earth could not even bear to look at her daughters, so she gave them to another woman to nurse.

As the girls grew, they began to glow. Day after day they grew brighter and brighter. The two shining daughters were devoted to their nurse. When she died, they were so stricken that they died, too. And light died with them.

On earth, humans grew afraid in the prolonged darkness. Thinking the nurse might have stolen the light, they dug up her body. But it had rotted away—all except the eyes, which mirrored back two women who were standing near the body. The people, thinking that they saw the dead goddesses in the eye-mirrors, took the eyes to a stream and washed them for five days and five nights. This made the eyes shine brighter, but the images remained. So they got a carpenter, who carefully cut out the images from the reflecting eyes. They jumped to life and became two young girls.

The girls were called Bomong and Bong. They were so precious that the people kept them inside at all times. But Bomong, dressing herself up in the brightest clothes and the most splendid jewelry she could gather, ran away. The minute she went out of the house, light shone all over the world. She went over the mountains and did not return.

Bong went to look for her, following her footsteps. But as soon as she came out, the brilliance of her light made rocks crack, trees wither, and people faint. As long as she was out, the heat was unbearable. She was a sun like her sister, but a much mightier sun.

After a council of people and animals, a frog hunter was set after Bong. He waited patiently, and when she came along he shot her in each side. Her death made the heat ease so that people could move about on the earth again. They still had Bomong's heat and light, which was sufficient.

The body of Bong lay for a long time where it had fallen, until a rat took it on his back and dragged it to Bomong. Seeing her sister dead, the sun wept in sorrow and terror—for she was certain that the frog would come for her, too. Bomong took a new turn in the sky and traveled on a path no one had ever seen her take. Then she found a place no one knew, and sat there and put a big stone on her head.

Because of the shadow of this stone, the whole world became dark.

Those who dwelled on earth were frightened. They started, humans and animals, to search for light. A rat, a wild bird and a cock were sent to find the sun. The cock had trouble walking, because his penis was so heavy, so he cut it off and it turned into an earthworm. His load lightened, he went on and found the sun goddess and begged her to return. "No," she said. "They killed my sister and they'll kill me. I'll only come back if my sister returns to life."

The cock went back with this news to the council. A carpenter was called and charged with remaking the body of Bong. He made it smaller and breathed life back into it. She was as good as new, only now she was a moon.

When the news was brought to Bomong that her sister was alive again, she flung the stone from her head and rose into the sky. All the animals rejoiced, especially the cock, who sang "kookoo" as he saw the sun, as he still does every morning.[9]

There are recollections of the Japanese sun myth here: A sister's loss causes the sun's withdrawal; the goddess hides under a stone, like Amaterasu behind the door of the Sky-Rock Cave; the mirror is the image of the goddess. But this legend, with its clear ties to Japan and Korea, is connected as well to another Asian region. The tale calls to mind the shamanic religion of Siberia.

In the massive literature on this religion, only rarely is the femininity of the Siberian sun mentioned. But the cosmology of the region is clearly enough summed up by the Siberian woman M. P. Molina: "Where it is warm, there are women in general; where it is cold, there is an old man." In scattered settlements across the Russian arctic and subarctic lived people of several different cultures, but all Siberians—Finnic, Turkic and Eskimo Siberians alike—believed in the femininity of the sun, which their shamans served and invoked.

It is known that Siberian and Korean shamanism are related, and that the Japanese *miko* is related to Siberian shamanism via Korea. But scholars have done little comparative study of these "sun cults," despite obvious links among them—the clearest link being the solar mirror that appears in all these related cults. Both Siberian and Altaic myths connect the sun goddess to mirrors.

Long ago, Siberian storytellers relate, there was no sun or moon, but no one minded. People could fly, and their luminous flight produced enough light and heat to keep the world comfortable. But some people began to sicken, and the world grew dark and cold. Full of pity, the creator sent a spirit who stirred the ocean with a pole ten thousand fathoms long. From the disturbed depths sprang two goddesses and their *toli*, or shamanic mirrors—the sun and the moon.

Even after Christianization, this vision of the sun as a mirror continued, but then it became God—not the shaman—who used the luminary as an omniscient mirror. The sun allowed God to see everything happening on earth; an eclipse was caused by God's cleansing of the mirror; the sun shone so brightly because God was too glorious to look at.

Siberian mythology holds clues for understanding that of Japan as well as Korea. The vision of the sun goddess hiding in the cave may have originated in the arctic, where the sun disappears for as long as several months; the Siberians, who said the sun was hiding, were not frightened by her absence. To bid her farewell each fall, the Tavgi Samoyeds, or Nganasans, butchered a white reindeer and hung its hide, head and hooves on a south-facing tree. When the sun-mother Kou-njami returned, another sacrifice welcomed her back. As long as she was above the horizon, in the short arctic summers, the Nenets did not shoot arrows—or, later, guns—into the air, even when hunting birds. The sun was the eye of the heavens, they said; they did not want to accidentally blind her.

The mirror of the sun goddess probably reached Japan from Siberia through Korea, for Siberian peoples not only told myths of a mirror-sun but constructed images of her as well. The matriarchal Khanty and Mansi built mirror-sun goddess figures from metal soup plates imported from as far south as Iran. Sometimes the plates were engraved, in which case the sun's face had odd hunting scenes or other decorations across it. A cloth body and a headdress were all that were necessary to make the plate into an image of the sun. Some wealthy women wore mirrors and similar metal ornaments in their own headdresses on ritual occasions when, as mothers of the people, they were identified with the great sun mother.

In addition to similarities in the myths of Siberia, Japan and Korea, there are similarities in ritual practice as well. One is that Siberian women as well as men can shamanize, as long as they are called to the difficult, usually dreaded role by the breakdown of normal consciousness that ceases only when the new shaman, in a new body constructed during her visionary trance, puts on the mantle decked with the sun goddess's mirror. Although in recent history Siberian shamans were men, they were originally women; the metal breast cups and women's hair braids are worn by all shamans in recognition of this.

In Siberian shamanic ritual, songs were sung to the sun goddess:

> At the campfire I want to shamanize
> To the center of the earth,
> To mother morning.
> Go according to the sun!
> To little mother morning
> Direct your steps!
> Children, children!
> Go with the sun! —Diszengi & Hoppal, p. 360.

Some of these chants to the sun-mother are extremely tender:

> O Lady my Mother, Show me my faults and the roads
> That I must follow! Fly before me, following a broad road;
> Prepare my way for me! O Spirits of the Sun who dwell in the
> South on the nine wooded hills, O Mothers of Light, you who
> know Jealousy, I implore you: may your three shadows remain high,
> very high! —Eliade, Shamanism, p. 321.

In all three areas, the craft of shamanism is traced to a magical female: in Japan, to Uzume; in Korea, to Pali Kongju; in Siberia, to a woman who mated with eagles. And, central to each tradition, there is the shaman's mirror. In a Samoyed initiation vision recorded by A. A. Popov, the shaman-to-be was given power by two women in a mirror-covered cave. What seemed to be a fire within the cave the shaman discovered to be sunlight, coming from a hole in the cave's roof. When shamanizing, the man mentally turned back towards this magical cave of sunlight, mirrors and luminous women. *Ibid.*, p. 41.

The Siberian shaman, like the *mudang* and the *miko*, must wear or hold the magic solar mirror; the sewn-in mirror on shamanic garb is the single most magical component of the Shaman's attire. In fact, Mircea Eliade points out, a shaman can dispense with any other parts of the regalia and still contact the spirits; without the mirror, however, no contact is possible. Among the Buryat, the shaman's sacred regalia includes a *toli*, or mirror engraved with twelve figures—the zodiacal animals controlled by the sun goddess as Mistress of Beasts. The mirror was adopted into shamanic costume almost upon its invention, as the Japanese *haniwa* portrait-statues attest.

The shaman wears the mirror of the sun goddess to trap sunlight, thereby inducing the goddess's attendance at the ritual. The mirror also allows the shaman psychic access to information otherwise hidden. The sun, the Siberians say, reflects everything that happens on earth. The mirror, therefore—the sun's image—can be used to find out anything, however distant. It is as though the sun is an all-seeing heavenly eye and the mirror, its double, shares in its visionary powers.

Sometimes the mirror is called "the white horse of the shaman": It is like a steed that conveys the shaman anywhere she wishes, to observe whatever is happening. Sometimes the mirror is, as among the Nganasans, the eye of heaven: The mirror can "see" things, the human eye is a mirror.[10]

Not only in Siberia, but across Europe, mirrors are seen in this magical way. "Scrying" is the art of divining the past, the future, or distant events in the present, through the use of a mirror surface. Ordinary mirror gazing is called catoptromancy; crystallomancy is the art of the crystal ball. Solar wells are used in hydromancy; cyclicomancy uses cups of dark liquid (blood is good; wine will do). Finally, onychomancy is the art of seeing the future reflected in the polished nails of a virgin. The ancient Celts used small crystal stones to tell fortunes; Greek doctors hung mirrors over sacred wells to diagnose illnesses. German peasants used mirrors to scry unmet spouses. The Aztecs used obsidian mirrors; the Mayans used quartz crystal; bowls of badger blood sufficed for the Pawnee.[11]

Mirror knowledge goes beyond seeing things distant in space or time; it extends to the self. Honesty and self-knowledge are symbolized by the mirror, which is why we call someone deep in thought "reflective." A Japanese proverb embodies this insight. "When the mirror is dim," it cautions, "the soul is unclean." European folklore is full of mirrors that tell the truth, no matter how painful to the listener; Snow White's wicked stepmother knew this when she approached her mirror to ask, "Who's the fairest of them all?"

Mirrors, that fairy tale makes clear, know everything: They know distant as well as near, future as well as past. And so, it follows, mirrors can change the future—they can be used in healing as well as in divination. To see how this can be, we must travel across half a world to the healing waters of the Egyptian desert, near the sun goddess's shrine at Dendera. There we'll discover how water, the earth's mirror to the sun, became infused with her healing properties and provided a means to alter the future.

Chapter Three

EGYPT:

DANCERS BEARING HATHOR'S MIRROR

The magic of mirrors has today been virtually lost, save in the odd superstition or metaphor. Churches are no longer hung with mirrors, which are considered utterly secular; homes, however, have them in plenty, as do shops and markets. Vast sheets of silvered glass decorate restroom walls—a far cry from the past, when tiny metal hand-mirrors rested on home altars, and temple rituals made use of huge mirrored sun-traps.

Today's glass mirrors are made from a process invented by the Phoenicians several millennia ago, lost, and rediscovered in Europe during the Middle Ages. During the interim, mirrors were made of metal in the style introduced to Greece from Egypt, where they represented the goddess Hathor. A typical early Egyptian mirror has the goddess's body forming the handle; from her head rises a shiny metal disc. The handmirror in this way reproduced the image of Hathor seen in tomb paintings and funerary statues, the solar orb surmounting her head. Worn like a headdress, the hieroglyphic sun-circle appeared sometimes opaque, sometimes clearly reflective; sometimes the sun appeared in the form of the ankh, originally a hieroglyph of the mirror as emblem of the soul.

The world's earliest known mirror was from Egypt: a slate disc from 4500 B.C.E. found in hi-Badari, some 250 miles south of today's Cairo. Dull when dry, it could be wetted to form a slick reflective surface. The earliest extant metal mirror was also found in Egypt, in a First Dynasty grave that dates between 2930 and 2700 B.C.E. Because of its ankh shape, it is thought to be Hittite in origin, for Anatolian engravings show such pear-shaped mirrors. After the Egyptians set up their own mirror factories during the Fourth Dynasty, which lasted from 2575 to 2415 B.C.E., the polished metal was cast as a circle—the solar shape[1].

Two huge displays of these mirrors could, until recently, be seen in the British Museum. In one were the small mirrors used for personal devotion and adornment; the other held foot-wide ritual mirrors. Dating from as early as the First Dynasty, the domestic mirrors had as handles the goddess—shown as a slender girl holding out a piece of fruit or a papyrus blossom to her worshiper. Sometimes Hathor's head alone formed the handle, in which case her cow horns rose on each side of the reflecting surface. As you looked into such a mirror, the disc of Hathor, balanced above her body, became your own face.

This Egyptian style of hand-mirror was reproduced for thousands of years. Long after the Pharoahs were gone, Greek and Roman mirrors showed a goddess in the same posture: one hand and one foot thrust forward, a direct gaze, a tender smile. Around the mirror atop her head were suspended, like charms, birds and cherubs and animals. Although the mystical meaning of the mirror was probably forgotten by this time, the hand-mirror was still made in the shape of the sun goddess.

Egypt's ritual mirrors were huge metal circles engraved with prayers and petitions to the goddess; one tells us it was created by the gods Ptah and Sokaris, under the king's direction, for Hathor. Just how the mirrors figured in ritual is no longer known, although there are a few hints. A painting in the grave of Mereruka shows a dance being presented in Hathor's honor, the dancers bearing mirrors. In Ptolemaic temples, the king is depicted handing Hathor pairs of ritual mirrors in order to obtain the power to rule. Votive objects shows "the time of mirrors," a ceremony at which humans offered mirrors to Hathor or held them up to her gaze.[2]

How should these paintings be interpreted? Possibilities present themselves: The mirror may have been worshiped as the image of the goddess; it may have been the means of her descent from the sky; it may have been used in the dances that were part of her rites. Or it may have been two or all of these—for, as Troy points out, the Egyptians were notable for their lack of "either/or" logic, seeing many possible answers as equally appropriate for any question.[3]

Egyptologists connect Hathor to the solar orb through her title as "eye of the sun." None, however, has pointed out that the mirror similarly connects her to the sun. Ancient texts point to Hathor's solar identification as well. The first mention of this primeval goddess, on the ancient Stone of Palermo, said she was worshiped "in the sun temple." Early hymns called her The Golden, Ruler of the Sky; they compared a king to her, saying he "shinest like Hathor" and that even "the gods turn their heads away in order to see her better."[4] Unfortunately, these descriptions have not been sufficient to sustain Hathor's identification as the sun goddess. Rather, the presence of the mirror in her rites has led to the limited interpretation of Hathor as goddess of sensual pleasure; she is said, for instance, to have ruled cosmetics, apparently because they are put on with the aid of a mirror. Demoted from a primary position among sky divinities to a secondary—even minor—place in the official pantheon, Hathor is often passed over with scarcely a mention in lists of Egyptian gods, the lioness of the sun severed from the source of her power.

How did this happen to Hathor? To answer, we must begin with the recognition that Egyptian mythology is a complex, often confused mosaic composed of fragments of many religions. In the Early Stone Age—the Paleolithic Period, when the Nile Valley was a grassy, well-watered land—Mediterranean- and bushmen-type people occupied the area; of their scanty material remains, little indicates their religion, but it is thought that some of their beliefs survived in the later culture. As the northern glaciers receded and the rising lands became drier, new light-skinned, short-statured people arrived from North Africa, as did a blond strain of middling height and the notably taller blacks. No written sources chart the beliefs of these new folk. But their totem animals are known through artifacts: lions, mostly, but sometimes cows, falcons, serpents. Ritual discs, too, have been unearthed from this Neolithic era; perhaps a foot across, made of stone circles carved with snakes, these evolved into the uraeus, the serpent-encircled disc seen on the heads of Egyptian solar deities.

Gradually, the nomadic hunters of the Nile settled into cities and towns, installing tribal deities in temples and beginning to trade with one another. The familiar forms of the Egyptian divinities developed: human figures with animal heads, or humans bearing the totem symbols of their animal selves. Out of these cities, small kingdoms arose—the later nomes of imperial Egypt. As centuries passed these were in turn consolidated into two great realms, Upper and Lower Egypt. Even later, these were united into one empire by the Pharoaic dynasties.

Despite political changes, religious toleration was so strong that each primary local divinity kept its own temples, its own mythology, its own territory. Hence entire cities were "dedicated" to goddesses, as Buto to Neith and Bubastis to Bast. Hence, too, the welter of creation myths, each centered on a local god or goddess. Conversely, we find deities with overlapping spheres of power—and a full dozen sun gods and goddesses.

Further complicating the theological picture were increasingly powerful cults of imported gods and goddesses, Ra among them. The now best-known Egyptian sun god was not even, at first, Egyptian. He was an import from the East, perhaps from Babylon. A Pharoaic craze for worshiping a male sun reached its peak at Heliopolis, "City of the Sun," where the Semitic Ra was installed as creator and primary god. Supported by the priests of the Pharoah, who wrote most of the hieroglyphs on which we base our knowledge of Egyptian myth, Ra was never more than a god of the courts, his worship "an excrescence upon the fundamental religion of Egypt, which indeed (it has) hitherto obscured."

Heliopolis was just one of the cities where Pharoaic priests took it upon themselves to systematize and, where possible, to synthesize competing stories of the gods; there are other pantheons—enneads—from other cities, with the deities assigned into hierarchies according to the strength and status of the ethnic communities they represented. Where there were several solar divinities, priests campaigned their own into primacy, but the others never utterly forfeited connection with the sun. Hence we have a god of the sun before rising (Anhur) and a goddess of the sun's heat (Sekhmet), a god of the dawn (Khepri) and the sun's-eye goddess (Hathor). We have a trinity of suns: Har-akhti in the morning, Ra at noon, Atum in the evening time. And we have a bevy of sun goddesses: Meht-urt, goddess of the place in the sky where the sun rises; the sky-cow Net; Bast, cat goddess of fertile solar heat; Mert or Mer-Sekert, goddess of the sun in the underworld; Uatchit, goddess of the illuminated northern horizon at sunrise; and the guardian-goddess Semanti, lady of light. Even Isis had solar connections, as her falcon-headed form shows.

Max Mueller argued that after 2000 B.C.E. sun-worship became so popular that every important divinity not otherwise assigned a cosmic identity was assimilated to the daystar. If this were so, it would be difficult to know with certainty whether a goddess was originally a sun deity whose worshipers were brought under the political domination of Ra's followers, or if late sun-crazed theologians simply dotted goddesses' heads with solar orbs to fill otherwise vacant pictorial space. Mueller, for one, believed the latter, arguing that sun goddesses were late historical developments. But even he admitted that all evidence points to Hathor's early and consistent identification with the sun.

To solve the problem of what the Egyptians believed, why not just consult the myths? Unfortunately, it's not as easy as that. Egyptian mythology does not exist in the relatively accessible form of, say, the writings of Greek tragedians or Roman satirists, or even in the later anthropological form of documents based on oral sources such as those in which Native North American mythologies are preserved. Rather, what we call Egyptian mythology is the projection of non-Egyptian scholars into the material and hieroglyphic remains of the ancient Nile civilization. A few "texts" exist, notably *The Pyramid Texts* and *The Book of the*

Dead; these prayer collections do not relate stories but merely refer to them in the context of a petition or holiday ritual. The recitation of Egyptian divine stories took place in secret, at certain sacred times; only the elect were permitted to hear. Only one myth is known to us in its entirety—and that, the myth of Osiris, was recorded by the non-Egyptian Plutarch. Through interpretation of cartouches and tomb paintings and mummy cases, through commentaries on prayer fragments, modern Egyptologists have constructed a system of myth that they believe at least substantively resembles that of the ancients. It is not clear, however, that this process has given the sun goddess her due.

The severing of the goddess from her solar vehicle began almost as soon as non-Egyptian writers began to record Egyptian ways. First were the Greeks, who traded extensively with the Nile culture. As Miriam Robbins Dexter has pointed out, there had once been solar goddesses in Greece, but religious synthesis had resulted in the rulership of the sun by male divinities—and in the limitation of the cosmic goddess's dominion to the moon. Later, Roman writers like Plutarch attempted to find parallels in Egyptian religion to their own Hellenized pantheon. What comes down to us through early literary sources is, therefore, often inaccurate, polluted by the writers' inability to perceive religious visions that differed drastically from their own.

For a millennium after the destruction of Alexandria, what was left of Egyptian culture lay beneath the desert winds, inaccessible to Europe. Then the eighteenth and nineteenth centuries brought the birth of modern Egyptology. It was a time of startling discoveries: Lost or previously unknown monuments and documents were reclaimed from the sand; the intensely brilliant tomb paintings were copied and analyzed; the Rosetta Stone unveiled its incomparable key to the meaning of Egyptian hieroglyphic writing; and virtually the entire movable thesaurus of Egyptian funerary ornament was consolidated for study and comparison—in London.

This was also the heyday of the solar-hero theory, which found in Egypt happy proof of its interpretation of the sun as the preeminent symbol of masculinity. Every god crowned with a falcon head was the sun; every god addressed as "shining" in so much as one inscription must be, too. The ennead with Ra at its head was triumphantly seized upon, offering as it did a sky god who was also a central divinity. In all this hectic activity, the sun goddess was ignored, despite the solar orb on her headdress, despite her falcon head, despite the prayers that addressed her as the "Lady of Light." Sometimes, albeit unwillingly, a goddess was admitted to have a "solar aspect," but the simple words *sun goddess* were not spoken.

The trend, once set, has continued. Even today, Egyptologists acknowledge only that Hathor is "the sun's-eye goddess," keeping her just a split hair from being identified as a sun goddess. Yet despite long centuries of neglect and misidentification, the Egyptian sun goddesses remain accessible through their symbols, their recorded rites, their remaining legends. Because of her particular symbolism—her connection with the mirror—we will concentrate on Hathor, but her worship by no means exhausted the devotion to the solar feminine in Egypt. A strong case could be made, for example, for viewing the Isis religion as the longest-lived link with the early Egyptian sun goddess. Her image, popularized during the Roman Era, shows a winged sky goddess; her brother-spouse Osiris was identified with the moon, suggesting that the original myth was of the moon's regular dismemberment and reconstruction by the sun's light.

But our interest here is Hathor, The Golden One, whose symbols are the mirror, the cat, and the eye. The cat as a sun emblem is widespread, as is the string game called cat's cradle because its intention is to capture the sun-cat. The snare that is set for the sun-cat is the web of its own movements through the sky, an image related to the sun-maze games of Scandinavia, at which we'll shortly look. South of Egypt, in the Congo, cat's cradle is played in the summer, for the people wish to force the tropical sun to rest from her blazing labors. In the Arctic, too, summer is the time for the game, but in this case the string is intended to snare the sun goddess Malina, to hold her so that winter approaches more slowly.

Hathor is related to the cat-goddesses Bast and Sekhmet—the sun as gentle domestic tabby and as raging lioness—both of whom were probably tribal totem-ancestors gradually drawn into the aura of the powerful Hathor. She herself may have been the sun-cat of pre-Pharoaic times, which the oldest texts say was female and which nightly fought with the serpent of darkness, Apep, killing it each dawn. Hathor was also said to have traveled from Egypt to Nubia to live in the desert as a wild cat—a lioness or a lynx. Though the story may reflect Hathor's origin near the mouth of the Nile, it may rather—or may also—be an image of the sun's annual retreat from her people, when winter comes to the world.

The story has been reconstructed from a papyrus of 310 B.C.E., apparently a copy of an even more ancient text. Ra, the verses tell us, was not idle in the sun goddess's absence. He had replaced her with another, apparently male, sun. "Hathor became angry against Ra, " one verse says, "after she had come back, when she found that I had put another in her place, and I had replaced her by a resplendent eye, I had advanced its place in my face." Outraged, Hathor demanded her domain back. Instead, the story goes, Ra turned her into the magical protective snake, the rearing asp or cobra called the uraeus, afterwards worn on the heads of divinities and Pharoahs as an amulet of strength.

Hathor was the sun's eye; "eye" and "asp" thus became synonyms. Meanwhile whatever god replaced the goddess continued in his new role. Probably this interloper was Horus, who appeared in the pantheon of Hathor's own city at Dendera as a minor god but who, at Heliopolis, was promoted above her. Conventionally, the goddess's name is read *Hat Hor*, "house of Horus," supposedly indicating that she carried the male sun deity in her womb or "house." If, however, the "house" is the round belly of the pregnant Hathor, whether she or the unborn Horus is truly the sun remains an open question.

An equally likely possibility, proposed by Egyptologist C. J. Bleeker, is that the name means "My House is the Sky." The second meaning is appropriate to the ancient sun goddess who, in one text, boasts that she is "the primeval goddess," Queen of All. Likewise the "eye of Horus," familiar from Egyptian iconography, is better called the "eye of Hathor," for she is sculpted wearing it like a necklace on her breast and in a little scarab on her forehead. The eyes of the dead were assigned to her, and appeared on the solar barque in which the goddess passed each night through the world of the dead; sometimes the eyes were doubled, forming the goddess's face.

The eye is connected, as we saw in Siberia, to that artificial eye, the mirror, one of Hathor's main attributes. The sun as the eye of the heavens is a frequent cosmological concept; the goddess as a pair of eyes is, throughout the Mediterranean, a frequent theological concept. O. S. G. Crawford, in his famous *The Eye Goddess*, interprets the eyes as an all-caring mother, always watching out for life on her earth. Sometimes they are painted with short, pointed, ray-like eyelashes, clearly indicating the eye-sun connection.

The eye has profound symbolic importance. Spells are cast with the evil eye; basilisks and gorgons petrify their victims with a glance. In the strange and wonderful way of magic, what kills can heal; therefore the eye is an amulet against harm, with the eye of Hathor being the earliest known of such devices. Knowledge as well as love rests in the eye, the mirror of the soul; conversely, blindness is a sign of true or inner sight. The connection between eye, sun and mirror occurs elsewhere as well. In Yorkshire, for instance, it was thought dangerous to walk anti-sunwise around a room at midnight, because if you then looked in a mirror you'd see the devil's face instead of your own.[5]

The Egyptian word for "eye", *iret*, was feminine in gender; thus the sun-as-eye was naturally female as well. Hathor was called "The Eye of the Sun," a title she bears in several of her most important myths. In one—where she appears as the lion-goddess Sekhmet—she comes close to destroying life on earth.

The story begins with Ra so senile that plots against his authority broke out on earth, as well as in the heavens. Furious, he hurled his eye at the earth, and "it went as Hathor," ancient texts say. The goddess transformed herself into a lioness and began to slaughter indiscriminately. On and on she went, killing without pause and without pity. No one could stop her until Ra commanded that vats of red ale be placed in her path. Mistaking these for blood, Hathor began to drink. She drank and drank until she was drunk; she drank until she fell over, stupified with drink. Only thus was humanity saved from extinction by the searing lioness-sun.

Other versions of the tale say the ale was spilled in Hathor's path. She paused in surprise—either struck by the similarity of the red flood to her dawn self, or seeing her own face reflected as in a mirror. The pause was long enough that she recovered her wits and returned to heaven, where Ra greeted the drunken goddess with, "Welcome home, oh pleasant one!"

In honor of the drunkenness that saved humanity, Hathor's worshipers assumed the goddess's identity for a single day each year. On that day, they got drunk—very, very drunk. The Feast of Drunkenness was celebrated at Dendera, the city in which Hathor led the ennead and in which her primary temple was located. At dawn, the goddess's image was brought forth to the temple terrace. At this signal, singing and drinking broke out through the city. Musicians beat their tambours; women danced around crowned with flowers; groups lifted flagons in honor of the sun goddess. And some of the women stripped off their clothes, for this is what Hathor was said to have done in another of her central myths.

Ra, it was said, was somehow insulted one day and withdrew from heaven; no one could convince him to return. Finally Hathor approached him and bared her breasts and genitals at him. Instantly his wrath disappeared, and Ra turned home calm as a blue sky. In another, similar story, it was said that a herdsman came upon Hathor in her true shape: a tousled, wild, naked woman. He was so terrified he almost lost his wits. Perhaps this naked wildness is why Hathor was sometimes called *nb.t htp.t,* "Mistress of the Vulva." It was in honor of this aspect of their goddess, and in imitation of her, that Hathor's female devotees danced naked in the streets of Dendera.[6]

Virtually the same ritual was part of the worship of the cat-goddess Bast in her city of Bubastis. That this gentle tabby-goddess was an aspect of Hathor is clear from the Philae text: Hathor was "kindly as Bast, as terrible as Sekhmet." The connection of cat and sun runs deep in Egypt. Bast is called, in some inscriptions, simply Rat, or "Female Sun"; and Horapollo says that the Egyptians described the sun as the pupil of a giant cat's eye.

Bast was honored in what Heradotus called "the greatest and most piously honored" of all Egyptian ceremonies. And no wonder—as he described it, the Bast festival was essentially a waterborne spring party. The celebrants floated on rafts and boats down the rivers. "Some of the women have rattles and rattle with them, and some of them play the flute all the way," he says. When they neared a settlement on the shore, "some of the women continue with their music while others shout opprobrious language at the women of the place, some dance, and some stand up and pull up their garments." The showing of the genitals, so reminiscent of Uzume's similar movement to draw back the sun in Japan, is apparently based on the vision of the vulva as seat of female power [7]; there may also be a visual pun (sun=eye=vulva) implied.

When the boatloads of happy worshipers finally arrived at Bubastis, they "drank more wine at this feast than in all the rest of the year," Herodotus tells us, estimating the crowds at three-quarters of a million people annually.

But this glorious occasion was not the only reason Bast was known and loved. Every Egyptian who housed a cat knew of the vast pet cemeteries at Bast's capital; every cat owner planned to send her pet's mummy there for burial. One of these cat coffins, now in the British Museum, is covered with beautifully interlaced wrappings that form a patchwork design; the body is topped by a carved wood cat's face with a friendly, albeit somewhat comical, expression.

Cats were relatively new to domestication at the time the cat-sun goddesses arose. Unlike the dog, who came to live at Paleolithic campfires as long as forty thousand years ago, the cat joined the human homestead perhaps five thousand years ago, after the agricultural revolution of the Neolithic. Stored grains attracted rodents, which in turn attracted wild cats. Someone set out a dish of cream, and a thousand years later, the still half-wild descendants of these rat-catchers were pampered Egyptian pets decked in tiny earrings.

So much did the Egyptians love their cats that a Roman soldier who accidentally killed one was ripped to shreds by the angry mob that gathered at the scene of the tragedy. Herodotus records the curious tale that when house fires broke out in Egypt, the residents allowed their homes to burn while they attempted to save the cats who, driven wild by the flames, tried to immolate themselves. Although this story is apparently based in fact, it is also clearly linked to the belief in the fiery nature of the cat-goddess.[8]

Bast was the gentle form of the feline goddess of the sun. Her statues show her crowned with the solar asp. In one now broken sculpture, Bast appeared with Medusa hair—a headdress of serpents, each one crowned with the sun. These figures of Bast are difficult to distinguish from Sekhmet, the lioness, called Lady of the Flame and Lady of the Scarlet-Colored Garment.

Sekhmet is known from images still found across Egypt, especially near the temples of Mut at Thebes and Karnac. These regal statues show standing women with protruding human breasts and lion's heads, who wear the sun as a headdress. Hundreds of these statues have been documented, many of them remaining in situ; no other divinity in ancient Egypt was honored with so many giant images.

Sekhmet was the scorching desert sun, Bast the gentle fertilizing sunshine. It is not known how early or late they became aspects of Hathor, the sun-goddess of Dendera, where still stands the temple that was one of the greatest sun shrines of ancient Egypt. Thirty miles north of Luxor it stands, its Hathor faces staring out at the sandy horizon. When Napoleon found it, the temple was half-filled with sand, with a village thriving on its rooftop. The site has now been restored, and the temple is again available to pilgrims and tourists.

Today's temple stands on the foundation of earlier shrines. Reputedly, architects of the first century B.C.E., at work on restoration, found a goatskin scroll of plans from predynastic—now prehistoric—Egypt. They were able, using these old blueprints, to duplicate the earlier temple—a rather eerie parallel to the constant replication of Japan's Ise shrine. Modern scholars doubt the tale. The temple as it stands is relatively recent, although ancient religious artifacts have been found within it.

From the simple Roman gate that marks the temple precinct, a ruined courtyard leads to the main facade of two dozen Hathor-headed columns. Just inside, a huge vestibule opens, its ceiling covered with sun symbols and a depiction of the sky goddess Nut arching over the zodiac. Even more impressive is the circular zodiac inside, where Hathor's head rises sun-like fom the horizon.

The sun's own light pours into the Hypostyle Hall through apertures in the ceiling, and the stone around these windows is carved with rays to reinforce the effect. Called The Hall of Appearances by the ancient Egyptians, this was the place where the goddess's statue, riding in her solar barque, was brought from subterranean crypts. Offerings of food were brought here, as well as sacred water from the temple's holy well. Nearby is a little sanctuary, a building entirely separate from the rest of the shrine. Only once a year—on Hathor's birthday, New Year's Day—did anyone enter it. And then it was but a single person, sent to accompany the goddess forth into the new light.

Surrounding this most sacred part of the shrine are dark hallways called The Mysterious Corridors, on which sacred writings are inscribed. Statues and bas-reliefs of the goddess abound, including one in which Hathor is shown wearing the menat, the miraculous necklace that was one of her symbols and that—like the Jewel from Amaterasu's necklace—was housed in her primary temple.[9]

It is probable that ritual mirrors were also kept there, for Hathor's celebrations are known to have made use of the mirror. Possibly they were used in divination; possibly they were held up to the sunlight; possibly they were part of the dances associated with Hathor's rites. Even the Pharoah was expected to dance when he came to Dendera, as one ritual song indicates—though it gives no indication of whether the dance was as bawdy as those associated with other sun goddesses:

The pharoah comes to dance
He comes to sing.
His heart is sincere, his body is in order,
There is no darkness in his breast.
Oh, his mistress, see how he dances,
O, bride of Horus, see how he skips.

The Pharoah's dance was part of the New Year festival, the high point of Dendera's ritual year, when the goddess appeared miraculously just in time to be bathed in the first light of dawn. Only a few—probably Pharoah and his priests—were in the inner temple on this occasion, but the mobs in the street were able to strain for a moment's glimpse of the goddess's image on the temple porches.

Even in the off-season, Dendera was a bustling city, for it had one of Egypt's most famous hospitals. Ruins called The Sanatorium are located near the sacred baths; papyruses tell us that the rooms around the baths were used by resident physicians who put patients into trance in order to cure them. The Dendera hospitals were a mixture of Lourdes and the Mayo Clinic: a place where the culture's highest medical science combined with a deep belief in the curative powers of the goddess's waters. Miracles were doubtless wrought there; they may have been medical, or they may have been magical.

The sun goddess was evoked in times of illness because she was an all-seeing eye able to detect the cause of illness, a mirror reflecting the soul's disease. She was also goddess of death—and, as such, was awarded the eyes of the deceased, *The Book of the Dead* tells us. Her power in the realm of death was so immense that she was the last called upon in the passage to afterlife: "Hathor... eye of Ra, dweller in his brow, face beautiful in the boat of the millions of years... make the bark of the sun great to sail forth the right and truth."[10]

As the Lady of the Sycamore Tree, the Lady of the West, Hathor sat in a tree at the edge of sunset. There she offered bread, fruit and water to the newly dead. The moment a bite or a sip, passed their lips, they truly died, for afterwards they were unable to return to the world of the living. The sun goddess, who dies each evening and is reborn each dawn, was seen as a fitting guide for the new dead, who do not know their way through the land of darkness. Each night, Hathor's boat floated across the watery realms of sleep and death, bearing the goddess through her night realm. This water, heated by her passage, bubbled forth from the earth at sacred springs. The thermal springs thus became shrines for the sun goddess, for their waters carried the healing powers of the goddess's dark side.

It was perhaps this sense of the sun goddess as ruler of darkness as well as light that inspired the Hathor shrine of the XI Dynasty found at Deir-el-Bakri: Hathor, in her cow form, is seen hidden in a cave. Similarly, the *Coffin Texts* mention the cave in which Hathor rests in order to renew herself for her annual epiphany.[11] This cave—together with the ritual self-exposure of women boating towards Bubastis, which recalls Uzume's dance, with the cat manifestation, which recalls "Grand-Aunt Tiger," and with the preeminent symbol of the mirror—ties Hathor's myths to those of Asia. And the healing springs at Dendera are a bridge between that complex of myths and that of antiquity's most famous sun goddesses, Sulis Minerva of Bath.

Chapter Four

IRELAND, ENGLAND, SCOTLAND:
"REST IN THY SHADOWY CAVE, O SUN!"

Thousands of miles from Dendera, we find a shrine virtually identical to it. There, a goddess of the sun was worshiped at a healing spring. She was named Sul—a word meaning both "eye" and "sun"—sometimes called Sulis, or Sulis Minerva. The goddess-patron of the only thermal waters in Britain, at Bath in southwest England, Sul was served by priestesses who tended an eternal flame and was worshiped by devotees for whom immersion in hot mineral baths cured ailments of mind and body.

The shrine is an hour's drive from London in the rolling Avon farm-lands. It is a short distance from Stonehenge, from Avebury, from Silbury Hill, from West Kennet Long Barrow—all shrines of pre-Celtic people. It's not far, either, from the splendid White Horse at Uffington, from the Cerne Abbas Giant, or from Chalice Well at Glastonbury, sites full of religious importance. From the Berkshire downlands across Salisbury Plain, the entire area was sacred to the Neolithic people of the island. It may be from this era that the sun goddess at Bath dates, for there is a Stone Age hill fort nearby at Solsbury (a name connected to that of the site's goddess) where some suggest midsummer fire rituals took place. The sun goddess seems to have been one of the primary divinities of the pre-historic peoples of England.

We can only conjecture about the early days of the shrine, for what we see in the city today are the ruins of the Roman temple to Sul and of the baths that surrounded it. When the Romans arrived in 54 C.E., Bath was already a healing solar sanctuary—or so the inscriptions to the sun, found in such number nowhere else in Britain, suggest. There is some indication that the Romans, having heard of Bath's glories, deliberately sought out the shrine. There may have been political reasons for taking over the shrine, as there were in the simultaneous destruction of the sacred grove at Anglesey; the Romans may have wished to co-opt a cult too powerful to suppress. The legions—agents of that *interpretatio Romana* whereby local divinities exchanged their original names and identities for Roman ones—dubbed the local goddess Minerva and began at once to enjoy the waters, even bringing in Etruscan soothsayers to increase that homey feeling. Sul's original name was not lost, however. Soon she was evoked as Sulis Minerva—her original name in the Latin genitive, joined to that of Rome's healing goddess, to mean "Minerva of the sun"—by the throngs patronizing the shrine.[1]

There is no sign the Romans built a garrison or other defenses at Bath; the site was given over to medicine, religion and commerce. As to Dendera, as to Lourdes today, pilgrims came from the edges of the Roman Empire to take the waters of Bath and to worship its lady. As the fame of the temple and its spring grew, so did the town around it. Then, after almost two centuries, the legions were abruptly pulled back to Italy to deal with political problems there. Flooding at Bath, which had caused the Romans difficulty from the start, grew worse. The classical baths silted up, the temple caved in, the site was abandoned. By the early Christian era, Bath was just a swamp at the edge of the Avon River.

But the springs continued to bubble up at the rate of a quarter-million gallons each day, sufficient for Henry I to notice and to build the King's Bath in the middle of the twelfth century, unwittingly placing it atop the old Roman reservoir. Local legends of a huge temple to the goddess remained as well, attested by the sixth century Saxon poem inscribed in the temple museum:

Splendid is this masonry
The Fates destroyed it
The strong buildings crashed
The work of giants moulders away.

Following such faint clues, antiquarians of the seventeenth and eighteenth centuries located the site of the Roman baths. Years of excavation at last revealed them, virtually intact, as well preserved by the mud as Pompeii by Aetna's ashes. Around the baths a resort arose, a planned community of architectural and landscaped treasures with names like the Circus and the Royal Crescent. Bath became a center of court life under the famous Beau Nash; it was as important to be seen there in proper company as to drink or bathe in the waters. The ruins were located in 1775, the Sacred Spring in 1878. The most splendid feature of the site, the Great Bath, was unearthed in 1880.

But the early excavators never located the temple itself. That was left for modern archaeologists, who in 1981 began excavations finished in 1983. The researchers found, north of the sacred spring and with a door opening to it, a highly ornate circular temple in the classical style.

Shortly afterwards, a modern museum on the temple site was opened to exhibit the treasures they had found. There the visitor can see the inscribed stones that show the devotion of her followers to the goddess of the thermal waters. "To the Goddess Sul, Lucius Marcus Memor, Haruspex, gave this gift," one reads. "To the Goddess Sul for the welfare of Gaius Javolenus Saturalis, imaginifer of the Second Legion Augusta," reads another.

There you can read the words of C. Iulius Solinus, from the third century C.E., about the springs: *Quibus fontibus praesul est Minervae numen in cuius aede perpetui ignes numquam canescunt in favillas.* "Over these springs the divinity of Minerva presides, and in her temple the perpetual fires never whiten into ash." There are the bas-reliefs and statuary, the bronze head of the goddess glowing in a dark corner, the bits of ornate pediments, the scale models. There is the Roman money found in the sacred spring, coins in the fountain. There, too, is the fountain itself, pouring under an arch of brick over a chasm. Stone, stained red by the iron-rich waters, forms the rim of the arch. The water foams out in a steaming flood, close to boiling, at incredible volume. It is primary water, from three miles below the Liassic-clay bedrock—ancient water, from rain that fell in Neolithic times, now being spewed back to the surface. Beneath the arch, in a little red-stained pool, are coins, even jewelry, for today's visitors enact the old rituals—perhaps instinctively, perhaps ironically, perhaps reverently.

From the museum one enters the Great Bath, a cool classical structure ringed with pillars. The arched roof they supported is gone, leaving the bath open to the air. The water undulates, constantly stirred by the water that streams in—steams in—from the spring through a stone channel to the pool.

From the Great Bath you move past the East Bath, a semicircular hot tub where bathers were immersed to the neck in healing waters and where you can see the continual floor-raising the silting problem forced upon the Romans; the Hypocaust, or steam-bath; the cool Lucas Bath; the tiny circular cold bath, where the Romans took the final plunge in their therapeutic tour of the shrine. En route you can dip your hands into the water as it flows through an ancient gutter, but swimming and drinking have been banned since the discovery, more than a decade ago, of encephalitis virus in the water. A new tap into the main spring, opened in 1985 amid great ceremony, means you can quaff a mug of the water in the Pump Room before departing. Shortly, it is hoped, it will again be possible to bathe in the waters, pumped into modern pools, but the Roman Baths themselves remain closed indefinitely.

The shrine of Sul is technically classified as belonging to Celtic Britain, but the worship of its goddess there probably preceded the Celts. More than four thousand years before the first Celts negotiated the English Channel, nomadic families ranged the hills of Britain, leaving scant traces of their passing. The first great era of migration began during the Neolithic, approximately 2500 B.C.E. Cultural ferment reached an even higher pitch in the following five hundred years, when the megalith builders arrived and began to build their distinctive tumuli, to set stone lintels upon uprights and to arrange stone circles across the islands.

The Bronze Age arrived between 2100 and 1800 B.C.E. with the Beaker people, named for their distinctive ceramic product, narrow drinking cups that were often buried with their owners. It was during the Beaker's time that mirrors began to appear in the graves of women, apparently images of the sun, who would guide the deceased through the realm of death. Mirrors, often splendid spiral-embossed ones, continued to be included in burials after the Celtic Halstad and La Tene settlers arrived, from 600 B.C.E. onwards. The arriving cultures did not eliminate all traces of earlier ones; rather, the groups slowly merged, the newcomers adapting many of the ways of earlier settlers. Thus the Celts—or Britains, to be more exact—that the Romans found in southwest England practiced rituals, celebrated holidays, perhaps even worshiped deities—of which Sul may have been one—with roots in the pre-Celtic past.

If little is known of the British aboriginals, almost as little is known of the Celts. They erupt into the historical and archaeological record with fierce and sudden energy in the first millennium B.C.E., speaking an Indo-European language and moving quickly beyond their original central European homelands into Turkey, into Italy, into France and Spain, finally into England and Ireland. By the time of Herodotus, they dominated all of non-Mediterranean Europe.

Their culture is difficult to detach from the others that influenced it, and nowhere is this truer than in religion. The Celts transmitted their beliefs orally. They had, yes, a rudimentary runic script, but the stories, epics, songs and ritual chants were stored not in libraries but in the minds of the practitioners, now often called druids, after Julius Caesar's terminology. Only after the Celts were conquered were their myths written down. First the Roman soldiers carved names of Celtic divinities on the bases of classically sculpted images; later, Christian chroniclers copied down oral narratives centuries after they were last recited in the original context.

Most inscriptions came from the continent, especially from France; little narrative myth is found there. In Ireland, conversely, no inscriptions have been found, for the Romans never invaded the small island. There is, however, a wealth of narrative material in compilations produced by scholarly Irish monks, works like *The Book of Leinster* and *The Book of the Dun Cow*. A thousand years later even more material—more than half a million pages—was taken down by the Irish Folklore Commission from the shanachies, the storytellers who had passed the old tales and ballads along for generations. The island of Britain stands midway between these extremes. Numerous inscriptions with Celtic names in Roman script have been found, while in the hinterlands oral narrative survived sufficiently long to be transcribed in such works as *The Mabinogion*.

These inscriptions and narratives form the basis of what is called Celtic mythology. But it is hard, from these varied sources, to construct a coherent system, in part because all the written material comes from the insular or island Celts of Ireland and Britain. Scholars must reconstruct how mythic motifs might have appeared in a continental context, must compare narrative description to statuary in an attempt to find the Celtic essence of it all. Lest one think this an easy task, remember that the Celts did not enter lands vacant of people; their traditions and myths were altered by contact with earlier settlers.

We cannot, therefore, say with certainty in what culture Bath's Sul originated. Solinus, in the third century C.E., was the first to write of her; he described a ritual in which priestesses guarded a flame that was never allowed to die out. Sul's name is found only at Bath, where it has the alternative form of Suleviae—the multiple Sul, perhaps a triple goddess like that depicted on one of the bas-reliefs found in the temple area. The fact that inscriptions to the Suleviae are found in France, south of the Rhone—where a multiple sun goddess is clearly intended—suggests Sul's name, at least, had Celtic roots.[2]

Sometimes Sul is called Brigid. "The high one"—a translation of Brigid's name that suggests her celestial nature—is known from numerous inscriptions and narratives, unlike most Celtic divinities, whose names appear only once. A title of that most familiar Celtic goddess is Sulevia. It thus seems likely that the goddess of Bath was the local version of the pan-Celtic goddess Brigid, known as Bride in Scotland, Briid in the Hebrides, Brigantia in Britain, Bridget in Ireland. A related goddess from Southern France is Belisama or Brigindo, a goddess of hot springs whose name has been derived from proto-Celtic *qval*, "to shine" or "to burn."

Strengthening the likelihood that Sul was a localized form of Brigid is the fact that, at her most famous sanctuary in Ireland, Brigid was worshiped in exactly the same way as Solinus describes the rites of Sulis: a corps of priestesses tended a sacred fire that was never allowed to die down. Also in Ireland, sacred wells are called Tobar na Sul or Tobar Brighde, with the same well often carrying both names. These wells are said to cure diseases of the eyes, like the British sacred well near Bridport—a town whose name incorporates Brigid's—where the sun's rays striking the waters at dawn fill it with curative energy.

To discover more about the Celtic sun goddess Sul, then, we can look to Brigid's legends. And therefore we must look to Ireland, for it was in Ireland that Brigid remained alive longest. *Na dein nos aquis no bris nos*, "Neither make nor break a custom," the Gaelic proverb says, and so it was with Brigid's worship. The conservatism of Irish folkways preserved many solar features of Brigid's cult by applying them to the new Christian Saint Bridget. Her feast was kept on February 2, Celtic feast of the triple Brigid; her solar myth was adapted into the tale of a saintly nun.

That Saint Bridget is a Christianized version of the Celtic goddess Brigid is widely accepted. If she is not, then the nuns at her abbey had some curiously pagan customs. Nineteen of them kept a fire perpetually blazing, tending it each one night in turn. On the twentieth night, the fire was left untended, and the nuns prayed, "Bridget, the fire is your fire, keep it ablaze." Apparently she did so, for the sacred fire is said to have flamed continuously from the founding of the abbey in the late fifth century until it was quenched by Henry de Londres, Archbishop of Dublin and an anti-Irish Norman, six hundred years later. Arguing that the sacred fire was clearly pagan, he doused it. As soon as he died it was relit, burning until Henry VIII forever extinguished the ashless blaze of Brigid.

An old Irish homily says that the girl who became Saint Bridget was the illegitimate daughter of the chieftain Dubthach and his slavewoman Broiscech. Her mother was stepping outside with a jar of milk when, pausing on the doorstep, she suddenly gave birth. The other servants ran to bathe the infant in milk. But the light that streamed from her was not dimmed by the bath, and the unearthly radiance followed her through girlhood.

Sometimes it was disconcerting. Once, when her mother was away, the neighbors formed bucket-brigades to quench what they assumed was a house fire, only to find the burning light coming from the cradle. Another time, Bridget was found playing with blazing cow-dung. When her rescuers tried to pull the burning material from the child, they found it cool to the touch.

Bridget, baptised a Christian and aspiring to sainthood, vowed never to marry. When the time came to consider a suitor, the girl simply refused. Her father insisted. She refused again. While they were arguing, a man named Beccan had the ill-wit to interpose. "Idle is the fair eye that is in the head, not to be on a pillow near a husband," he said.

Bridget pointed to her eye and it popped out of her head. As it lay there on her cheek, she pointed at Beccan. "There is your delightful eye," she said. His eye popped out onto his cheek as well. Terrified, Dubthach promised Bridget she would never have to marry. At that, she popped her own eye back into its socket. The unfortunate Beccan was, however, not similarly healed.

Freed from marriage, Bridget took eight nuns and founded the Abbey of Cill Dara, the Oak Church, near a sacred tree in the midlands of Ireland. In County Kildare, the abbey site is still accessible, although all vestiges of Bridget's convent save a round tower have disappeared. The lands around the convent, said to have been vast and rich, were won by Bridget through trickery. The local chieftain agreed to give land to her, but only as much as her cloak could cover. She put the cloak on the ground and it began to grow and grow, spreading itself upon the hills for miles until the shocked man gave the nun what she wanted. This mantle became famous: *A Bhrigid, scar os no chionn, Do bhrat fionn dom anachal*, sang the poet who wished Bridget's protection "like your bright mantle over my head."

When she had no hook on which to hang this mantle—which was white, the only color Bridget wore, even to the veil that covered her unshorn hair —she always had a sunbeam. One day Bridget fell asleep in heavy rain while tending her sheep. When she came back to the convent, she found no fire to dry herself. A ray of sunlight suddenly shot through a window. Bridget, thinking it was a rafter, hung her cloak on it. The sunbeam grew strong as a board, and the cloak hung there until it dried. Thus, even in her saintly disguise, the old solar goddess showed her power over the sun's rays.

From the first, the Abbey of Cill Dara was a healing center. Bridget bathed frequently, and the water in which she bathed effected miraculous cures—especially in cases of eye disease. The connection of Bridget with cures of blindness is found again and again. One day, for instance, it is told that she awoke at dawn to see sunlight drenching the green Irish plain. She wished to share the splendor with her friend Daria, a nun blind since birth, so she kissed her eyes. Instantly the woman could see. She gazed in pleasure at the landscape for some time, then asked Bridget to make her blind again, lest the beauty of earth blind her to the beauty of the spirit. With a wave of her hand, Bridget removed her friend's vision.

This saint-goddess had an unmistakably solar nature, as her life history, replete with solar images, has shown. In addition, the Irish association of Brigid—and women in general—with the sun produced lovely poetic images. An early poet prayed to "Bridget, shining virgin! Bridget, torch and sun!" A tenth century prayer to the Virgin Mary called her "o masterstroke of women, o chart of the sea-path home, o fair-tressed lady, o branch over wood, o bright sun!" And a Gaelic song collected by A. Carmichael addressed the sun goddess directly:

Hail to thee, thou sun of the seasons,
As thou traversest the skies aloft;
The steps are strong on the wing of the heavens,
Thou art the glorious mother of the stars.
Thou liest down in the destructive ocean
Without impairment and without fear;
Thou risest up on the peaceful wave-crest
Like a queenly maiden in bloom.

The same folklorist, working in the village of Barra, recorded the old woman storyteller Mor MacNeill as saying that, "In the time of my father and my mother there was no man in Barra who would not take off his bonnet to the white sun of power, nor a woman in Barra who would not bend her body to the white moon of the seasons."

In ritual as well as in poetry, Bridget the saint—and behind her, Brigid the goddess—was connected with the sun. On her feast day, no spinning or other work that required twining and twisting was allowed, nor anything that demanded the turning of a wheel—prohibitions also enacted on sun-goddess holidays in Scandinavia. Rush swastikas or eye-shapes were woven, sun-wise from left to right, to protect the home against fire.[3] And rituals were held at sacred wells, of which there are some three thousand across Ireland. These wells often have solar names and solar myths.[4] Called Tobar Greine or Tobar Brigid—that is, "Well of the Sun" or "Brigid's Well"—these small pools were sun-traps that lured the goddess to earth on certain days; they were also called "eye-wells," for they were held to be especially effective in curing eye diseases. The sun in Ireland, as in Siberia and Egypt, was connected both with the mirror-well and with the eye.

One Tobar na Solais, or "Well of Light," is at Killineer, near both Bridget's Kildare sanctuary and the solar tumulus of Newgrange. Another healing well, at Belgatheran in County Louth, had the same name. It is, alas, no longer magically functional, having been angered when butchers dropped viscera into it. As the insulted well disappeared from the earth's surface, never to return, the country folk saw hundreds of candles blazing farewell. Tobar Kilna-Greina, the Well of the Sun's Shrine in County Cork, was said to have been the abode of a woman who, disguised as a fish, would answer questions put to her; she too disappeared when there was an insulting lack of decorum at the rituals. Despite the departure of its oracle, the well's "pattern" continued to be practiced for centuries: one walked nine circuits sunwise, then laid a white pebble called "a stone of the sun" on an altar in a nearby stone circle. Yet another well, at Ardaugh, in County Longford, was said to trap healing powers not only in its waters but in the moss around it. A local legend of no particular intrinsic interest tells that once three nuns were seen at the well, accompanied by a spotted cow—a folk recollection of the triple sun goddess appearing with her cosmic totem.

The West of Ireland is particularly rich in sun wells. In County Clare, Tobar Greine springs forth from under an ancient dolmen. Nearby is the Lake of the Sun (Lough Graney) in the Mountains of the Hag (Sliabha Echghta), haunted by a mythic Lady Sun's Daughter, Gillagreine. Near Gort, County Galway, is a tiny Tobar na Greine, "Well of the Sun," "just a little wee spot in the rocks," according to local antiquary Tom Hannon. "People in my younger days went there on Easter morning at sunrise. They said you could see the sun dancing there, but I've never done it. I met an old lady who saw the sun giving off rays which seemed to dance, long ago when she was six." This spring ritual of visiting sun wells on Easter morning was common across the isle of Ireland and Britain, as well as on the Isle of Man. The British poet Sir John Suckling, aware of the folklore about the sun goddess dancing on Easter, compared a woman to her:

> And oh! she dances in such a way
> No sun upon an Easter day
> Were half so fine a sight.

When there wasn't a well nearby in which to watch the sun dance, people set out pots of water to catch the sun's first Easter rays; they then agitated the water to make the sun's reflection dance on walls and ceilings. In rural Scotland, the sun was said to whirl around like a wheel and to glow with rainbow colors. These rites derive from the Celtic spring feast of Beltane—from *bel*, "white, bright"—when it was believed the reborn sun whirled three times when rising. On earth, in honor of the sun's rebirth, new fires were kindled on hilltops.

Other wells hold other festive associations. At Liscannor, in Ireland's County Clare, is the famous *Daigh Brighde*, "Brigit's Vat." According to Maire MacNeill, author of a massive study of Irish midsummer festivals, the site is—with Puck Fair and the Crough Patrick pilgrimage—one of the longest-lasting survivals of Celtic ritual. And the well is still held in high regard. Two big circular paths, one above the other, are trod by the prayerful before they enter the protective stone hut. Its walls are lined with crutches and holy cards, special offerings—a typed prayer to St. Bridget someone has framed—and dozens of plaster and plastic statuettes not only of Bridget but of the entire Catholic pantheon. At the far end of the little enclosure, the well pours its water down the hillside, ruddy, cool and quick. An empty glass sits on the side of the well; the taste is bitter, for the water is full of minerals.

In County Donegal, Tobar Bride is a famous healing well that is particularly effective against toothache, if the petitioner leaves a little white stone as a substitute for the aching tooth. The old name of the well is still remembered, though it has not been used for a thousand years: Tobar Aibheaqg, "Well of Fire." It's also remembered that the well was dedicated to a goddess; nearby, at Tobar Brigid in Sligo, where an ancient swastika is carved into the stones near the well, a sun-wise procession moved around the sacred water each February 1. In County Limerick, the Tobar Breedia's curative waters should be drunk for best effect; moss gathered from the well can also be used for healing, if first boiled in milk and then used as a poultice.

The required ritual is virtually identical at all the solar wells across Ireland: preliminary prayers, followed by sun-wise walking circuits of the well, commonly made three times. After this, the petitioner drinks the wellwater, then leaves a token on a nearby tree. A holy card suffices today, but strips of paper or cloth, or little carvings of the afflicted limb, were popular in ancient times. Finally, the pilgrim makes circuits of other holy sites—trees, stones—in the area, often adding a pebble to a stone-heap nearby. More vigorous pilgrimages entail crawling, walking on the knees, or wading through rivers and streams. Usually the patterns are kept either on St. Bridget's day or for some special intention; many of these latter have to do with head or eye diseases, over which virtually all Bridget wells were held to have power.

The cure was effected through sympathetic magic: The sun was an eye; the sun's eye was captured in the water; the water could make eyes bright as the sun. This connection of sun with eye is something we have already seen in Egypt, India and Siberia. As Miranda Green has argued, the eye is a natural solar image, with lashes radiating from a central orb.[5] There was a Greek notion that inside every eye was a fire, which illuminated objects as the eye observed them. The eyes close in sleep; when the sun closes her eye at sunset, night blankets the world as though an eyelid has shut. If the sun is an eye, this magical thinking goes, then the sun's glance captured in water can create sharp, clear vision for other, earthly eyes.

Just as Minerva was the name given to Sul in Bath, and Saint Bridget was given the identity of the Celtic goddess Brigid, so Brigid herself may have replaced an even earlier sun goddess in Ireland. In the parish of Kilkeering, County Roscommon, a well was discovered by a virgin named Caolainn. A man happened to admire the woman's beautiful eyes, whereupon she gouged them out and threw them at him. The virgin then groped her way to a sacred spot, where she pulled rushes from the pond. Where the plants had been uprooted, water gushed forth. When Caolainn wiped her bloody sockets with the rushes, her eyes grew back. The identical story is told of three other wells —at Killinaugh, County Cavan; at Dunleer and Farquhart in County Louth. But in these cases the woman was said to have been Bridget, not Caolainn.[6]

Who is this Caolainn? Why does she presume to create the sun-wells? The answer is that, just as Saint Bridget took rulership of the wells away from her namesake-goddess—and the Virgin Mary has taken some from Bridget—a pre-Celtic divinity originally owned the sites and was assimilated to the Celtic Brigid. The legend from Kilkeering points the way: The original owner was the Cailleach, known across Scotland and much of Ireland. She is not one of the Irish Tuatha de Danaan, deities of the family of the goddess Danu, usually interpreted as gods of the Celts; her tenure on the island preceded theirs.

To unravel this puzzle we must move beyond written sources, for the earliest peoples of the islands left no history and few monuments, although they amalgamated with the later-coming Celts to form early Irish society. They did leave place-names and the stories connected with them; they left a few words; and they left a huge tumulus directed at the winter sunrise. Piecing these clues together, we can discover the pre-Celtic sun goddess.

Was she the Cailleach? Yes, and no: The Cailleach was one of a pair of goddesses, the one who ruled the "little sun" of winter while a sister goddess, Aine, "light and heat," ruled the summer. Aine's name, too, appears at solar wells—like that at Ballybreist, County Limerick, near the hill dedicated to her, Knockainy—and legends told of her are identical to those of the Cailleach. The gentle goddess Aine, "the best-hearted woman that ever lived," and the "meager blue hag," as Milton called the Cailleach, are one goddess—a goddess who magically restored her youth each year, going into a cave and emerging young again, bringing life back to the worn and wintry world.

"The bright one," as the goddess Aine is known in Ireland, was the fairy queen of midsummer. Then, *clears*, or straw-topped poles set alight, were carried in procession around her sacred mountain Knockainy (Cnoc Aine). A legend says that, once, the villagers forgot the ritual, and the whole mountain caught fire. Another tale tells of a group of girls who stayed behind after the procession on the mountaintop; there they met the goddess herself. She showed them her magic realm through a ring that she took off her hand. In Donegal, folklorist Sean O'hEochaidh reports, Aine worked spinning out sunbeams and making gold cloth from the thread. There in Donegal, too, the story remains of how Knockainy's alternative name is Creig na Cailli, "Hag's Crag," for Aine's other half was the hag of winter; there, too, is the remarkably unremarkable tale that a younger girl named Aine, only daughter of a farmer near Teilionn, disappeared into the mountain when spoken to harshly.

In Ireland, Grian—T.P. O'Rahilly translates the name as "Sun"—was Aine's sister; their mountains Knockainy and Cnoc Grene rise near each other in Limerick, where the word *cailleach* means "dark of the sun" and *aine* means "warmth." Where we find Grian, we find the Cailleach: a hooded woman, a veiled woman, sometimes a nun. She rode a magic horse over land and sea, through the daylit world and the night-sea-journey. Sometimes, rather than riding a horse, she became one: the roan mare, Lair Derg; she was also the horsewoman Macha who lived in a crystal *griannan*, a sun house.

In Scotland, the daughter of Grian was Grianaig, the Cailleach, who used a magic wand to flog down any vegetation that might think to grow in winter. There she was best known as the Hag, whose name day on March 25 was, until 1599, celebrated as New Year's Day. And on the Isle of Man, until recently, she fought with her sister over possession of the world: In the celebrations when the "little sun" gave way to the "big sun" on May 1, younger men fighting on the side of the Winter Queen always lost to the forces of the May Queen.

Although summer is pleasant in northern Europe, winter seems more memorable; it is the name of Grian that comes down to us as the Gaelic word for sun, not that of Aine. And the legends of the winter-hag far outnumber those of her summer sister. There are many versions of her name: Cailleach Bheur in Scotland, Cally Berry in Ulster, the Cailleach ny Groamch in the Isle of Man, the Hag of Beare in Ireland. In Britain, she was Black Annis, a blue-faced cannibal with long white teeth who snatched people from their firesides, and who guarded a well and a cave in Argyll. She was said to crouch among the branches of an old pollard oak, the last remnant of a huge forest, which grew out of a cleft in the rock at the mouth of her cave, an opening she dug out of the solid rock with her fingernails.

She was ugly. She had one eye in the middle of a blue-black face, an eye of preternatural keenness. She had red teeth and matted hair "white as an aspen covered with hoarfrost." Over her hair she wore a kerchief, and over her gray clothing was flung a faded plaid shawl. Her behavior was as unpleasant as her appearance. She hired her farm workers for six months, with the stipulation that none would be paid who could not outwork her. Looking at the hunched old thing, many a man fell for the trick and paid with his life, dying of overwork trying to keep the pace she set. So strong was she that she carried boulders in her apron; the ones she dropped became mountain ranges. Beinn na Chailleach, a Scottish mountain, is one of those named after her; "hag mountains" are always extremely prominent aspects of the landscape and usually cloud-covered or stormy.

She was vastly ancient, the Irish Triads tell us: "The three great ages: the age of the yew tree, the age of the eagle, the age of the Hag of Beare." She could endlessly renew her youth. All the men she loved—and they were countless—died of old age as she went on growing young again, finding another young man to share youth with.

Like Aine, she was a spinner: the Spinning Hag. Because of her, it was important never to take a spinning wheel out of the house after nightfall or to spin at night, for she would punish those who turned the wheel when the solar wheel was still. In Donegal the story is told of a woman, spinning at midnight, who saw a hag come in her door. The traveling folk, she thought, and spoke in welcome. Soon she was complaining to the hag of the difficulties she faced in finishing her work in time for the weaver. "No fear, " said the old woman. "Let me take it away, and tomorrow I will bring you it all, complete. I will charge nothing, but if you do not know my name, I will take all the yarn you have."

The woman, thinking it a bargain, gave her the wool, and off the hag went. But when she was gone, the woman could not sleep for thinking of how to find the hag's name. The next morning she sought advice of the town's wise woman, who told her to go to Binn an Eidhin at nightfall, to sit under a rock, and to listen. And so she did, and soon she heard the song:

> Spin ye, spin ye!
> Little knows the woman
> For whom ye spin:
> My name is the Spinning Hag !

The next day, when the hag came with the spun wool, the woman cheerily answered her question. "Your name is the Spinning Hag!" And the Spinning Hag, furious at being outwitted, demanded the woman fix dinner for the fairies who had done the spinning.

And so she did, but the dozen beauties who came ate all the dinner, then all the oatmeal stored for winter. Then they cast around for something else to eat. Spying the woman's husband, they tied him up, thinking to make a further meal of him.

Desperate, the housewife rushed back to the wise woman. "Tell them Binn an Eidhin is on fire," she said, "and when they give you three hairs put them up the chimney." And so the woman did. When the fairy women heard her calling "Binn an Eidhin is on fire!" they screamed and raced out the door. But soon enough they discovered her ruse, and back they came.

They called into the door. "Open the door, man of the house."

But the man of the house said, "How can I, tied hand and foot?"

"Open the door, spinning wheel." And the spinning wheel said the same thing.

"And you, woman of the house, are you bound?" they asked.

"I am not," she said.

"Well, take these three hairs and bind yourself!"

And the fairies put three hairs under the door, and the woman put them up the chimney.

"Are you bound yet?" asked the fairies.

"I am," she said.

"Tighten, tighten," said the fairies. And the hairs called out, "How, when we are up the chimney?" And the Hag and her maidens left in a fury, and never came to the woman of the house again.

Virtually the same story is told in Scotland, where the tradition of the hag in the sun survives in children's rhymes like this one:

> There was a wee wifie row't up in a blanket,
> Nineteen times as hie as the moon;
> And what did she there I canna declare,
> For in her oxter (armpit) she bure the sun
>
> 'Wee wifie, wee wifie, wee wifie,' quo' I,
> 'O what are you doin' up there sae hie?'
> 'I'm blawin' the cauld cluds out o' the sky. '
> 'Weel dune, weel dune, wee wifie! ' quo' I.

There in Scotland, in Badenoch, it is said that a hunter and his two dogs, caught in stormy weather, took shelter in a hut. After a moment a cat entered—a miserable, weather-beaten cat who, upon seeing the dogs, begged the hunter for Highland courtesy, that he not set the dogs upon her. She gave the hunter a long hair, asking him to tie the dogs. A cautious man, the hunter tied the hair around a beam, keeping the dogs free. The cat made herself comfortable by the fire, where she began to swell to incredible size.

The hunter casually remarked upon the change. "Aye, aye," the cat said, "as my hairs imbibe the heat, they naturally expand." When she was enormous, she suddenly resumed human form and turned upon the hunter, whom she accused of breaking the mystical contract between those of his profession and the animals they hunt. She sprang at his throat with the fury of a tigress, and the dogs in turn attacked her. "Fasten, hair, fasten," she screamed, and the hair obeyed—snapping the roof beam. The dogs tore off one of her breasts, but she escaped, transforming herself into a raven to do so.[7]

In this story we detect what both Katharine Briggs and Robert Graves claim was one of the primeval goddess forms worshiped in the islands: Cat-Anna, the cat-goddess worshiped in Connaught, in the far west of Ireland, at a cave called Clough-mach-righ-cat. There she gave oracles, but also vituperative answers to tricky questions. The same cat winter hag appeared in Leicester, where, to mark the arrival of spring on Easter Monday, people dragged a dead cat before a pack of dogs, calling this the "hunting of Black Annis." Like the Korean tiger-goddess who threatens the sun, and the fierce Egyptian Sekhmet who devours humanity, the winter hag of the islands has an alternative identity, or familiar, the cat.[8]

It is clear how Aine can turn into the Cailleach. Every woman knows how to grow old. But how does the Cailleach renew her youth, turning again into Aine? That, folklore tells us, is done through magic and through dance. A celebration called Cailleach an Dudain, "old woman of the mill-dust," still danced a century ago in Scotland, enacted the ritual. A woman and a man holding a magic wand danced, more and more obscenely, until the man waved his wand at her head. She fell down at his feet as though dead. Lifting her left hand, the man touched it with the wand; the limp hand moved from side to side. The man began to dance around, touching the other hand, the feet, the legs—each becoming alive to the touch. Soon the woman's limbs moved, but her body remained inert. Kneeling above the woman, the man breathed into her mouth while touching her heart with the wand. Suddenly she sprang back to life, and the two danced even more energetically than before.

The dance reflects the Scottish tradition that the Cailleach kept a maiden—named Bride—prisoner in the high mountains of Ben Nevis. But her own son fell in love with the girl. At the end of winter, he succeeded in eloping with her. The hag chased them across the landscape, waging fierce storms as she went. To defend his prize, the son turned upon his mother, chasing her until he put out one of her eyes, whereupon she turned into a big gray boulder. In the west of Scotland the pursuit is said to begin on the day of vernal equinox, when light and dark of are equal length. In some versions of the story, as that from the Isle of Man, a holy well is involved; there, the son's horse creates a healing spring. In another version, the Cailleach fails to put the stone cover on a holy well, which bursts its bonds and forms a lake while the horrified hag turns to stone.

That the Cailleach and the Bride are identical is made plain in Scottish folk custom. Throughout the country, the last sheaf cut at harvest is called either the Maiden or the Cailleach; when called the Cailleach, the harvest sheaf is often used to prepare the ceremonial bed for Bride on her day, February 1. Legend, too, declares them to be the same: each year, on the eve of Bride's day, the Cailleach is said to travel to the Isle of Youth to find the Well of Youth there. As dawn breaks the next day, she takes a drink of the miraculous water and turns instantly into Bride. As she does so, the dull grasses turn green, and white spring flowers blossom instantly.

The longest extant version of the freeing of the summer sun from her imprisonment was recorded in 1859 by folklorist Hector Urquhart; John, the tinker of Inverary, was the storyteller. It begins with Brian, a prince, who wished to marry a henwife's daughter. He was forbidden to do so until he found the most marvelous bird in the world.

Brian set off to do so. He marched along the road for a long time, until he came to the Cailleach's house. There he stayed the night, and in the morning arose to find it snowing fiercely. He looked around and saw a fox putting on his shoes and stockings.

He protested, but to no avail. The only way to get his shoes back was to take on the fox as a servant—and, shortly thereafter, to agree to ride the fox as a horse.

The fox, who turned out to be a fast mount, took Brian to the home of the Giant of Five Heads, Five Humps and Five Throttles. There, the fox said, he would find the marvelous bird. And the fox told him magic words by which he could trap the marvelous bird. All went well: Brian became the giant's servant, found the bird, and stole off with it. But, alas for Brian, he could not resist peeking once he'd gotten away from the giant's house. The bird screeched. The screech woke up the giant.

The giant caught poor Brian, dragged him back to the house, and offered him a choice: to steal the White Spear of Light from the Realm of Big Women, or to have his head mounted on a stake in the yard.

"I would rather go steal the White Spear of Light from the Realm of Big Women," said Brian. And so it was. As he set off, he met the fox again, who told him that to steal the White Spear of Light was ten times harder—twenty times harder—than to steal the marvelous bird of the giant. Undaunted, Brian went on, riding the fox as before.

They went to the country at the back of the wind and the face of the sun, the Realm of Big Women. But, alas, Brian again was caught, and this time the Big Women gave him this choice: to become a spark and be burned to death under the bellows, or to steal Dia Griene, the sun goddess, from the gathering of the Fionns.

"I will go steal the sun goddess," Brian said. "A man is kind to his life."

Off he went. He met the fox, and the fox told him what he most dreaded to hear: that stealing the sun goddess was so hard, that though many had tried, not a single one had returned alive. Nine guards guarded her, and she dressed herself in a dress like no other dress in the world—except the one the fox had, which she gave to Brian. So Brian disguised himself as Dia Griene, and the guards all gave way so Brian could enter the sun goddess's chamber. There he spent the night with her.

The next day Brian and the sun goddess escaped, leaving through the window. The fox took them towards the Realm of Big Women. As they approached, Brian wondered why he should give up the goddess of the sun just to gain the White Spear of Light for the giant.

"I will make a sun goddess of myself, and you can give me to the Big Women," the fox said. And she turned herself into a sun goddess, and Brian traded her for the White Spear of Light. Then Brian and the sun goddess set off, leaving the fox behind.

In a few days the fox caught up with them, as they neared the house of the giant. "Isn't it a shame," said the fox, "to trade the White Spear of Light for that filth of a marvelous bird." Brian saw no other way. But the fox did: She would turn herself into a White Spear of Light.

And so she did, and Brian left the giant's house with the marvelous bird, the sun goddess, and the real White Spear of Light. But when the poor fox caught up with the couple, she had no teeth: The giant had used her to chop down a tree and had smashed up her mouth.

They traveled until they came to a roadside spring. There the fox made a sudden demand: that Brian use the White Spear of Light to strike off her head. If he did not, she threatened, she would kill him. "A man is kind to his life," said Brian, striking off the head with one blow. And the head fell into the well, and up from it rose the son of the king who was father to the sun goddess—Dia Griene's brother. And so they all went together to Brian's house, and Brian and Dia Griene celebrated a wedding that lasted a year and a day.

In this story the fox—the Cailleach in disguise—reveals both her ability to transform herself into the sun, and her eagerness to help Dia Griene to her wedding. That they are the same figure is clear. The fox has a dress identical to Dia Griene's; she is able to transform herself into Dia Griene. The winter hag and the summer princess are even more clearly identified in the legend, related by J.G. Campbell, in which the hag appears to the heroes Fionn and Ossian, who are appalled by her ugliness and refuse to let her sleep with them. But their comrade Diarmaid pleads for her, and she joins Fionn and Ossian as they sit by the fire. Soon enough she "sought to be under the warmth of the blanket together with Diarmaid," and soon again turned into "the most beauteous woman that men ever saw."

Similarly, in the famous Irish tale of Niall and his brothers, the hag at the sacred well and the blossoming maiden are one and the same. In that tale, the young men approached a sacred well guarded by a woman of great age and hideousness. In return for a drink of the well water, she demanded a kiss—probably, in the original, somewhat more—from each of the thirsty men. Each recoiled in dismay, except for Niall, who fulfilled the Cailleach's request.

Instantly she transformed herself into a maiden of surpassing beauty. Struck with wonder, Niall asked, "Who are you?"

"Royal Rule am I," the woman answered.

In yet a third tale, the five Luagaid brothers were hunting and became lost in a snowstorm. Each, in turn, stumbled upon the same hut; each, in turn, was offered shelter in return for sleeping with the hag who was custodian of the place. Each, in turn, declined. And each, in turn, was tossed out again into the stormy night.

Finally the last brother, Luagaid Laigde, arrived. Unlike the others, he had sense enough to agree to share the woman's bed. When he did, she transformed herself into a woman whose beauty, the story emphasizes, was "that of the sun shining in May." When Luagaid made love to her, she conferred upon him the kingship of Ireland.

Finally, there is a version of the "Hag of the Hair" in which three sons were born to a man. He assigned a tree and a well to each boy, saying that if anything should befall them, the well would dry up and the tree wither away. The eldest boy, leaving home to seek his fortune, found a little hut with an old hag inside. He asked hospitality, but she said he could enter only if he tied his dogs. He had no rope; she gave him a hair. He tied the dogs, the hag grew huge, and she called to the hair, which snapped the dogs' heads off.

At home, when the tree withered and the well dried up, the father knew one son had been killed. The second son went out to seek his fortune, and the same befell him, and his tree withered and his well dried up. At last, the third son set out to find his fortune. He, too, found the little hut, and there was the hag awaiting him. She complained of the dogs, he said he would keep them under control, and she said he must tie them. He said he had no rope, and so she gave him a hair of her head.

But this brother set the hair into the fire. The hag heard the hair crackling in the blaze and asked what was the noise, but the hero just kept his dogs close to him and did not reply.

Then the hag, moving close to the fire, began to swell up. "Old woman," said the hero, "you are getting big."

"You are the last," she said, "and I will have you!" Then she called for the hairs to tighten, but they could not, and so the dogs were able to bring the Cailleach to bay and the boy to force her to revive his brothers.

The magical transformation of winter goddess into summer goddess always takes place in a cave, or in the cave-like hut of the hag. Black

Annis had her bower, a small cave in Leicester that Lewis Spence described as

> a round cave about ten or twelve feet in diameter. It is now nearly filled up with soil. Children who went to play on the Dane Hills were warned that Black Agnes, or Annis, lay in wait to snatch them away to her cave, where she would scratch them to death.... In old Leicester it had long been customary on Easter Monday to proceed to Black Annis's bower to witness the diversion of trailing a dead cat before a pack of hounds.

The ritual, Spence suggests, was originally a springtime cat-hunt, which resulted in the ceremonial killing of the winter hag.[9]

There are always caves in stories of the Cailleach. There is the cave inside Binn an Eidhin where lives the Spinning Hag of Donegal. There is Uamh Caillich Bhig Ruaival, the Cave of the Hag next to the Ruaival River, in Scotland; in that country too is the Cave of Gold, which no one can find, where seven cowhides of shining metal are forever hidden. There are legends in the west of Ireland that St. Patrick—who, as Maire MacNeill points out, stands in for another, earlier male figure—penned up a hag in a cave, from which she escaped as a beautiful woman[10]. The saint was also said to have extinguished "a baleful light in a cave"—a cave that was dedicated to Brigid. The hag's cave was the place of transformation; an ancient Gaelic poem praises it as the place in which the winter hag transforms herself endlessly into the young spring: "Rest in thy shadowy cave, oh sun! And let thy return be in joy!"[11]

This cave is within a mound of earth, another song tells us:

> This is the day of Bride,
> The queen will come from the mound;
> I will not touch the snake,
> Nor will the snake touch me.

This mound, as well as the other sun-symbols in these stories—the cave, the mirror, the transformation of old woman into young—points the way to an explanation of one of the archaeological mysteries of Ireland, indeed of Western Europe. Standing on a ridge overlooking the Boyne River Valley, twenty miles north of Dublin and near the famous hill of Tara, is a six-thousand-year-old artificial hill—a mound—faced with white quartz. Inside that hill, down a corridor of stone, a shaft of sunlight pierces the gloom each year, traveling into the recesses of the cave to illuminate spiral carvings. The light then retreats, not to enter the cave again for a year—until the next winter solstice.

This is the tumulus at Newgrange, one of the great monuments of the megalithic civilization that also created Stonehenge. Built in approximately 4500 B.C.E., it predates Stonehenge and the Pyramids of Egypt—making it one of the oldest ritual sites in the world and the world's most ancient astronomical observatory. In use for uncounted years under the megalith builders, it passed into use as a ritual cemetery under the Celts, who called it Brug na Boinne. Then, for almost a thousand years, it lay forgotten save in the legends of the countryside. The mound, like many pre-Celtic sites, was believed to be the habitation of the fairies, the *sidhe*. This superstition saved the tumulus from destruction, though erosion pulled down the white stone facing, blocking the entrance to the interior cavern.

Newgrange is one of a number of similar sites located within a few miles of each other on the hilly banks of the Boyne. One is of special interest: Loughcrew, where sun worship is attested and where we find the Hag's Chair, a megalithic monument. Loughcrew is most renowned for the carvings that spiral across its rocks. Set in the Mountains of the Hag—the Sliabh-na-Cailleach—its 90-foot prominence offers a spectacular view of nearly half of Ireland's counties. Twenty-five burial cairns are found there, many of them sculpted with sun wheels. Some of these wheels, like those in Scandinavia, which we'll discuss in Chapter Six, are spoked. Others are concentric circles; these appear particularly on the Hag's Chair, a nine-foot-long stone with a hollowed-out seat. Finally, the Loughcrew monuments include many "mirror emblems," in which the solar disc has a handle; in Sweden these are held to be engravings of actual sun-mirrors. George I. Flom, an early interpreter of the Loughcrew stones, believed the sun symbols on the stones showed a dual solar divinity: "the one as a light and heat-giving power, the other as declining at the end of day." The megalithic civilization of which these mounds are relics has frequently been held to have worshiped the sun; others argue that, no, a goddess was chief deity. The French megalithic scholar Dechellette, for instance, argues that the rayed suns on the Loughcrew monuments represent the body of a goddess, not the sun. These difficulties are resolved simply. The carvings represent both the goddess and the sun.

The connection of the sun goddess with the Brugh na Boinne may resolve arguments that have raged for centuries about the ritual purpose of Newgrange. In the 1700s the antiquarian Charles Vallancey suggested that Newgrange was an Anglicized version of a Gaelic phrase, *an uambh greine*, Cave of the Sun, somehow pronounced like "new graney." His theory was rejected; today archaeologists say the name merely refers to the use, some centuries past, of the cave for grain storage. It was, in this interpretation, a "new grange," a new granary. However primitive his etymology, however, Vallancey seems to have hit upon the likeliest interpretation of the ritual significance of the cave.

Scholars derided Vallancey for having made the common mistake of tying the tumulus to the Celts. Whoever they were—and that is certainly far from settled—the megalith builders were not Celts, whom they long antedated both on the continent and in Ireland. Whoever they were, they were impressive engineers and architects. If the architecture of Stonehenge is stirring, the contained beauty of Newgrange at least equals it. And the engineering that created a cave from 220,000 tons of rock, oriented precisely to the moment of winter solstice dawn, would be difficult to duplicate even today.

During the early days of antiquarian interest in Newgrange, entrance to the cavern was blocked. When the litter of fallen rock was removed, spectators gasped at the splendid spiral petroglyphs that have earned the site special fame. But more than a century passed before Newgrange's real significance, the solstice miracle, was rediscovered. Neighborhood legends that told of the entry of light into the cave were dismissed as fanciful fairy stories. Although, early in this century, the caretaker brought selected friends into the cave each solstice morning, officially the tumulus was designated a passage grave, a mound covering a cemetery.

In the 1960s Michael and Claire O'Kelly began their painstaking survey and reconstruction of the exterior of the mound; it is to this period that replacement of the white quartz facing dates. The well-preserved interior remains in its original, unretouched but virtually pristine condition. The O'Kellys cleared debris away from a small square hole above the entrance; this "roof-box" allows light into the cave on solstice morning. Discovery of the roof-box led to the confirmation, in 1969, of the long-held belief that the sun entered the tumulus on December 21. That day the O'Kellys and several colleagues, blessed with a fine day, occupied the tumulus at sunrise and proved the truth of folklore.

Official skepticism did not immediately cease. Rather, it was next suggested that changes in the obliquity of the earth's ecliptic meant the entry of light was mere coincidence, that the earth's wobble would have blocked the sun four thousand years ago. The image of primitive rock-haulers intent on weighing down bones with boulders died hard, but in 1974 the scientist Jon Patrick announced that, indeed, the sun shone into the tumulus at its construction, and that "it will continue to do so forever, regardless of secular changes in the obliquity of the ecliptic." The genius of the builders had designed the roof-box wide enough to incorporate any such changes, a fact that provokes the unsolved question of whether this was mere accident, or whether the megalith builders knew about the earth's wobble—something science only this century has learned.

Once the entry of light into the tumulus had been confirmed, the search was on for an interpretation. Because the solar religion is attested as part of the megalithic complex, it was assumed that the site had to be related to a solar divinity. This, in turn, was presumed to be male. The assumption of a sun god led immediately to today's most common vision: that on solstice morning, this deity sends a shaft of fertilizing light like a penis into the interior of the earth-mother's womb, reenergizing the forces of vegetation that will spring forth a few months later. Lack of any proof that the megalith builders conceived of the sun as masculine has not stopped this from being generally accepted as a sound reason to build a ritual site oriented towards the solstice sunrise.[12]

The male-sun-god theory presents some problems. Why would the megalith builders have staged the mating of sun and earth when the sun was old and weak, rather than at a time when the sun was virile and powerful? Why would the sun's penis be so oddly proportioned: 6 inches wide and almost 70 feet long? Finally, why did the sun's penis have to stretch to the back of the earth mother's alleged womb? And what significance, in this cosmology, would the light's touching of the spiral symbols have? Only the presumption of the sun divinity's maleness would blind theorists to the obvious difficulties this interpretation presents.

As we have seen, however, these difficulties arise only because of the misinterpretation of the sun's gender. Nothing about the structure points to a god rather than a goddess. And Newgrange's spiral carvings—known throughout megalithic society as symbols of the goddess, often indicating her staring eyes—have been showing for millenia the cave's real occupant.

Assuming a feminine sun only adds to the mystery of Newgrange. If the sun's entry into the cave is not a fertilizing act, what then is it? The sun enters the cave for five days, two before and two after the day of solstice itself. The builders seem to have wanted to ensure at least one successful day during the often cloudy Irish winters. Only on solstice morning does the sun reach the back wall of the tumulus, making that day clearly the central one. At least half the time, solstice dawns in lashing rain, and the assembled guests stand within the cavern to witness total darkness. The cavern is at least dry, for the designers thoughtfully built grooves to carry off the constant Irish rain. But when the electric lights that now provide interior illumination are turned off, a cloudy day brings not even a dim light into the interior.

Should the day be partially clear, with wispy clouds on the horizon, those keeping vigil will see a pale florescence creep slowly across the floor of the cave to lay there wanly for twenty minutes before fading. It is a cool light, not sufficient to see the faces of the other watchers in the cave. But at least it is not darkness. When the sun rises into clear skies, however, the light is no cool dim wand. At approximately 8:45—for in Ireland the sun rises late on midwinter mornings—the site supervisor leads the elect up the green hillside to the entrance. Up the wooden steps over the elaborately carved entrance stone they climb, descending to a narrow opening that leads up a corridor of huge rocks, four dozen ten-foot megaliths. Some 63 feet long, the corridor rises slowly above the level of the entrance.

Inside, the chosen twenty arrange themselves against the dry rock walls and wait breathlessly. At 8:55, a dim strip of light suddenly appears on the sandy floor of the cave. The watchers gasp, for the light seems to arrive in a rush, not to creep into the cavern. For a few moments the inch-wide strip rests there. Eyes begin to adjust to the new brightness. Then, the light begins to change color and to widen. Within moments a wide strip of butter-yellow light blasts across the cave, reflecting upwards sufficiently to illuminate the rough corbeled arch twenty feet above. The light glows like fire.

The sunlight pours in, warming the cave's occupants with its color. One by one they kneel in the sand and put their hands into the light. Everyone is surprised, for far from being as warm as its tawny color suggests, the light is cool. Everyone peers down the corridor into the light. Almost everyone weeps. There is little talk; the feeling of a sacred presence is so strong that words evaporate.

Slowly, slowly, the light begins to retreat. Curiously, it does not fade; it backs away. The strip of light grows thinner. Then all of a sudden there's no light inside the cave. Instead, there's a puddle of light in the doorway. Then the puddle of light moves up the corridor. It is like watching footsteps or, as site superintendent Clare Tuffy likes to say, like watching the earth turn. Slowly the sun leaves the cave. Slowly, the watchers leave the cave.

It is 9:30, and the sun is a finger's width above the horizon. The light—after the cave's dark interior, if you have been in there staring at a wisp of light for more than half an hour—is dazzling. It seems liquid;

the world seems drenched in it. Witnesses report an odd sensation of knowing, for the first time, that there is light behind them as well as in front of their eyes. There is a feeling that light and air are separate—the sense that light is rarer, more precious. And there is the added sense that the sunlight is a living, conscious entity, a feeling that begins in the darkness of the cave but does not end for hours, sometimes days, afterwards.

Impossible as it may be to know for what ritual intention the tumulus was constructed, the sense of reverence towards light, shared by today's participants, must be similar to that felt by Newgrange's builders if they kept vigil inside the tumulus. Although it is tempting to imagine that they constructed the shrine with this in mind, there is no way to know if they ever occupied the cave during solstice mornings. And effect on human beings is not likely to be sufficient reason for such a literally monumental effort. It is more likely that magic connected with the weakening sun of winter and the restoration of its powers was intended.

What was this magic? When the tumulus was reopened after its centuries of disuse, huge basins hewn from stone were discovered in the three chambers that open off the cave's main chamber—into the farthest of which the sun's light shines on solstice. Although charred human remains were found in the basins, suggesting cremation rites, the bones dated from long after the mound's construction. The designers of Newgrange may have had something else in mind for these basins.

Martin Brennan[13] is convinced the basins were put there to hold water. Water inside the cave would thus form a solar mirror and provide one explanation for this monument: It was built to focus the beam of the sun's eye onto an image of her beauty. And, in fact, there is such an image in the cave. On the wall at the rear is a triple-spiral petroglyph whose spirals would have been reflected in the water the moment the sunlight hit it.

But even without water in the basins, the stone spirals themselves would have served—indeed, do serve—the same purpose each solstice morning.

If one sees the sun as an eye, rather than as a solar penis, a different vision of the meaning of the monument emerges, one more in keeping with its actual construction than the theory now current. Imagine the sun as a woman, rising late on solstice morning. Her single eye slowly peeks above the horizon. She finds it drawn somehow to a tiny opening in a mound. Peering into that opening, her gaze is drawn into an inner cave.

Along the corridor her eye travels, until it can gaze no farther. And then, she discovers a spiral design. For seventeen long minutes, the sun goddess stares at the twisting spirals on the back wall. There she recognizes—finds mirrored—her own beauty. She finds herself delighted, restored, by the amazing experience of knowing herself.

And thus the builders of Newgrange worked a miracle. By forcing the Hag to see the beauty of sunlight captured within the cave, they broke the bonds of winter and freed the captive summer.

Each year the young sun would return, only to grow old again, to become the Cailleach, the blue hag who eats people each winter. So each winter, from the time of the construction of the Cave of the Sun until time's end, the thin ray of light that comes into Newgrange on winter solstice must be there—not to help her people remember the miracle of the seasons, but to make that miracle happen. Like Amaterasu—who goes into the Sky-Rock Cave in an ugly fury but, forced to admire the beauty of light, emerges radiant—the goddess of Newgrange is transformed. It is the same story: The sun is drawn into her cave and emerges, escapes, with all the beauty of sunlight itself.

Part Two

THE SPINSTER ON THE STONE

O mother sun, to us here, to us here!
O father cloud, to Prussia, to Prussia!
Prussia's hills are alight with flames;
our hills are running with streams, o mother sun!

Blow, wind, blow the cloud from us here to Prussia!
Bear, o wind, the rain from us here to Prussia!
We have had enough of rain!
O let there be sun again, O mother sun!

Rise, mother sun, rise! So small, we shepherds,
and short, our jackets of fur. We are so cold, so cold.

—Folksongs from Lithuania and Latvia

Chapter Five ☀

THE BALTS:
DEAREST GODDESS ON THE AMBER MOUNTAIN

They tell this tale on the edge of the Baltic sea. Once, they say, the world was spring-young and the stars were still unborn. It was then that the sun goddess Saule fell in love with the moon-man Meness.

Only one creature, a frog, objected to the match.

"As it is, Saule dries up our favorite swamps each summer," she said. "What will happen when she has children of her own? She'll be worrying about them when she should be worrying about us. She'll blaze hotter and hotter. We'll all be killed!"

Soon all the frogs believed her. The pond was in a panic.

A delegation was organized to ask the highest god to call off Saule's wedding. The croaking delegates hopped across the world until they found the god's house. He wasn't home. But Saule was.

"I am warming the whole world safely now and will continue to do so forever, " she snapped. "How dare you talk this way? You are vermin! I never want to see you again!"

The frogs admitted that they had no reason to doubt Saule and that it was unjust to stand in the way of her happiness. Afterwards, not a single frog could look the sun goddess in the eye. So they stayed in the shade and only came out at night—as they do to this day. [1]

This is only one of the hundreds of myths surrounding Saule, the sun goddess of the Baltic Sea. And these myths include some of the most tender and affectionate of all Baltic myths, for Saule was much beloved by her people, who maintained her worship for the better part of two millennia on the shores of the amber sea. This worship began in prehistory, as Saule's story begins in the primeval world before creation as we know it.

This world at the beginning of time was paradise. "It wasn't the day before yesterday when Saule was engaged," a Latvian folksong stresses. "Saule was engaged when the earth was created." When her wedding day arrived, Saule decked herself out in silver crowns and necklaces. Meness opened the great silver gates of morning, then lifted Saule's wedding wreath, claiming her as his love.

It was endless springtime. The sun and the moon lived together in a pretty little house at the edge of the world. Each day they traveled the skies side by side. They had countless children, the countless stars. *Dainas*—folksongs that originated in the religious liturgy of the ancient Balts—tell of Saule's happiness. "Rise up, dear moon, rise up, the brightest," the sun sang to her husband. "I am already a long time out of bed and I light for everybody in the world, old and young, small and tall." Sometimes Meness served as Saule's charioteer, driving the sun-chariot as the goddess lit up the surface of Earth, her eldest daughter. It was a time of peace and happiness; there was never conflict, there was no betrayal.

Among Saule's many children there was one who was the most brilliant, the most beloved. She was Saules Meita, the sun-daughter, the morning star who was almost as beautiful as her mother. Even the sons of the highest god came calling, riding from the other side of the world to rein in at her door. Saule looked forward to her daughter's marriage. She planned to give Germany to Saules Meita for her private preserve, and so for centuries Saule shone especially bright on the cattle and brown horses of that land.

But it was not to be. For there was evil in this Eden. The moon was a faithless love who would break the heart of shining Saule.

It happened this way: Saule had to rise early each day to light the world, and Meness grew weary of accompanying the goddess on her rounds. When he failed one morning to join her in the chariot, Saule took no notice. But the moon-man was not sleeping. He was planning, in Saule's absence, to seduce the beautiful long-haired daughter of the sun.

Meness said to the sun-daughter as she passed, "O, stay and wait, I have to tell you many thoughts. The first thought is about the dark night, the second thought about checkered clouds, and the third thought is about the shining Sun."

Did he rape her? Did she go willingly? Some say he was the guilty one; others say the morning star herself desired the glamorous moon, her stepfather in this version. In either case, incest ended the world's primal bliss.

When she returned, Saule immediately knew something was wrong, someone was missing. Weeping tears of amber, Saule cried, "I see, count or no count, that one star is missing—the one that rose first, sank last, shone brightest." Although she searched throughout heaven, Saule could not find where her daughter had gone, the one she called her white lily. When Saule realized why—that Meness had violated both her child and her trust in him—she took a sword and struck the moon across the face, leaving scars that can still be seen today.

She was heartbroken. In her apple garden, she wept bitterly, singing, "The golden apple has fallen from the apple tree." The sun-daughter was no less wretched. Her garland of innocence was stained. For three years she gathered withered foliage, crying, "Where, o mother mine, shall I wash my apparel, where wash away the blood?"

Saule could no longer live with Meness. No more would they travel side by side through the sky. Instead, Saule went her own way. Sometimes she rose when the moon was still up; then she kept to the other side of the world until he set. And always, she kept her daughter glowing by her side—the star we see at dawn and dusk—so that Saules Meita would be safe from the incestuous moon.[2]

The amber-weeping Saule was chief divinity of the Balts, who lived on the eastern shores of the sea named for them. Creating light like thread, Saule is the first spinning sun goddess we will examine in detail, the others being in Scandinavia, Eastern Europe, and the Americas. The vision of sun as spinster leads us to unravel connections with other images: snakes and spiders, stones and crystals, dwarf smiths who forge magical necklaces, magical rites like maze dancing and ball playing. Like the mirror, the spinster sun sits at the core of a complex of solar images. We will begin our exploration with Baltic Saule because of the vast literature that is devoted to her—literally hundreds of thousands of poems and songs, probably the richest extant treasury of sun goddess literature anywhere.

The very name of the Balts includes that of their goddess: *balta saulite*, they call her in a tongue that allows for more passionate tenderness than ours, "darling little white sun." *Saules mat*, they say, "mother sun," or sometimes *Saulite mat*, "little sun-mother," and *Saulite sudrabota*, "small silver sun." The affectionate folksongs, the *dainas*, addressed to Saule show loving delight in a goddess who daily blessed her thankful world with light:

> Saule wears silken garments,
> with a silver crown,
> with a silver crown,
> made of gilded leaves.

> Saule crosses the lake,
> brilliant as tinsel,
> a crown of gold on her head,
> and polished slippers on her feet.

Goddess-mother Saule
reached her hand above the river.
Her shawl, her gilt shawl,
slipped from her shoulders.

Saule, the *dainas* say, was a beautiful matron who decked herself with silver jewelry and danced in silver shoes; in her honor, Lithuanian women at festivals wore red embroidered dresses and silver-gilt head-dresses. Red and silver were Saule's special colors: Red forest berries were her dried tears; the tree in which she slept flowered red each morning as she rose; she was a red apple setting in the west. Or she was a silver apple falling from a tree; she sailed a silver sea, scattering silver gifts; she sowed the earth with silver.[3]

She lived in a silver-gated castle over the hills at the world's end. Each day she rose early from the mouth of a well and mounted her char-iot drawn by wild brown horses with stars covering their backs. "They never tire, they never grow weaker," she boasted of these horses, "and I have no time to let them rest." She herself did rest, for a moment at noon, when she took a nap on a cot of roses in the middle of the sky. As she traveled, Saule watched the world beneath her; like other sun deities, she was a watchful eye in the sky. When something was lost, the owner invoked Saule; she helped find wandering livestock and even located lovers for the lonely.

She was intimately addressed by her children below. The story is told that a Latvian farmer was walking in his rye field. Seeing how hot the day was, he lifted his hat to Saule and begged her to set, so that his young daughter could rest from her farming labors. But before Saule could answer his request, the girl's father-in-law called up to her. "Saule," he said, "you seem to be rushing! Go slower! Stay late in the sky! My daugh-ter-in-law has much work to do and needs the extra light!"

Similarly, Saule had work to do herself. Each morning, for instance, she had to decorate the treetops with appropriate ornaments. "The fir tree gets the gloves and socks," she said. "The birch, the green wool yarn; the oak tree gets two silver rings." She had to clip the forest's ceiling with golden scissors. She had to watch over everything, like a good mother or housekeeper. Sometimes even Saule couldn't find time for it all, as one *daina* complains: "O, Mother Sun, what are you doing? The silken mead-ows haven't been mowed, the golden hills haven't been harrowed!"

At night, Saule dismounted and watered her horses in the Nemunas River, then tied them to a tree growing out of a gray boulder at the world's end. Hanging her silken garments to glow silver in the twilight, she bathed in the sea. Then she slept in an apple tree; during the night, spirits of dead Balts journeyed to her on horses or birds or smoke. Late at night, she boarded a golden boat to travel east beneath the earth to her rising place. "Whoever says that Saule walks on foot," a *daina* tells us, "is lying. Across the forest, she travels in her chariot; across the sea, she glides in a boat."

All of these details are captured in the folksongs of the Balts. These *dainas*—without question the greatest cultural treasure of the Lithuanians and the Letts of Latvia—have been recorded and collected for almost two hundred years. The Lithuanian national archives hold more than 105,000 *dainas*, with 30,000 melodies, including ones that influenced Chopin, Schumann and Schubert; in Latvia, nearly one million songs are registered. Before being transcribed, these ancient songs were carefully preserved in folk memory; the first *daina* collected, in 1632, was recorded identically three hundred years later. Rubulis claims that "the songs are so extensive and true that historians base textbooks on them." Even the songs and proverbs themselves reinforce the need for accuracy. "You cannot cast out a word from the song," it is said in Lithuania, while a *daina* singer claimed that—

> I sing the song as it has always been,
> It has not originated in my own mind.
> Having been composed by the old people,
> It is sung anew by me.

Credit for the conveyance of Baltic oral literature through the generations must go to the women of Latvia and Lithuania. Scholars agree that most of the songs—73.3 percent, according to Karl Bucher—were composed by women. And the entire repertoire was memorized and performed by them, for women were the villages' main singers. At Latvian celebrations, groups of women stood across the room from each other, alternating songs. As a group's turn came, two singers would join hands in the center of the group and serenade each other while the rest hummed accompaniment. Group and solo singing was also part of daily work; as women did laundry, as they spun and wove, as they cooked and cleaned, they sang. And much of the time, they sang to the sun goddess.

> I open the window to Saule,
> I look out at Saule.
> Ah, it's too short, this life
> that I live in her light!

Perhaps because singing was a women's art in Baltic lands, the magnificent songs to "Dearest Goddess"—as Latvian poet Eso Benjamins translates the affectionate diminutives used of Saule—remained steadfastly in the repertoire. We find in these songs a powerful connection between female generations. Throughout them we find being the mother of a daughter, and the daughter of a mother, as primary poetic experiences. To be a daughter was, according to the *dainas*, a special gift, surpassed only by giving birth to one. "Let us both think, Dearest Goddess," one *daina* says. "If the child is a son, he'll become a soldier. Should I throw him in the river? If the child is a daughter, she'll sing us sweet songs."

There are genres of song among the Balts that are not found in other Western literature but that are deeply true to female experience. There is, for instance, the derogation of neighbors' daughters in comparison with one's own. There is the more tender "orphan song," sung by a woman whose mother has died:

> Saule and my own mother,
> You are both so pale.
> I see Saule and
> I mourn my mother.

Many of the *dainas* addressed to Saule praise her as a mother—specifically, the mother of daughters. But the many *dainas* devoted to the daughters of the sun unfortunately also present the greatest puzzle in Baltic literature, for the texts are full of contradictions. In some songs there is one sun-daughter, Barbelina; in others two or three; in yet others the daughters are innumerable as stars. In some songs, indeed, the daughters *are* stars, the morning star Austrine and the evening star Valkyrine. Again, the maidens are diminutive suns, traveling in their mother's path and climbing rose trees to the sky. Sometimes the sun maidens stay at home to keep house for their mother—not always adequately, as one *daina* says, leaving the floor unswept and the table covered with food scraps, running away to Germany to play instead of doing the farm chores.

We cannot definitively sort through these confusions, but we can pick out some connecting strands in the myths of the sun-daughter called Saules Meita, the "Sun-Maiden." The most loved child of Saule, she was also the goddess's double:

> Yesterday Saule was brilliant,
> but today she is so vague.
> Yesterday's sun was Saule herself—
> today it's just the Maid.

In defining the relationship between Saule and her daughter, a Lithuanian folktale is instructive. It tells of a king who wanted to know why the sun was sometimes red when she rose and set. "Go to the sun's mother," the king told his coachman, "and find out."

"But I don't know where she lives!" the coachman objected.

"Go find out, or I'll hang you from the apple tree!" said the king.

The coachman was miserable. Travel to the mother of the sun? No one had ever done that.

Out in the stables, a horse noticed his downcast manner.

"What's the matter with you?" the horse asked.

"Why, just that the king wants me to find the mother of the sun and ask her why the sun gets red when she rises and sets! And if I can't, he'll hang me from the apple tree!"

"Well," said the horse, sighing slightly, "we'd better get going."

The coachman mounted the horse and traveled for three days and three nights, until he came to a river so wide no one could possibly cross it. There on the shore the coachman collapsed in frustration. His tears, falling into the water, attracted a huge fish.

"Why are you crying?" said the fish. The coachman related his sad tale. "Get on my back," said the fish, "and I will take you across the water."

So the coachman and his horse got on the fish's back and crossed the water safely. Four more days and nights they traveled, finally reaching the most beautiful palace in the world, the amber-studded palace of Saule. There they found the sun's mother shaking out the bedding.

She was very friendly. "What do you want, stranger?"

The coachman related his sad tale.

"You'll have to wait until Saule returns for the night," the mother of the sun told him. "You can ask her then. Meanwhile, you can wait in the kitchen." And so the coachman went to wait in the sun's kitchen.

He was so tired he fell asleep. But he woke up quickly when the sun returned, for the entire house started to glow with light and warmth. He overheard the sun's mother addressing her daughter.

"There was a man here looking for you," she said to Saule. "His king sent him to find out why you are red when you rise and when you set."

Saule turned red. "Where is this man! I will burn him to cinders!" she shouted.

The coachman's hair stood straight up.

"O, he left when he found you weren't home," said the sun's mother. "But what is the answer to his question, young daughter? Why are you so angry?"

"Mother," the sun goddess said with exasperation, "you know very well that there's a princess in the middle of the sea more beautiful than I!

When I rise and see her I get so mad I turn red! And when I must pass over the sea at night before I set, I see her again and turn red again!"

The coachman overheard, and he was out the window like a flash. His trusty horse took him over the land, and the fish helped them over the water, and soon he was home to answer his king's question. The king was mightily pleased and gave the coachman a bucket of gold coins as a reward. The coachman was mightily pleased and took the coins to the stable to show his horse.

He did not get to enjoy his good fortune for long, for almost immediately the king summoned him back to the palace. "What was I thinking, to let you go?" he said. "You did so well on your last errand that I have another. Find that beautiful princess and bring her to me."

Now the coachman's heart sank to his boots. How could he find a princess in the middle of the sea? Shoulders drooping, he went back to the stables and got his horse ready for the journey.

The horse was in good spirits. "We found the house of the sun's mother; we found out why Saule is red," said the horse; "And we can find the princess."

They traveled across hills and plains searching for many and many a day. Then, just when they had given up hope, they came upon a stork's nest perched in an old oak tree. As they were riding by, the nest began teetering.

"It's going to fall!" shouted the coachman. He rode up and caught it. Another instant and the nestlings would have been smashed on the rocks.

Above him, he heard the sudden pounding of wings. "You saved my children!" the stork mother called down. "Can I ever repay you?"

"You don't happen to know how to find the princess more beautiful than the sun?" the coachman asked.

"Well, yes, I do," said the stork. "I fly over her every day." The stork gave the coachman directions. She also told him that the princess slept in a palace surrounded by other princesses, but that she could be distinguished by the ring she wore. If he stole the ring, the princess would obey him.

Off went the coachman and his faithful horse. And indeed they found the palace in the middle of the sea, and they found the princess in the middle of her maidens, and the coachman took the maiden's ring from her, and she followed him back to his king. And that's how the king got to marry the princess, and how his coachman got to marry the king's sister and be showered with golden coins.

The princess in the middle of the sea is a doublet of the sun's daughter. Saules Meita is described in Latvian folksongs as sleeping on an island in the sea, wearing her magical ring. She also—and more often—appears in Baltic and Scandinavian folktales as a princess on a glass mountain. Originally, this was an island or mountain of amber—called *glese*, Tacitus says and *glaesum*, according to Pliny, in Northern European tongues.

A typical version of the tale starts with a young man named Hans at the edge of a forest pond, where he saw three women swimming.

When they saw him watching them, they sprang from the water, changed into ducks, and flew away. But Hans was infatuated, so he built a hut near the pool and awaited the maidens' return. He searched the pondside until he found three garments, one of which he took into his hut. Shortly afterwards, he heard a voice call, "Let me in, I have lost my garment." One of the duck-maidens entered and, grabbing Hans' own cloak to cover herself, begged him to give her her dress back. He refused, and ran home to get his mother. But halfway there he remembered he had not locked the chest where he'd hidden the dress.

Back he went, but too late. The girl was gone, the dress was gone, and all that was left was a note written in golden letters: "I live on the Crystal Mountain."

Hans set out. He asked everyone where the Crystal Mountain was, but no one knew. At last he found a magic hare who led him to the mountain road, then vanished. Hans wandered down the road until he came to a dead horse, over which a bear, a wolf, a raven and an ant were contending. "Divide this among us," said the animals. Hans gave ant the head, raven the entrails, wolf the bones, and bear the flesh. In return, each of the animals gave Hans something magical: from ant, a foot; from wolf and bear, a hair each; and from raven, a feather. Thus equipped, Hans set off for the nearby castle on the summit of the Crystal Mountain.

When he reached the mountain's base, he began to climb. But the glass was smooth as a mirror, and he kept sliding back. He changed himself into a bear, and he carved steps into the mountain until glass splinters made him bleed. Then he tried being a wolf and hanging on with his teeth, but he wounded his mouth on the glass. Finally, he changed himself into a raven and flew to the top of the mountain.

There he found the maiden peering out a window. She told him that her mother was a witch who kept her imprisoned. Hans, turning himself into an ant, crept into the old woman's bedroom. When she came in to sleep, he bit her all over her body. This he did for three nights running.

The witch knew this could be no ordinary ant, so she trapped him as he was crawling out from under the bed and forced him to resume his human shape. Then she demanded to know what he wanted.

"Only your daughter," said Hans.

"You must earn her," said the witch. And so she set him some tasks.

The first was to eat an egg without breaking the shell. That was easy: He turned himself back into an ant, crawled in, ate the egg, then crawled back out. Using a bit of chalk to stop the hole, be brought the egg to the witch.

"Good," said the witch. "Now go to the great forest, cut down all the trees, and split up all the wood."

Hans went to the forest. It was so huge he became tired just looking at it. He lay down under a tree and went to sleep. When he awoke, there were thousands of cords of wood stacked neatly.

A voice in his ear said, "I came and did the work while you slept, and I will help you again." It was the voice of his beloved maiden.

He went back to the witch and reported the work done. "Good, " she said. "Now I will kindle it into a blaze, and when the wood is flaming you must leap into it. If you can't, you also can't marry my daughter."

The next day Hans went to the forest and piled up all the wood into a huge bonfire. The witch lit it. As the flames grew, Hans grew more hesitant to jump into it. He made several runs at the fire, but stopped short each time.

At last he heard the voice of the maiden, calling, "Spring now! Spring!" and so he did. As he leaped into the middle of the flames, the burning brands separated so that Hans stood without injury in the flames. As the flames died down, a new city was revealed with a castle in the middle of it, and there lived Hans and his maiden, happily ever after.

The witch? She was never heard from again.

The story of the princess trapped on a mountain or an island occurs throughout northern Europe. Latvian folk songs tell of the sun maiden entrapped on an island; in some tales, in fact, the princess is imprisoned on a mountain rising from the sea to form an island. Sometimes, as in Germany, the maiden holds a single golden apple, which the hero must take to free her; or she is surrounded by flames through which the hero must pass; or, as Rapunzel, she helps the hero by letting him make a rope-ladder of her own golden hair.

Perhaps of the most familiar of European folktales, these are no mere fairy stories but the remnants of a complex solar myth of the sun and her daughter. The dual sun goddess whom we encountered in Ireland is paralleled here, suggesting a winter-summer dichotomy. Whereas the Irish sun goddess hides in a cave in snake form, the Baltic sun-to-be rests in human form on an island or mountain. Sometimes the island is in the sky: In Baltic tales, the trapped princess is named Valkyrine, lady of the evening star, daughter of the sun. Throughout its many variants, the story —replete with solar images, including egg, tree, fire, mirror, rings and golden hair— have at its essence the freeing of the summer sun from winter's grasp.

Should we need more confirmation that the imprisoned maiden is the sun, we can look to an ancient Baltic story. In 1431, the missionary Jerome of Prague, one of the earliest outsiders to visit Lithuania, discovered the Balts worshiping the sun, which they said had been imprisoned in a tower and freed by means of a huge iron hammer. "The signs of the zodiac," Jerome's informants told him, "brought help to the sun, and broke the tower with the huge hammer, and restored the liberated sun to men, and therefore that which had been the instrument by which mortals had received light was worthy of veneration."

The image of the sun as a maiden imprisoned in a tower or hiding, as the *dainas* say, "at the bottom of the deep rock pit," is tied to the image of her release from this entrapment. And the freeing of the sun goddess was cause for celebration. Among the Balts, celebration took place at *kaleda*, winter solstice, the day on which the heavenly smith Kalvis remade the sun. Using a magic hammer, he forged a golden cup to be filled with the sun's liquid light. Then she returned, the reborn Saule, urging on her horses with silken whips as she rode an iron-wheeled chariot over the hilltops of dawn.

The opposite solstice was also an important Baltic feast: *ligo*, celebrated on June 24. The festival's name comes from a word used as a refrain in the seasonal songs: *Ligo* comes from *ligot*, "to sway" or "to sing." Another common solstice refrain was the Latin word *rota*, "wheel." The words suggest both the wheel dances that helped Saule through her seasonal paces and the fire-wheels that were part of solstice festivals throughout ancient Europe.

On *ligo*, it was said that the sun goddess rose crowned with a braid of red blossoms to dance on the silver hills wearing silver shoes, very much as the sun goddess danced in Ireland and Scotland. On this festal day, Saule changed colors; she hopped and jumped like a lamb:

> Saule leads the dance
> beside the vast forest.
> Give me, Mother, a golden belt
> because I want to run and watch.

At *ligo*, people sought out streams that flowed towards sunrise in which to bathe themselves; water catching the sunbeams at sunrise would bring health and beauty. The women donned braided bridal wreaths—even married women who, on this day each year, could be free in dress and behavior. Everyone walked through the fields, singing and calling down Saule's blessings on the crops. The sun goddess sang along with them: "Saule sings *ligo* all night; the fathers sing *ligo* in the sheep-fold."

Finally, celebrants gathered around bonfires to sing the night away. Many of the *ligo* songs were teasing jests that allowed the accumulated tensions of village life a ritual outlet. But everything ended on a note of harmony and hope when the farewell *daina* was sung: "Bless, O god, the place where we ate, where we drank. May here grow two rye-ears at the end of each stalk."

From the festival of *ligo* through the harvest season, Saule reigned as a queenly mother. But, like the Cailleach Bheur, she finally grew old and needed to be restored—or replaced by her daughter. This transition may not have been a smooth one; the old sun may not have readily given up her place. In the Lithuanian folktale of the red sun's anger, we find a sun goddess envious of a princess, perhaps her successor, certainly more beautiful than she. In the *dainas*, similarly, there is tension between Saule and her daughter:

> Each morning Saule dresses
> the little fiance.
> She says as she dresses her:
> Take heart, you are very young.
> My self, my old self, I have no power,
> except that I have so much gold.

Donald Ward, an expert in divine twinship who has written on the *dainas*, finds behind these songs a myth in which the sun maiden, promised in marriage to the two sons of god and abducted by the moon, is held captive by the sun until liberated by the twins. Is the moon-man, then, Saule's collaborator when he rapes her daughter? The *dainas* suggest an ancient myth in which a sun mother and her daughter—the morning star, or the dawn, or the year's new sun—feel rivalry as well as love for each other. Perhaps at one time the matron was replaced each year by the maiden. The *dainas* may faintly recall the struggle between them, with the male stars tipping the balance in the daughter's favor. But the *dainas* never tell the whole story. They never say what happens once the sun maiden is married; she is always a bride, never a wife. Time has stopped;

there is a static quality to the relationships. Perhaps this is what gives the songs their charm: The relationship between Saule and her daughter is caught at a poignant point of strain.

The *dainas* and folktales of the Balts are particularly important to understanding European sun-goddess mythology because they derive from a very ancient stratum of European culture. Although the *dainas* were recorded relatively late, they are by no means modern. Lithuanian and Latvian separated linguistically in the eighth century C.E., but the pantheon is identical in the two countries; the myths therefore must date to the period of unity. This mythology seems untainted by the imagery of southern religions, for the Balts were the last European people to be Christianized, and they held fast to their beliefs for centuries after being officially converted in 1387. The deep conservatism of the Baltic people, that same cultural conservatism that led to the preservation of the *dainas*, swung into action, producing a syncretisic Christianity incorporating pagan beliefs. Right into the twentieth century the Baltic people practiced what Marija Gimbutas calls "a dual faith," in which many old ways were preserved; for instance, women were charged with keeping alive the ancient sacred fire in each household.

Who were the Balts, these conservators of sun-goddess culture? They emerge in the archaeological record during the Mesolithic Era (8000 to 4000 B.C.E.) when the northern part of Europe was occupied by agricultural tribespeople whose lives were regularly disrupted by raiding battle-axe nomads, the early Indo-Europeans. In the western part of the region—now Poland—the original tribes mingled sufficiently with the invaders to form a mixed culture that Tacitus called the Aisti; these Old Prussians and Curonians had similarities to the Germans and Celts, with whom they had extensive contact. At least, that's what scholars who have attempted to reconstruct this prehistory believe; the culture itself, unfortunately, was utterly lost as Slavs and Germans subdued the land over several millennia.

The north and east, today's Lithuania and Latvia, was home to an unmixed form of the battle-axe culture. The nomads here either encountered no agriculturalists or eliminated them. While the western Balts were being absorbed and then eliminated, their eastern neighbors were conveying an ancient culture virtually without modification into the historical period. In Lithuania, this archaism is especially notable. There, the national language is the only living Indo-European tongue that preserves forms from the most remote past. While English, modern Greek, even Gaelic—all descendents of the same original language—have simplified themselves over the generations, Lithuanian has retained a complexity that makes scholars compare it to dead languages like classical Greek and Sanskrit, to which it is the closest living relative. If Lithuanian retains archaic forms of the Indo-European language, its speakers may have conveyed intact into history more than just the language forms of that ancient culture. The presence of a sun goddess, rather than a sun god, among them is therefore especially intriguing.[4]

Commonly, the Indo-Europeans are described as invaders who swept down from the north into the European Mediterranean, into Anatolia, and into India between 2500 and 1500 B.C.E. They are thought to have carried with them a sky-father cult that was forcibly melded ("married") to indigenous Great Goddess religions to form such complicated pantheons as those of ancient Greece and Hindu India. Apollo, this argument assumes, represents a vital Indo-European concept: the masculine sun, appropriate emblem of a patriarchal, sky-oriented people.

But a sun goddess among the Balts raises suspicions: If the language is so ancient, might not Baltic mythology be closer to the original Indo-European than are classical Greek myths? Ralph Mannhardt argued so at the end of the last century, claiming that the original Indo-European sun myths were preserved as in amber in Lithuania. Donald Ward is willing to grant that the myth of the sun maiden and her twin lovers "unquestionably dates from the period of Indo-European unity," but persists in assuming that the maiden represents only the dawn; thus, he suggests, dawn goddesses like Indian Ushas, Greek Eos and Roman Aurora could descend from the original culture.

But if the maiden, why not the mother? Sun goddesses survive in most Indo-European language areas. Was the original Indo-European sun divinity a goddess?

It is possible that Saule's presence in the Baltic pantheon merely means that her worshipers had fallen under the influence of the spinning sun goddess of the nearby Finno-Ugrians, who were not of Indo-European origin. But the infection seems to have raced throughout the Indo-European tribes: northwest of Saule, the goddess Sunnu ruled the Scandinavians, and there was a female sun among the nearby Germans; there were sun goddesses among the Indo-European Hittites and Slavs. Even in Britain, where the Roman legions imported their Mithraic Apollo, the sun goddess was still visible in Sul. The tradition from which Saule springs, therefore, is as strong as that of the Apollonian sun among the Indo-Europeans—perhaps stronger, for Marija Gimbutas points out that Lithuanian and Latvian folklore has the same value for determining the beliefs of the ancient Indo-Europeans as their languages do for reconstructing the mother tongue.[5]

Or was Saule, and the other sun goddesses we find in Indo-European areas, a breakthrough from the strata of what Gimbutas calls Old Europe? There is some reason to believe so: The presence of the dual sun goddess, and the myth of the captive sun maiden, is in Ireland connected with a pre-Celtic, probably pre-Indo-European, divinity. Symbols of the sun goddess are shared with those of the Neolithic Old European bird-headed and serpent goddess. Some apparently Greek figures, rooted in an Old European strata, share these same stories and symbols. Was Saule an Old European goddess penetrating through an Indo-European overlay, or the Indo-European sun goddess herself?

Perhaps both: A sun goddess among the Indo-Europeans could have encountered and melded with an Old European sun goddess to form the beloved Saule. This is suggested by the fact that a sun goddess can be found in the Baltic area's archaeological record very early, during the Mesolithic. Among the Balts, Saule was sometimes envisioned as a pot that held liquid light. The most ancient ceramic pieces from the area seem to convey the same idea for, Gimbutas tells us, they were decorated with obvious solar designs as well as complex "incisions of diagonal lines, triangles, and rhomboid patterns" that form "a radiating sun." Other pots that may represent a sun goddess are the so-called face-urns, found in the Vistula River Basin; these show the head of a woman wearing a beaded necklace and have sun symbols on their lids. Some of the face-urns have little handles that form ears, to which beaded earrings were attached.

This pot-goddess evolved into a goddess of amber. The Baltic artifacts of greatest modern appeal are the amber ornaments found in Baltic burials as early as 5000 B.C.E., during the Mesolithic. The next age, the Neolithic, was marked by production of amber discs punctured in the center and marked with two intersecting lines forming the rays of the solar wheel. Such discs were made as late as 1800 B.C.E.—still the Neolithic on the Baltic shores, although Southern Europe had moved into the Bronze Age centuries earlier. Almost all Baltic amber artifacts from this period are from graves, where amulets of the resin jewel were placed, apparently to aid the deceased in the afterworld. The common practice of burying Saule's jewel with the dead—sometimes carved into horses like those that drew her chariot—suggests that the sun goddess's protection was sought for the traveling soul. Amber may have also represented a promise of rebirth, for the substance "animates" thread and other light objects like an organic magnet, once rubbed enough to generate electricity. Electricity, in fact, comes from the Greek word for *elektron.*

Even today, most of the world's amber comes from the Baltic coast. In ancient times, Baltic amber was traded throughout the early Mediterranean; so valuable was it that Pliny saw a tiny amber figure selling for more than a slave. At first the Balts traded with near neighbors like the Uneticians, who had such a great hunger for amber that almost 80 percent of their excavated graves contained the gem. But the tenth century B.C.E. found all Europe clamoring for the jewel, as were the peoples of North Africa and the eastern Mediterranean. This created a boom economy along the Baltic, complete with the sudden importation of the finest luxury goods the Bronze Age had to offer—and the eruption of the previously backward Baltic lands into the full flower of the first great age of European history.

Archaeologists excavating the amber routes have found traders' hoards, containing treasures of bronze mixed with amber beads, in stashes along north-leading rivers. In some cases, the amber was worked before it left its homeland, but in other cases amber was brought raw to factories as far south as Italy. As the vogue for amber increased, it was fashioned into hairpins, into lamps, into sculptures of ritual and artistic importance. These amber items decked the persons and households of their owners during their lifetimes; commonly, at least some amber went to the afterworld as well. In Etruria, in Mycenae, in lake dwellings in France and Switzerland, at Stonehenge, in the Egyptian pyramids, in Phoenician graves, the tear-shaped beads of the crying sun goddess have been discovered.

A common Greek tale from this era was that amber was gathered in the Garden of the Hesperides, where golden apples of immortality grew; the jewel was therefore credited with bestowing eternal life, although how this belief withstood the continual deaths of amber-owners is not easily explained. A more famous story is the Greek one that Phaeton, son of Helios, borrowed his father's chariot one day but, unable to control the sun's horses, fell to his death. His sisters, the Heliades or sun maidens, wept endlessly for him until turned into poplar trees standing over a stream, dropping amber into the water. Sophocles, too, believed that amber was produced by sisters weeping for their brother—in this case, the Greek hero Meleager. In the first story, Baltic myth shines through: Saule, the apple sun, sleeps in a tree in her own garden. In the other, the connection between the sun, women's tears, and amber remains, suggesting the story had been conveyed southward from a Baltic original, especially since transformation into trees is a typically Baltic motif. The rather obsessive relationship between sun maidens and their brother hints, too, at a potentially incestuous relationship, as do the *dainas*.

The sun's amber is at the center of a web of solar images. The jewel is a fruit, a golden apple, to be harvested from the solar tree. But it is also a stone; stones, especially amber, were used as spindle-whorls, and spindle-whorls were worn as jewels; the sun goddess was a lady in a necklace who sat spinning on a stone. The goddess had long, often golden hair: the comb to prepare wool is one of a spinners' basic tools, and the goddess's golden hair thus became a shining web. Hair and yarn are morphologically connected to snakes, which similarly connect to sun's rays; Lithuanian folklore stresses this connection with proverbs like "If you kill a snake, the sun will cry," and "If someone kills a snake, it will not die until the sun has set."

There are other features to this complex. The sun-spinner was a spider, the sun her round body, the sunbeams her web. Light was gossamer webbing across the sky; the sun was a rolling ball of yarn. The sky was a silken skein; it was a fabric cloak that had to be laundered with rain. Although all of these images derive from the Baltic. We will also meet them in other areas of Northern Europe and North America where the spinster goddess attacted solar imagery to herself.

Of these connected images, one of the most vital is the connection of spinster and stone. "Mistress Sun sits each morning on a rock and spins for hours before dawn," a Scandinavian song tells us. The stone on which the goddess sat was not separate from her; rock was, magically, the goddess herself. Gimbutas reports that, to the Balts, all stones were feminine; boulders shaped like female torsos were especially sacred, but any one with a flat surface could be called a goddess. Rocks were often carved with sun symbols or drilled with holes called footprints, presumably those left by the dancing Saule with her silver shoes; these footprints, when filled with milk, were cups, for light was a nourishing liquid. By extension, rock-hard ceramic is the goddess's material; she herself can be a pot full of milk. In Lithuania, huge stones were cut smooth and set up in shrines to attract goddesses to do their spinning there. In the *dainas*, both Saule and her daughter spun and wove. In one song, Saule wove cloth beside the Dausava river, carding with a comb of gold and passing thread with a shuttle of silver. In another, the sun maiden carded wool at the top of a glacier stream; she wove wool, while her mother wove silk.

The Sun Maiden weaves shawls
in the middle of the sky.

Two are solid gold,
the third is solid silver.

Saule's light-spinning gave rise to other metaphors: She was a weaver of human beings, the divine ancestress who created new fleshy clothes for the spirits of the dead. As Mother Sun, she was responsible for feeding her children; therefore the sun was sometimes a jug of milk, sometimes and more primordially a mother's full breast. This single breast could be detached from the goddess's body; the sun was then a cup or sun-pot, the sun herself a potter. As mother of life, the sun-goddess was also mistress of death; she spun out the length of each day and divided time into months, seasons, years, as she divided lives into youth, maturity, old age. Thus she was a fate-goddess, foreteller of a future that she, in fact, controlled.

The Dearest Goddess
sits spinning
her strands
on the mountain
top.
Will she
mate me
with an ass?
Or will it be
the man
I want?

The goddess on her stone used a spindle to make light. This tool, in its earliest and simplest form, was a rock or a pebble. The earliest form of spinning, some eight thousand years ago, was simple enough. With no tools at all, short yarns were created from a mass of wool simply by twisting the fibers; this is the simplest form of spinning. Soon enough, though, it becomes impossible to maintain the twist manually. But the addition of a bit of weight to the yarn's end allows the spinner to lengthen it indefinitely. As the weight—the spindle "whirl" or "whorl"—spins at the bottom of the thread, it twists the fibers emerging from the mass of wool. The skill of spinning with a whorl involves allowing just the right amount of twist to travel up the yarn to the point of emergence. It is also important not to allow the spindle-whorl to turn in the opposite direction, thus loosening the twist in the already-spun yarn or—worse yet—breaking it. Notched, crochet-hook-like spindles were invented to avoid this problem.

Fiber and whorl—both of these spinning symbols are connected with the sun goddess. The round sun is like a spindle, anchoring the strands of light; light rays jut from the sun like hair or yarn. The many injunctions against dancing widdershins or anti-sunwise in circle dances, as well as magical solstice prohibitions of various sorts, are clearly designed with the image of the spindle-sun in mind; worshipers did not want the spinning sun to untwist or break the skein of light.

Spinning is an apt metaphor for the production of light, for it was in the past a constant, apparently endless, activity. It is perhaps difficult today to realize just how omnipresent spinning was in earlier cultures. Every inch of every thread used to weave every garment had to be wound by hand. At any moment during the daylight hours, some woman of the family would be spinning. Sometimes she would sing as she spun; sometimes she would tell stories, a form of entertainment still called "yarn-spinning" in her honor; sometimes she would let the repetitive motion lull her into a meditative trance and she would speak prophecies. The woman with her ceaseless spinning was both the model and representative of the spinning sun goddess.[6]

Among the Balts, the connection between the sun and spinning is very old, and the sun-stone, amber, forms the link. Spindles of amber have been found in the most ancient burial mounds in the region. Sometimes amber discs—drop-spindles—were also placed in the grave, perhaps as concrete prayers to the sun goddess to spin forth the lost life in another body. No doubt some of these spindles were used before being buried, for amber was considered a magical substance for a spinner; as the light never tangles in the sky, so an amber spindle protected the new thread from snarls caused by unhappy or malicious spirits. Finally, the amber took the form of beads and necklaces.

At first, necklaces were not intended as ornaments but were simple conveniences, for when spinning women stopped for another task—to change a baby or to knead the bread—they would twist their work, amber drop-spindles and all, around their necks. This evolved into the necklace, originally strings of spindle-beads hung on thread. Such beads or spindles are the most widely distributed of ancient artifacts; thirty-five thousand years ago, Cro-Magnon people wore beads. Even the most practiced eye cannot absolutely tell the difference between beads and spindles-whorls, so interchangeable are they in shape. In many countries even today, huge necklaces of spindle-whorls are worn as magical ornaments. So it's not surprising that the spinning sun goddess has as one of her magical attributes a necklace of amber, gold or other precious substance.

The spinster on her stone is common to all peoples of the Baltic coasts; she crosses cultures, appearing among Finno-Ugrians and Russians as well as among Balts, Germans and Scandinavians. Although the image could certainly spring from the same archetypal source in different lands—as it probably did in North America—it is likely that in Europe the sun-spinster's mythology was conveyed with her craft, passing from group to group together with new spinning implements and the technology that went with them. If this is so, the oldest form of the spinning sun goddess was probably an indigenous deity of the subarctic, a goddess whose worship preceded the coming of the Indo-Europeans, who brought their own sun goddess with them. This ancient presence is hinted at by the spiral dances of the Troy Towns in Scandinavia, where a spring ritual that freed the sun maiden was enacted. From the same era as these stone mazes date other artifacts suggesting an early sun goddess. Across Sweden, Norway and Denmark we find petroglyphs and petrographs—rock carvings and paintings—of chariots, discs, wheels, footprints and "sun daggers" in the shape of spindles. These mazes and carvings help us as we unravel the tangle of cultures in the sun goddess mythology of northern Europe.

Chapter Six

SCANDINAVIA:
THREADING THE MAZES

In 1882, a marvelous prehistoric maze came to public attention. At Wisby in Denmark, it centered on a natural limestone cave from which lines of boulders were arranged in a spiral. Each spring, young men of the village would "imprison" a girl in the maze's center, then lead her forth triumphantly from captivity. The game was of ancient origin, and its late survival hints at earlier ritual prominence.

The same festal event was traced across Scandinavia, in Germany, and into Britain. Where we find the springtime dance, we also find the maze, built of pebbles or boulders, or cut into the living turf. Although the myth behind the ritual is lost, the maze dance was important enough to survive through a millennium of Christianity. At Saffron Walden in Essex, England, the maze was still danced in the seventeenth century; a girl occupied the center and a boy raced through—"threaded the maze"—to rescue her. In Brandenburg, Germany, a similar maze was threaded each spring until the last century, and early this century the maze was still chalked on pavements in provincial Europe each April 1.

In Scandinavia, the mazes were called Troy Towns, *Trojaburgen*. While it might seem that the game would be connected to the eastern Mediterranean war and the epics it spawned, such is not the case. *Trojaburg* derives from an old Scandinavian word for "twist" or "turn." Soon after the discovery of the Wisby monument, Ernst Krause, a German scholar, theorized the connection of the mazes to a ritual of winter's passing and the liberation of summer. He claimed the maze and its name were traces of an early, pan-European sun myth centering on a female divinity.

In Italy, just a decade before Krause announced this theory—and unknown to him at the time—a pitcher had been discovered that supports this interpretation. The Etruscan pitcher of Tragliatella shows in detail a ceremonial dance. In it, a woman offers a round object—a globe, or a ball of twine—to a man. Nearby, a group of seven dancers and two horsemen celebrate. From the tail of one of the horses comes a labyrinth on which are roughly painted the words *truia*, "Troy," and *mi felena*, "I am Helen."

A few centuries after the pitcher was made, the Roman Pliny saw vestiges of turf mazes in the Italian fields and expressed puzzlement at their "Trojan" name, *ludus Troia*. But the name wasn't Trojan, and we still don't know what it meant. The Etruscans who trod these mazes and could have explained the name had been conquered by the Romans. All that survived was the maze's name and the ritual's date. The ritual continued to be practiced for centuries. During the Roman Republic, the "Play of Troy" was still held, a vernal equinox pageant in which young men danced bearing arms. But the goddess to whom they originally danced had been deposed, and the connection of the maze to both her ball of yarn and to the solar orb had been lost.

As in Rome, so elsewhere. The springtime maze was danced across the north, from Iceland to Russia. More than a thousand of the intricate designs—Shakespeare called them "quaint mazes in the wanton green"—have been discovered in England where, despite their apparently classical name, the turf was cut and the mazes threaded long before the Romans brought Mediterranean myth and culture to the island. Often these British mazes were said to have been made by Volund or Wayland, a smith-god linked to the Baltic sun-forger Kalvis. The sacred designs themselves were often incorporated into churches erected on sacred pagan sites. Many of these were dedicated to Mary the Mother, believed to be present within the mosaic labyrinth set into the church floors.

Krause believed Trojaburg to have been a northern ritual that spread south, perhaps even giving its name to the famous war. Such an arctic or subarctic origin is supported by the fact that the labyrinth accurately maps the sun's turnings in the northern sky. In temperate zones, the sun rises and sets in relatively regular fashion, east to west, but in the far north it spins through the sky quite differently. On summer solstice near the Arctic Circle, the sun begins its daily motion due north and comes to rest again—it does not set—in the same place. As the year progresses, it moves farther and farther south, so that by midwinter it rises and sets within a small arc directly to the south—if it rises at all, which above the Arctic Circle it does not. The sun's yearly pattern, then, forms the widening arcs of a labyrinth.

On the pitcher of Tragliatella, the labyrinth is shown together with the ball held by Helen. The juxtaposition is important, for the ball is the reverse of the labyrinth. While the latter is unskeined light, the ball is light condensed, ordered. The two images are in turn connected to the great Spinster Sun, webbing the sky with light that spins forth from her limitless orb. And it suggests a double perspective on the sun as orderer and creator, a subject we shall explore throughout the rest of this section.[1]

It is not known when the Scandinavian mazes were first constructed. It may have been as long as six thousand years ago, for worship of the sun goddess in Europe's far north reaches into prehistory. Although the people who gave their name to the region were Indo-European, they were not the first to occupy the area. That these earlier residents were sun worshipers is not disputed, but no one has previously questioned the gender of the solar divinity. A pre-Indo-European sun cult is known from rock paintings and carvings in Norway and Sweden that center on solar imagery. The great expert on Norse mythology, Hilda Ellis Davidson, categorically proclaims the rock-artists of early Scandinavia to have been sun worshipers. But, like other scholars, she assumes evidence of a solar cult to be evidence of a male sun deity. Backing up her presumption, she cites the presence of bulls, boars, stags and other male animals on the rocks. She ignores, however, the preponderance of female symbols on the rocks. These point to a goddess, rather than a god, of the sun.

Scandinavian rock-art is found scattered in often inaccessible locations over a six-hundred-mile-long region. It falls into two categories: earlier, usually northern, work similar to southern European rock-art and interpreted as hunting magic although including solar symbols; and later, usually southern, petroglyphs depicting the symbols and rituals of a Bronze Age religion centered on sun worship. This Bronze Age lasted more than a thousand years, from approximately 1600 to 450 B.C.E., a span equal to that from the Dark Ages to the Industrial Revolution. There is every likelihood that changes and developments occurred— including the evolution of spinning, which in Scandinavia grew up independently of the rest of Europe. By the middle of the Bronze Age the craft was sufficiently established to be used as a metaphor for the production of light by the cosmic goddess. After the invention of spinning, the area remained stable enough in terms of technology and religion that it is considered to have had a unified culture. That culture, its art suggests, honored the spinster sun.

Spinning implements abound on the rocks: Clearly depicted are combs, hooks and spinning wheels. Other engravings show a long pointed object cut at one end by a knob or cross-bar; scholars have named these "sun-daggers." Daggers? No one has been able to explain, through ritual or myth, a connection between this weapon and the sun. Even Davidson, searching for the martial cult appropriate to a male god, expressed frustration at finding no evidence of any such thing. But the carvings may never have been intended as daggers; they look more like clothespins seen sideways than weapons. As spindles, however, they are perfectly intelligible; any modern spinner would recognize the form. If the "sun-daggers" are interpreted as spindles, surrounding symbols become intelligible. A famous carving from Ostergotland, for instance, shows thread winding from the tip of a "dagger"; another shows the "dagger" spinning a pig.

Spinning tools, although frequent, are not the only female symbols on the stones. The sun's footprint appears, recalling its presence on Baltic stones connected with spinning goddesses. The footprint is always a female symbol: More precisely, like the shoe, it represents female genitalia and sexual desire. Shoes are thrown at newlyweds or tied to their car bumpers to bring the bride fertility; the old woman who lived in a shoe had so many children because of the hugeness of her sexual appetite; Cinderella's slipper represents the attraction or "fit" between her and Prince Charming. In addition to this sexual meaning, the footprint indicates where divinity has touched the earth. Saule, dancing on silver hilltops at summer solstice, leaves such footprints. The footprint stands for the fertile power of a goddess, and the surrounding symbols make plain which one: The footprint appears next to the solar disc or with the sunbarque; sometimes two close-set footprints transform themselves into the solar wheel.

The wheel represents the solar chariot; alone or carrying the solar disc, it appears frequently on Scandinavian rocks. Even more frequent is its corollary vehicle, the boat; one carried the goddess during the day, the other at night, when she traveled beneath the earth through the realm of the dead. The ship appears in the petroglyphs surrounded by solar symbols: footprint and spindle and solar wheel. Placed as they are in conjunction with the footprint and the solar circle, these vehicles can be interpreted as connected to the sun goddess.

Even more impressive than Scandinavia's carvings are the bronze sculptures excavated from its bogs. The most famous of these was found on the Danish island of Trundholm in 1902 and called in early published reports the chariot of the sun goddess; later this was shortened to the chariot of the sun. Dated to 1200 B.C.E., it may have been ritually broken and buried in the bog, where the tannic water preserved the splendid object. It has six wheels: Four support a bronze horse, while the final pair carry a solar disc in a rude chariot—a wagon, really. The disc, composed of two convex plates, is still partly covered on one side with incised gold carved with concentric circles; the other face was bronze, carved with spirals, leading Miranda Green to posit a presumption of solar duality, of a "light-faced" and a "dark-faced" sun. No driver was found with the chariot, but she came forth from a bog in nearby Fardal: a bronze, gold-eyed woman who crouches, naked except for a pleated miniskirt. Her right hand, held above her, is pierced to hold reins or a whip; her left hand squeezes her breast in a nurturing way, reminding us that the sun is often seen as a milk-filled breast. Around the goddess's neck hangs a necklace like that found on Baltic sun-pots and worn by her descendents Freja and Frigg. [2]

Upon these Bronze Age roots was grafted an Indo-European mythic stock that, as we have seen from the Balts, may have included a sun goddess or solar twins. This is assuming that the Indo-European invaders, arriving in the area around 400 B.C.E., did not dispense with the earlier inhabitants entirely. Some would claim the latter. Scandinavian mythology is frequently cited by structuralist theorists as profoundly representative of the tripartite division discerned in all Indo-European societies by Georges Dumezil, following a model he originally devised to explain Indic texts: Scandinavian kings, earls and farmers in turn enacting the functions of sovereignty, force and fecundity. Dumezil seems to have imagined a clean slate on which this triply functional society was writ, while others—including specialists in Scandinavian mythology, like Eugen Mogk—presume some influence from the pre-Indo-European dwellers on the land. The fact that the Bronze Age symbolism of the sun goddess is carried forward into the written texts argues against the blank-slate theory.

The sun goddess whom we find in written literature was called Sunnu (or Sunna)—we get our word *sun* from this goddess. Her people spoke Indo-European languages; their descendants are today's Germans, Dutch, Danes, Swedes, Norwegians, Icelanders and English. These diverse tribes shared religion as well as language, divinities as well as rites. Written documents of their beliefs come to us mainly from the Scandinavian colony in Iceland; we know of continental German beliefs only through the notes of occasional invaders like Caesar and from modern folklorists like the Grimm brothers. How much is essentially Indo-European, how much derives from Bronze Age Scandinavian beliefs, is yet to be determined.[3]

Sunnu's story is told in the Eddas, our major sources for Norse mythology. The Elder Edda consists of a mere thirty-four poems on mythological subjects; lost for generations, it was rediscovered in

Denmark in the Middle Ages. No single person wrote the poems; they were composed years, decades, even generations apart by poets trained in traditional tales and in the traditional ways to tell them. The tiny volume is all that's left of a presumably vast oral literature, the quality of which is hinted at by the beautiful surviving poems. The Elder Edda is one of the most important sources of information on Scandinavian mythology, but learning about Norse deities from it alone is impossible. The poems were composed by and recited for people deeply familiar with the material; the style is allusive rather than narrative. We are left to piece together stories from a riddle line there, a portion of song there.

Poems of the Elder or Poetic Edda are referred to in the later, or Prose, Edda compiled by the Icelander Snorri Sturluson in 1220. Designed as a handbook for poets, the work was based on oral tradition and genealogical records as well as on early poetry. Lucky for us that Snorri wrote when he did, for the myths he recorded were on their way to extinction. The Vikings remained unconverted to the new religion of Christ until the early Middle Ages, but when the change came it was a bloody one. Civil war raged across the subarctic subcontinent until a council met to decide the religion of the land. Christianity, the Viking elders decided, was the only choice; otherwise the bloodshed would continue, for the Christians had pledged to exterminate the old religion and, if necessary, its adherents. Private worship of the old deities was, however, permitted in the safety of individual farms.

Neither the Poetic Edda nor the Prose Edda contained much information on female divinities, concentrating rather on gods and heroes; both Eddas, however, concur in their description of the sun goddess. One of the earliest deities, she was made when sparks left over from earth's creation leapt into the sky. "Sunnu shone from the south," says the Elder Edda, "on the world's bare stones, and from the ground there sprouted leeks."[4] The new sun, having no special place in the sky, wandered about. To stabilize the world, she had to be given a palace: Forseti, the overhead sky. The gods, meeting in council to determine the sun's route, also made places for the moon and stars, then divided time into afternoon, dusk, midday, months, years.

Another story says that the sun goddess was the daughter of Mundifoeri, a man of overweening pride. Mundifoeri had two beautiful children—so beautiful he named them Sol and Mani as if they were equal in beauty to the luminaries. Angered by his arrogance, the gods punished him: They took his children from him and put them where their names suggested. The boy drove the moon's chariot, the girl the sun.

Although the story of Sunnu's birth is found in the Norse Eddas, they are virtually silent on her daily journey. To supplement this sparse information, we must turn to the idioms and folktales of the neighboring and related Germans, collected by the great folklorist Jakob Grimm.[5] The sun's day, German tales and songs tell us, started when she awoke and spun light for a few hours. Then, with a clap, she announced herself to the sleepy world. Or she laughed aloud as she rose above the horizon, for she was the joy-bringing goddess. "When you see the sun so glad," a German poem says, "You must own the fine day is hers. You thank her, not God."

On special occasions, the sun danced as she rose; in Norway the celebration of the sun's dancing on Easter carried on into Christian times, like similar celebrations of the dancing sun goddess among Gaelic peoples. It was polite to bow to the sun when first you saw her, saying, "Hail to thee, Lady Sun, all the world's delight!" She saw you do this, for the sun was a big eye in the heavens; in swearing an oath, you tipped your fingers in her direction as proof of your intention to keep your promise.

After rising, the sun climbed—or flowed—upwards. Traveling through the sky, Snorri tells us, Sunnu was pulled by two horses: Arkakr, or Early-Waker, and Alsvidr the All-Swift. A kind of ventilation device or wind-bag, called Iron-Coolness, placed beneath the horses' shoulders, kept them from overheating themselves or the earth: "Arkakr and Alsvidr hence draw up wearily the Sun's weight, and under their collars the kindly gods set in ancient time Svalin ("the cooling"), a shield for the shining goddess. Mountain and sea would set on fire if it fell beneath."

As the day dragged on, the sun became weary. Late in the day she sat down exhausted in a chair on the horizon. This was the most sacred time of day. As Sunnu sat—or, as we say, as the sun set, for this myth forms the backdrop of our language—she entered a blissful state. *Solagladen*, "the sun gladdens," the Germans said, meaning she glittered for joy. Sometimes the sun goddess would bow as she set. Sometimes she would bathe or dive into the sea, hissing and steaming as she set. After Sunnu sat, it was bad luck to say that she was gone; you could only say she was resting.

And she had good reason to rest, good reason to hurry across the sky, for she was pursued constantly by a fierce wolf who sprang each morning from the Shores of Iron. In some poems he is called Skoll; in others he is the terrible Fenris Wolf itself, the wolf that will end the world. Ahead of Sol ran Hati Hrovitnisson—which means Hate, son of the Mighty

Wolf—trying to bite the running moon. When the luminaries were caught and eaten, the Song of the Shaman-Woman, or Voluspa, tells us, the end of the world would be at hand, the time when the maiden sun would die in the teeth of the wolf.

Voluspa's words were ominous: "Dark is the sun. The Earth sinks below the sea. No bright star now shines from the heavens, only smoke and menacing fires." With the coming of the Doom of the Gods—Ragnarok, in Icelandic; Gotterdammerung, in German—the world as we know it would be destroyed in flame and sorrow. And the gods? They too would die. The Scandinavians believed even the greatest divinities would die when the end of time arrived, when the dark goddess Hel would rise to devour creation. Grim as this prediction seems, it included rebirth after the holocaust. This the shaman-woman also foresaw. As dark as her earlier vision was, this one is beautiful: "I see rising a second time, out of the waters: the Earth, green once more. An eagle flies above rushing waterfalls hunting for fish from the craggy heights."

Not only would the earth be reborn, but the gods in their own beautiful forms would be reborn, too. And the sun would rise again anew. At the very instant of death, Sunnu would give birth to her new self, her daughter. These are the words of the prophecy: "Sunnu will have a daughter before she meets the wolf's fangs, and that girl, when the great gods die, will ride her mother's roads."

Max Mueller found in the familiar story of Little Red Riding Hood a folk reminiscence of the goddess's perpetual pursuit by the wolf—for, like the sun, the little girl rises from the wolf's mouth at the end of the story, complete with her sun-red hood.[6] The story of the sun's death by devouring also occurs in the Lithuanian tale that the demon Tiklis follows the sun, attempting to eat her and end the world.

When the sun dies, her daughter is there to replace her. The daughter is a star, patiently awaiting her turn to shine; a German word for stars, *sunnelin*—"little suns"—shows their role as baby luminaries, as does the Holstein tradition that a new sun rises each day, the earlier day's sun having been cut up into stars by cosmic spinsters. This mythology recalls that of Saule, replaced at winter solstice by her star-daughter. In these cosmologies, the sun goddess must be endlessly reborn; the daughter who will replace her is now visible as a star.

The fact that the sun goddess becomes pregnant and gives birth to these daughters raises the possibility that, for the Indo-Europeans, a sun goddess and a sun god rode together in the sky chariot. The Scandinavian god Dag (Day), who rode in a chariot adorned with precious jewels, is mentioned once in the Eddas; in the Gothic language there were both male and female words for sun. It is easier to imagine an Old European sun goddess surviving among Indo-European tribes if the invaders were already predisposed to believe in a female sun deity. In this case, the sun god would have simply dropped away among the Scandinavian tribes when, moving into the territory of the petroglyph artists, they encountered a mythology resistant to elimination.

It seems likely, among the threads that make up Norse mythology, that the death of the sun derives from a far northern original, based on the sun's actual annual departure to the south. The myths of the captive or devoured maiden seem to reflect the region's annual reality. Farther south, days shorten in winter, but the sun does not entirely disappear; only in the Arctic can the sun be described as a hostage to the season. In fact, German folklore suggests that the "hiding" or death of the sun was a regular occurrence. German tradition remembers something called the "key to day," which could be stolen and hidden in a river; this would keep the sun goddess prisoner. The sun, it was also said, could disappear in anger, hiding at the bottom of a cave, or in a well, disguised as an eye.

A longer story, echoing the Baltic legends of the rescue of the Sun Maiden by the Twin Gods, comes from the *Historia Danica*. King Alf, it is said, went off one day with his friend Borgar to win as his bride the beautiful Alfhild—a title of the maiden sun goddess. He was very young and exceedingly fine to behold, with hair as silver as the sun herself. Alfhild herself was so beautiful that if she took off her veil no human eye could endure her radiance. She was also inaccessible, captive in a palace-prison guarded by two dragons. Other men had tried to win her, but they had not only failed their quests but lost their lives. Their heads stood on poles all around the palace.

But Alf was stronger than his predecessors. He did battle with the dragons and vanquished them. He would have soon captured the maiden, but her mother intervened. Dressing Alfhild in men's clothes and armor, she pushed her out the back door of the palace. Alfhild ran away, surrounded by a band of female warriors. When she reached Finland, she turned and faced her pursuer. They did battle, and he struck her helmet off. Alfhild, admitting him the victor, agreed at last to wed.[7]

The story follows a pattern that we have already seen in Celtic and Baltic lands: The maiden summer is freed from captivity despite the opposition of the winter hag. And what, exactly, is the role of the hero in all this? Among the Balts, the twin Sons of God saved the captive Sun Maiden; in Scotland, a woman died and was revived by a young man in a dance. In Japanese myth, a bawdy dancer brought the sun out of her cave retreat; in Egypt, drunken women exposed themselves to passersby on the birthday of Hathor; the unsmiling dark sun of the Cherokee, whose myth we will soon consider, was revived by young men and women dancing together. A basic theme in these myths is that the power of sex releases the sun from captivity; it is sexual activity that allows her to be renewed. Human lust is needed, at certain vital moments in the year, to provide the magical impetus for the sun to move ahead in her path. The hero, then, is useful for his role in encouraging female desire, necessary only to stimulate the goddess's own energies.

Because this idea is so widespread, it is probably impossible to know how it came to be woven into the tapestry of the Scandinavian sun goddess. If, as we have argued, Norse mythology combines the traditions of the Indo-European settlers and their conquered forebears with traditions adopted from neighboring peoples, an indication of this complex ethnic background is found in the multiple names given the solar deity. Alfhild, bride of Alf, is one. Snorri gives us other names: "Sister of the Moon, Wife of Glenr, Fire of Heaven and the Air, Sun, Glory, Ever-Glowing, All-Bright, Sight, Fair Wheel, Healing Ray, Doubtful-Beam, Luminary." The Norse sun goddess was called Shadowless Shining and the Good Light, "the lofty flickering Flame of the World's Hall," or "Glenr's god-blithe Bed-Mate."

Among the solar names are several pertaining to dwarfs: Afradull, "elf-beam" and "elf-ray," because she petrified them with her glance; Dvalin's Playmate and Dvalin's Delight, Dvalin being a dwarf she killed. Across Scandinavia, the sun goddess was connected with dwarfs; the Scandinavian version of the glass mountain story, for instance, says that a captive dwarf, stealing a ball, began the adventure. The reiterated connection is, however, puzzling, for although dwarfs were said to be the sun goddess's servants, she is said to have killed them with her glance. Often she turned them to stone; the Troy Towns, where the ritual of her freeing was enacted, were also called Troll Towns, and the stones were thought to be petrified dwarfs. This suggests enmity between sun and dwarf. Were the dwarfs the very creatures responsible for building the labyrinth in which the sun maiden was kept prisoner? Or was the dwarf the same solar enemy who, in other areas, appeared as the devouring frog who threatened the sun? Yet there are some stories that suggest a positive connection between sun and dwarfs: In these stories, the dwarfs were her servant-smiths, fashioners of the key to day and of her magnificent solar necklace, honored by the erection of stone circles. The name *troll* comes from an archaic root meaning "to roll or to spin," clearly showing the connection with the rolling sun. Hence the troll or dwarf is both like and opposed to the sun, in a complex of associations that we shall explore further when we discuss the connection of snake and sun in North America.[8]

Not only did the Scandinavian sun goddess have many names, but many goddesses—even mortal women—were compared to her. Scandinavian poets frequently used solar imagery in describing their heroines. "My sun-bright lady," one poet sings; another tells of a "sun-bright maiden," yet another of a "bright-faced" one. The Valkyre Swanhild was "lovely to see as a ray of sunlight," she had "sun-bright hair," and "the sun in a cloudless sky is not so fair." The divine Gerd was so beautiful that when she "raised her hands to unlatch the door in front of her, a beautiful light shone from them both so that earth and sky and sea were the brighter for it."

Heroines were not alone in being spoken of this way. In addition to Sunnu, two other Scandinavian goddesses, Freya and Frigg, were continually connected to the sun. They were so frequently given solar attributes or placed in the solar vehicle that it is difficult to determine whether they were originally paired sun goddesses—mother and maid—whose identities were later denied, as male sun gods became fashionable, or if they were goddesses to whom solar imagery naturally accrued because of the femininity of the Norse sun. In either case, the imagery that surrounded them partook of feminine sun imagery: cats and amber, necklaces and spindles, dwarfs and chariots.

The maiden goddess was Freya, called der vana solen or "the beautiful sun" in a Swedish folksong. Like other solar goddesses, she was associated with cats, who pulled her chariot. These cats, to Freya's people, controlled the sunshine. In Germany, if it rained when a woman planned to do laundry, she suspected a cat was angry at her; if a wedding was rained upon, it was because the bride forgot to feed a cat. Like Hathor, another cat–sun goddess, Freya was extremely popular. She had innumerable temples; her worship lasted until the early Middle Ages. After Charlemagne destroyed her last remaining temple, at Magdeburg, Germany, the goddess was degraded into a devil, her priestesses into witches—hence the current Halloween connection of broomstick-riding hags with Freya's servant, the black cat.

In her cat-chariot, Freya rode out after battles to choose from among the slain those whom she wished to specially honor. Thus, she acted as one of the Valkyries, the shield-maidens who appeared in the Darradarljod as weavers who created war from their bloody tapestries; in some texts, Freya is referred to as the chief of the Valkyrie tribe. Valkyries, surrounded by a sun-like ring of flame, often appear in Scandinavian legends that parallel the Baltic sun-maiden stories we have previously seen. In stories of the Valkyrie Brynhild, for example, we find her asleep on a glass mountain far in the south, where the captive sun lives in winter, surrounded by fire and protected by a dragon, which the arriving hero is required to kill. Ernst Krause calls this figure—Freya/Brynhild—the sun-maiden incarcerated by the demon of winter. The same motif occurs, of course, in Snow White, in which the maiden is seen in the company of dwarfs and is freed by an arriving hero.

Freya's legend is replete with solar images. She was said to have taken as lover her brother Freyr, the fertility god. In another story, she married Odur and bore two jewel-like daughters, Hnoss and Gersimi. But then the faithless Odur disappeared without a trace. Freya searched and searched. Finding nothing, she began to weep. The stones on which her tears fell became jewels: on land, gold; in the ocean, amber. At last, weary of mourning, she donned the wings of the falcon, the sun-bird, and left her Scandinavian homeland. She became a wanderer, looking every-where for Odur. In the many lands through which she passed, she acquired many names: Mardoll, light of the sea; Horn, the spinning flax-woman; Syr; Gefn; Skialf; Thung.

At last she found Odur deep in the tropics under a flowering myrtle tree. She convinced him to return north with her, like the spring sun returning to the Arctic with green leaves and summer trailing behind. A famous poem describes Freya's return; it is replete with solar images, including the female lasciviousness inspired by her return. Out of the morning lands, it says, beautiful Freya came; the white frozen moorlands turned green and blooming as she passed.

> Out of her gold locks
> shaking spring flowers,
> making chaste housewives all
> long for their heroes home,
> loving and love-giving
> came she to Scoring.

A variant of the story involves Syrith, an alternative name for Freya. In the story, Syrith appears as a golden-haired woman so beautiful that no one could look her in the face. Imprisoned in a mountain wilderness by a giant who forced her to tend his goats (hence her name Syr Fen Tanna, Syr of the Crags), she was found and freed by Odur. She, however, declined to return his love, despite traveling to his parents' home to live.

In exasperation, he finally announced that he would marry another maiden, at which time she changed her mind and agreed to wed.

Another such a sham-bridal occurred in Freya's mythology when giants demanded that Freya wed their king, Thrym; instead of Freya, the gods sent Thor, "in bridal veil/And with the ornate Brising necklace." When the moment of truth came, Thor took the hammer brought to bless the marriage bed and used it to kill the giants. Apparently the ruse worked only because Thor was wearing Freya's necklace, which so dazzled the giants that they failed to notice his red-gold beard.

This necklace is of great import in Freya's mythology. Like the Baltic pot-sun goddesses and the Bronze Age chariot-driver of Fardal, Freya wore a fabulous necklace, the Brisingamen—whose name derived from *brisingr*, "fire." It came into her possession this way: One day as she walked along the border of her realm, she saw four dwarfs, including the fated Dvalin, making a necklace that shone like the sun.

"Sell it to me," she told the four little black men, "and I will give you a fortune in silver."

"Not for all the silver in the world," the dwarfs answered.

"What treasure will buy it for me?" Freya asked.

The dwarfs, smiling to each other, answered that only one would do: that she sleep with them all, one night for each. Greedy for the necklace, Freya agreed.

When she returned home with the Brisingamen, though, she could not wear it without eliciting comments and questions, so she wore it only at night, when she slept. Loki, the trickster, knew what happened with the black dwarfs. To cause trouble, he slipped into Freya's bedroom while she slept. Then, transforming himself into a flea, he bit her on the cheek. Sleepily, the goddess rolled away, giving Loki access to the fastener on her neck. He slipped off the necklace and stole away with it.

But Freya would not be deprived of Brisingamen for long. When she discovered the theft, the goddess turned herself into a war-maiden named Gondul and waged battle until her treasure was returned.

Norse mythology's other vestige of the solar feminine occurs in the figure of Frigg, Queen of Heaven, a spinning goddess with a star-jeweled distaff who created golden light and wove the clouds. Her legend is remarkably similar to that told of Freya: Friggs includes dwarf-made necklaces, tears of gold or amber, the departure of the loved one, spring returning with the goddess's smile.

To have her necklace made, Frigg stole part of a golden statue of her consort, Odin, and brought it to a group of dwarfs, who melted it down to create the world's most beautiful necklace. This new ornament at first enchanted Odin. But then he discovered the ruin of his statue; suspecting a connection with the new necklace, he became obsessed with finding the thief. He began to persecute the dwarf smiths, demanding to know who had brought them the gold for the jewelry. The dwarfs refused to betray Frigg, so Odin found another way: He started to cast a spell on the statue itself, to empower it with speech.

Just when it seemed the secret would be out, Frigg's servant Fulla located a dwarf willing to destroy the statue to keep the goddess's secret—and all he wanted in return was Frigg's smile. He destroyed the statue. Frigg smiled at him. And furious Odin disappeared, like Freya's husband Odur. Frigg searched through all the world for him, weeping tears of gold. At last he relented and returned; Frigg smiled, and that smile brought back summer.

It is possible that the necklace of the sun goddess preceded the tales about it; the stories may have been invented to explain the sculptural tradition of showing goddesses with necklaces. The necklace might have stood iconographically for glories, rainbows that sometimes circle the sun; it could simply represent the solar corona, so visible during an eclipse. Or it may have had some mythic meaning that is now lost. In some very ancient pots from Old Europe, the goddess wears no necklace but has several slits in her throat. Perhaps only the goddess's head was thought to illuminate the sky, as in the Seneca myth we shall soon examine. Whatever its source, the fabulous necklace of fire or light is part of the sun goddess's treasure.[9]

The Norse sun-goddess myths we've so far examined are all from Scandinavia. But related traditions can be found southwards, in Germany. Because there the Norse myths were not written down, we have only folklore to inform us of beliefs about the sun goddess. Luckily, some crucial tales have been preserved. In one, the sun-woman was sent to the sky as punishment for having a hard heart. As she was hanging out her morning laundry, an execution procession passed. Looking at the accused, she scathingly said he probably deserved death. Immediately all her laundry fell to the ground; she was never able to hang it again; when she died she was imprisoned in the sun.

Here the sun, the sky's divine laundress, is demoted to a cursed human, as she is in another tale as well. It says simply that a man was cutting wood and his wife spinning on Christmas Day—the solstice festival when such tasks were forbidden—and as punishment were transported to heaven, where they must forever work at those tasks. The man cuts wood in the moon, the story tells us, while the woman sits in the sun spinning. Frau Sonne, she is called, the spouse of Herr Monne.[10]

In addition to these traces of the German sun goddess, we find her in the two supernatural beings associated with the solstices: the spinning Frau Holle and her evil twin, Berchta (Perchta), known throughout German, Austrian and Swiss folktales and folkways. Of the two, Holle— her name derives from *holde*, "kind"—has the more pleasant legends attached to her. Sunshine came from her hair as she combed it, snow from her shaking out a feather comforter; rain was her thrown-away laundry water, clouds her laundry hanging out to dry. She was a splendid white lady who appeared every day at noon to bathe in a fountain; she was a grandmother, a white ancestress like Saule; children were said to spring from her fountain. She lived in a cave in the mountain, or she lived in a well and people visited her by diving in.

Holle's solar connection is evident in the game of Hupf-oder Hinkspiel, in which children climb upon each other, the one at the bottom of the pile being called both Dame Sun and Holle. "Where does the goddess live?" they sing as they play. "Up there, above. What is she doing? Spinning silk. How light? As her own hair." The game recalls the hollow mountain in which Holle lives, sometimes described as Venusburg or the Mount of Venus, an earthly paradise guarded by dwarfs into which, should humans wander, they will be sensually entertained but eternally trapped.

Holle is a German form of Freya. Both have as emblems the ladybug or ladybird beetle; the Germans call this insect the sun-calf or sun-chick, and say that it lives in the sun. While our children tell the ladybug that her house is burning and that she must save her offspring, German children instruct the bug to fly into the sky and make more sunshine. Cloudy days, in German folklore, are the result of somebody's killing a ladybug.

Frau Holle's carriage was drawn by the red beetles. One story says that, kidnapping a little girl who loved to play with ladybugs, she brought the child to heaven and kept her there for five years. During that time, Frau Holle sat constantly at her spinning wheel outside her front door. When she had made a beautiful linen bridal dress for the girl, Frau Holle brought her home. There the girl learned that, for the five years she'd been gone, a war had been raging in which she would have doubtless been killed.

Sometimes Frau Holle rode on the wind in a wagon or chariot—the same solar chariot that appeared at Trundholm. This chariot was, throughout the Scandinavian and Germanic worlds, connected with spinning goddesses. An otherwise baffling tale from the early Middle Ages is explained by the long-lasting connection of solar ship and spindle. The villagers of Kornelmünster, it was said, built a mock boat to humiliate the weavers in the neighboring village of St. Trond. Set to guarding the boat, the weavers were unable to protect it—or themselves—from naked women who danced around it until the weavers were roused enough for additional pleasures. The ship was banished for the disorder it caused.

Throughout Germany ship processions marked the beginning of spring; so much license accompanied the events that the Church banned them. Vestiges of similar, mock-boat, ceremonies occurred in historic times throughout Scandinavia, where they were part of summer solstice ceremonies and were accompanied by ritual obscenity on the part of women—something we have seen in Japan and Egypt that restored or renewed the sun goddess.

Chariots and the sun's gold are connected in one famous story told of Frau Holle. Once, it is said, she had to have her chariot repaired. It had a broken lynchpin, and the craftsman who worked on it had to chip out bits of wood from the wheel's hub to insert the new pin. When Frau Holle had flown away, he found the bits of wood he'd chipped out turned to gold.

Holle loved to shower gold upon the unsuspecting. Once a man walking in the hills came upon Frau Holle stripping flax. He wished her good evening and, in friendly fashion, she asked him to help himself. No thanks, he said politely, he had more than enough flax already. He bade her farewell and walked home. There, he found something stuck in his shoe: a bit of Holle's flax, hardened into gold.

Flax was Holle's special plant; she gave it to humanity so that we could make linen. It happened when a poor farmer came upon her mountain sanctuary. Generously, she offered him anything in sight. Surrounded as he was by precious jewels, he nevertheless asked only for the blue flowers Holle held. He had chosen wisely, she said, and disappeared.

The man returned home and sowed the seed of the blue flowers in his field. When the flax had grown, Holle returned to teach the family how to make linen. The family grew rich. After many years, the ever-fresh bouquet that the old man treasured began to fade. The man, knowing this meant he must die, went back to Holle's mountain sanctuary and disappeared into it.

In the Aargau, Frau Holle was a golden-haired goddess who lived inside a mountain. There in her halls unborn babes slept, surrounded by candles; she fed them on flower nectar and, when a woman wanted a child, Holle sent one off. Should the baby die immediately after delivery, she put it back with the other flower-fed unborn; but if it lived several weeks before dying, it was placed at the heart of the mountain to be fed on Holle's special honey.

Holle's connection to the spinster sun is especially marked on her feast day, winter solstice. It was Freya's feast among the Norse, who forbade spinning and other rotating tasks for the twelve days when the sun took its midwinter rest. Among the Germans, on Jul or Moddernatt (Mother Night), Holle checked the quality of each woman's fiber craft. A careful spinner would wake to find Holle had left her a single golden thread. Or, inspired by the neatness of a woman's workplace, Holle would sit for awhile and spin, leaving the distaff full of thread of supernatural fineness. Sloppy spinners, however, would wake to find their work even more disordered than they left it: the threads tangled, the wheel itself shattered.

Holle also rewarded industrious spinners by filling their reels while they slept; but she set afire the spindles of the lazy. Women who dropped spindles into water became Holle's favorites for the year and would be showered with gold. As a goddess of fiber arts, Holle's natural blessing was, "So many hairs on your head, so many good years," her curse the opposite, "So many hairs on your head, so many bad years."

Holle had an unpleasant side; she could transform herself into a troll-woman with long teeth. In this guise she was more commonly known as Berchta, whose name means "the luminous," possibly referring to the brightness of sun on snow. During Jul, the feast she shared with Holle, Berchta was called the flat-footed queen because one of her feet became oversized from pushing the pedal on the spinning wheel so hard. Sometimes, the solstice divinity was conflated with St. Lucy, who was said to have had a bird's head and to eat babies in winter, and on whose December feast day there was to be no spinning.

Like other sun goddesses, Berchta was known for her towering rages. In Orlagau, she visited neighborhood spinning rooms and gave empty reels to the women with orders to fill them up in a quarter-hour; when the women could not, she tangled all the floss. At Oppung, she stood outside a house where merrymaking was in progress and handed through the window twelve empty reels. She demanded that they be spun full immediately. A clever girl filled them with unspun flax, wrapping a few threads about them to disguise the ploy, and, somehow, Berchta was fooled.

In Langedembach, she persecuted an old woman who was one of the town's most industrious spinners. Warned by her son not to spin on Berchta's day, the woman said, "She brings me no shirts; I must spin them myself." The window was pushed open and Berchta looked in. Seeing the woman at work, she threw her a couple of spindles and demanded they be filled. The woman wound a few strands around each spindle, then ran outside and dumped the lot into a creek. Once again, Berchta was appeased.

On Berchta's feast day, Twelfth Night, a pancake supper was served. Pancakes are a traditional offering to sun deities, their round shape echoing the luminary's. But Berchta's feast had special rules: Any leftovers had to remain on the table for the goddess. Otherwise, she would find a meal by cutting open the stomachs of the sated sleepers, using a plowshare threaded with chains as a surgical needle to repair the flesh. In some German villages, it was traditional to serve only very greasy food on Twelfth Night, with the idea that the grease would make Berchta's knife slide off instead of piercing the stomach.

The period between Christmas and January—the time of Holle's circuit of the land and of Berchta's rages—was sacred to the goddesses; from this German tradition comes our twelve days of Christmas. During this fortnight, in northern lands, the sun seems to stand still; the dramatic loss of light—almost ten minutes daily—slows down, but the growth of light is not yet perceptible. During this sacred time, no rotary actions were to take place; sleighs were used instead of wagons; grinding between millstones was forbidden; and, of course, women had to cease spinning with the wheel.

One famous solstice rite survived into Christian times in Scandinavia, where the sun goddess appears disguised as St. Lucia, "Saint Light," just as Berchta survives as St. Lucy. Until the last century, St. Lucia's feast day was celebrated by a girl's riding on horseback through the town accompanied by boys who personified dwarfs killed by sunbeams. The feast is still celebrated on December 13, the date of winter solstice before the change to the Gregorian calendar. At dawn on that morning, the eldest daughter of the home—called the Light Bride, or Lussibruden—dresses in white and puts a lit candelabra on her head to represent a supposed Christian saint who had the power to bring sunlight. Thus attired, she wakes up each family member and serves them buns called Lussekatter, "light cats." She sings a hymn: "Lo, 'tis the Queen of Light, clad in garment white, wearing a crown of light." This same St. Lucia, incidentally, was said to have torn her eyes out and served them up on a platter to her fiancé—which cannot help but recall St. Bridget's curious behavior regarding her eyes and courting men.

On summer solstice, the opposite feast, the opposite behavior was in order. Instead of refraining from spinning, women were to set wheels afire and roll them down slopes into water. If the wheel made it all the way to the stream to be doused, a good harvest was promised. In England, where Scandinavian influences survive, the same feast is still celebrated today, using rolls of cheese instead of fiery wheels. A similar ceremony could be conducted out of season when the need arose—when an epidemic struck or other disaster befell. In the Germanic solar ceremony of the "need-fire," a blaze was kindled by the friction of a wooden axle rotating in the nave of a wagon wheel, left to right, in the sun's direction. A spinning wheel could also be used to kindle this fire. To assure the success of the act, all house fires had to be doused and relit from the new fire. The ritual is found wherever Scandinavian influence spread, including in Scotland and Ireland.

Although the Germanic year was divided into halves, there are traces as well of a third solar goddess. Ostara, whose name means "movement towards the rising sun" and who became Eastre in Anglo-Saxon, provides our name for the festival of resurrection. On this day the sun was said to dance or leap three times as she rose, and bonfires were built in celebration. Women clothed in white were said by Grimm to "show themselves" in clefts in rocks or on top of mountains; it is unclear whether this meant they appeared suddenly or, like other female celebrants around the world, exposed their naked bodies.

Finally, our custom of Easter eggs comes from Ostara's festivals, where decorated bird eggs representing the sun were common, but egg-shaped stones could be substituted. The rolling of painted eggs down hills—still common today—was, like the solstice wheel, a magical act to encourage the springtime sun to roll forward into happy summer. Although these festivals were most common in Germany, there are British survivals of them as well, such as at the megalithic site at Drewsteignton in Devon, where the egg-shaped rocks were said to have been set up by three spinning women one morning before breakfast.

The egg as a symbol for the sun is omnipresent; we still order eggs "sunny side up." Although the Germans may have derived the image through archetypal logic, it is also possible that they adopted it from the neighboring Finno-Ugric people, to whom the sun was the cosmic egg laid before the earth's creation. Norse language and mythology, like Greek and Celtic and Baltic, is Indo-European, but several millennia of proximity to non-Indo-European cultures meant that symbols and legends were shared with such neighbors as the Hungarians and the Finns. In the resulting mythological stew, it's not easy—or, sometimes, possible—to distinguish each ingredient's origin.[11]

And nowhere is this more true than in the area that we'll now explore: Russia and Ukraine, which combine elements of Indo-European and Finno-Ugric myth and ritual. The Indo-European part of the mix comes from the Slavs of central Europe, whose sun goddess is familiar, in residual form, in the story of Cinderella. The name of this "elf of the cinders" comes from an old word meaning "to sparkle," and especially signified the sparks thrown off by forging iron. Like other sun maidens, she was—in the most familiar version—held captive by a wicked stepmother, but gets free to lure a prince through her glass slipper. In various less-known versions she lives naked in a cave or at the bottom of a well. She wears a coat of catskin or of golden chimes; she is said to wear "sun shoes;" and her beauty is said to shine like the sun. In other myths, this Slavic sun goddess Solntse lives with her moon husband in a three-room house: She has her own room; so does he; and the children bunk together. Sometimes this sun goddess appears as Matushka Krasnogo Solntsna, the Mother of the Red Sun; in this case she is seen as a pregnant woman, the sun apparently her round belly.

In Serbian folklore, the sun goddess appears as the spinning maiden Papalluga, a sort of Cinderella. She brought down an unfortunate fate upon herself when, dropping her spindle into a ravine, she caused her mother to turn into a cow. Happily, the cow could still speak and help her daughter; unhappily, the father remarried a wicked, jealous woman. The first thing this stepmother did was to order Papalluga to spin a ball of hemp overnight—or be killed. Papalluga's cow-mother came to the rescue, chewing the hemp and producing fine linen out of her ears. The stepmother caught on, however, had the magical cow killed, and commanded Papalluga to pick up a load of scattered millet. As she was doing so, the girl was visited by birds, who brought her magical clothes and assisted her at her task. And so Papalluga was able to dress in fairy garments, go to church, and catch the eye of the prince. Three times this happened, until Papalluga found herself at church, dressed and shod in pure gold—but then, you know the rest.

The dual sun goddess in these Slavic tales usually appears in the forms of girl and witch (in the Cinderella tales, the mother figure is further divided: kind mother or fairy godmother, and evil mother or stepmother). In Russian folklore, the witch is the monstrous and powerful

Baba-Yaga, who lives in the forest in a house built on spindles and who flies through the air in a mortar, rowing with a pestle—tools used to prepare flax for spinning. The first part of her name means "grandmother" or simply "woman," and derives from the name of the Hittite goddess Kubaba, whose solar attributes we will consider in Chapter 11. Yaga, the latter part of the goddess's name, has defied definite translation, but there is a convincing link to the Sanskrit for "snake." The snake, often a solar symbol, appears in Baba-Yaga's legend as the stovepipe of her infamous oven, the one in which she both creates foodstuffs and burns up those who infuriate her. Through its fiery heat, the stove is connected to the sun in its productive and destructive capabilities. Proverbs tell of the connection: "During the day my stove heats me, and at night my mother. It is warm in the sun; it is good by the mother."

Baba-Yaga's legend invariably revolves around a young girl whom she traps and holds prisoner, but who escapes. In one of the most famous, the witch's young counterpart is Vasilisa the Fair, a spinster woman whose alternative identity is a frog, a feminine solar symbol and also the symbol of Baba-Yaga herself. A common version of the Vasilisa story has the girl seeking light from Baba-Yaga and held prisoner while she performs mundane household tasks. These done, Baba-Yaga gives her the light she seeks; Vasilisa then goes forth carrying the light and attracts the attention of the king by her splendid spinning and weaving. Baba-Yaga and Vasilisa thus suggest a pair of solar divinities like Saule and her daughter.[12]

In addition to Slavic influence on Russian legend, we also find that of the Finno-Ugrians, who in Russia are predominantly Voguls and Ugrians. Among the former, metal plates—possibly mirrors—from Troitsa, center of the sun cult, were the sun's image; among the related Ostyaks, tin rayed plates were hung in holy trees during the sun's winter absence. The Ugrians called their sun goddess Jumala or Zlotababa, Golden Old Woman; her gold statue, worshiped into the sixteenth century, was said to utter clanging tones like the rising sun. In 1549, the German Baron von Herberstein visited a Ugrian shrine where he found a golden goddess rather like the familiar Matrioshka dolls-within-dolls; it enclosed a smaller figure, which enclosed one smaller still. Offerings of gold were hung in the sacred trees by worshipers; when enough was accumulated, a new outer figure was forged. As late as 1967, in the village of Tiumen, treasure-hunters were informed that Jumala still existed, but she was hidden to protect her from materialistic depredations. Another golden goddess is recorded in the thirteenth-century *Novgorod Chronicle*, which says that both Finns and Ugrians sacrificed to her in the city of Perm.

Joanna Hubbs connects this sun goddess with the pan-Russian figure of Mokosh, a spinster goddess depicted as a large-headed woman holding a spindle, honored by women who embroidered her image on ceremonial cloths. The spinning creator goddess appears in the north of Russia as an embroidering woman, Koliada, who remakes the world at winter solstice:

> The first thing she embroidered was the moon,
> The shining moon and then the stars.
> Then she made the beautiful sun,
> The beautiful sun and the warmed clouds.
> And after them the wet pine trees in the forest.

The embroidery she creates is replicated in the magnificent ceremonial cloths of Ukranian and Russian women, worn by brides as part of their bridal headdress, used as shrouds for the dead, hung on sacred trees on cultic occasions, and wrapped around bread placed on the home altar. Patron of spinners, this goddess is shown in embroidery carrying the sun and surrounded by her creation. In northern Russia, where the naturalistic goddess becomes utterly abstracted, her lozenge ideogram symbolized the vulva as well as the sun. Her connection with the sun is made even more apparent in the seven-to tenth-century C.E. temples analyzed by B. A. Rybakov, a Soviet archaeologist: The bronze images incorporated the solar disc for the goddess's head, or represented her by the sun disc alone.

No myth survives in Russia of this Ugrian sun goddess, but we find a myth about her among the related Hungarians.[13] For them the sun was an egg in the sky laid by the fairy queen Tundr Ilona, who took the shape of a swan for the occasion; children honored her in springtime by "making a sun"—throwing eggs into the air. In the sun lived Xatel-Ekwa and her daughter the dawn, Xoli-Kaltes. When the mythic hero World-Scavenger came to her residence, Xatel-Ekwa was out riding the sky, mounted simultaneously on three horses. Coming home, she ignored the man except to give him to her daughter, who decided to bake him. Just before he died of the heat, Xatel-Ekwa took pity on him and freed him from the excessive dawn.

After the Christianization of Hungary, female saints stood in for the sun goddess. As in Scandinavia and Germany, one was St. Lucy, whose Hungarian name was Luca, "light," and who spent winter solstice testing girls on their spinning abilities. Sometimes, too, the Virgin Mary also substituted for the sun goddess. On Marian holidays, the virgin's face was said to be visible in the sun as it rose, while at summer solstice it was said, "Where the sun lieth down to rest, so shall Mary." And folklore had it that there was always at least one sunny spell every Saturday, for that was the day Mary laundered her babe's diapers and hung them out to dry.

In Hungary, as in the rest of Eastern Europe, the sun goddess was honored by fiber crafts; some of the most beautiful artifacts from that area are the embroideries of which Mary Kelly has written. Spring embroideries, she points out, showed the goddess with upraised arms to bring solar energy to earth; summer was celebrated with a figure of the goddess in frog posture, giving birth, or with her hands lowered to protect the growing crop. At harvest, celebratory red cloths were decked with solar symbols, and, finally, in winter, the goddess was shown with her daughter, who would soon take her place.

Finno-Ugric sun-goddess traditions can also be found among the Finns. And among the Finns, the Saami—the Lapps—are outstanding for their preservation of folkways of the feminine sun. Among them we find two goddesses, Beiwe and her daughter Beiwe-neida, who pass through the sky in a sled of reindeer antlers. Third in order of precedence among the deities, Beiwe—Paive to the Norwegian Saami—was a wonderful being who brought back greenness to the earth in arctic spring, who made new plants grow so the reindeer-cattle could prosper and reproduce.

Because she was the special goddess of fetal reindeer, the appropriate sacrifice was a white female animal—preferably a reindeer, although a ewe or nanny goat could be substituted. If no white female animal were available, one that did not satisfy the ritual requirements—a brown female one, for instance, but never a male—could replace it, as long as it was covered by a white cloth or had a white thread drawn through a puncture in its right ear. After killing the animal, the Saami cut a consecrated piece from each of its four quarters. These were threaded on a stick, which was then bent into a ring and hung behind the tent. The blood of the sacrifice was used to consecrate wooden globes and rings, and plaits of birchwood tied with ribbon. More birch was used for hoops in which the hide and bones of the animal were placed in token of their dedication to the round Sun Mother. When sacrifice was made by the Saami, a special prayer was said to the Sun Mother on behalf of the insane; Rafael Karsten suggests that this was because madness was thought to be caused by the sun's winter absence.

Sometimes sacrifices took place because of special prayers that needed answering; they also occurred regularly at the solstices. On winter solstice, or on the day when light first appears in the Arctic, the Saami smeared their doors with butter, so the sun could eat the rich food with her hot beams and so begin her yearly recovery. On summer solstice, "sunrings"—twists of leafy branches—were hung about, and buttery "sun-porridge" was sacramentally eaten. Prayers were offered that the sun virgin would "pour her merciful rays over the reindeer, and everything else."

Like so many other people, the Saami saw the sun goddess as an eye in the sky that could locate missing persons. A herder lost in the wilderness would form a sun-ring from a bit of wood. The ring had a handle, forming an ankh-like figure through which the sun's rays could beam. The lost one, holding up the ring, prayed to Beiwe not to set, not to leave him lost on the darkening tundra, not to allow night to come before the ground-hugging tents of home appeared on the horizon.

This aspect of the Sun-Mother as helper of the lost must have particularly endeared her to the nomadic Saami, who spent so much of their time away from their settlements, watching reindeer cattle. The sun-ring appears again in one of the most vivid Saami symbols of the sun deity: the shamanic drum, which, in the north, shows a single sun-ring, sometimes with rays; and, in the south, a central circle with sunbeam lines radiating out to the edges of the drum to show the sun goddess's omnipresence.

The drum represents one thread of the Saami sun-goddess symbolism, the spinning wheel another. In sacrifices to Beiwe-neida, the Lapps placed flax or a spinning wheel on the altar to represent the goddess. Although once racially distinct, the Saami have lived in contact with the Finnic peoples for so long that they adopted the Finns' language and many of their mythic ideas. The Saami sun goddess, traveling in her antler sled through the sky, may have originally been separate from the spinning sun goddess of the other Finns, the Balts and the Scandinavians, but the Saami adopted spinning symbolism so long ago that it is impossible to completely untangle the threads of convergent cultures.[14]

Aside from the Saami, the other great treasury of Finno-Ugric sun goddess information comes from Finland itself. There mythic stories are no longer scattered through folklore as they are among the Germans—or as Finnish myths were a mere two hundred years ago. But the threads of Finnish myths are gathered in a massive compilation of legends, recitations, charms and curses called the Kalevala.[15] Traveling through Karelia and Savolax in the early part of the last century, Elias Lonnrot gathered the songs and stories of the remote villages in what must be that century's most impressive feat of individual scholarship. Diligently, Lonnrot then arranged the bits of lore. Piecing together characters, themes and subject matter, he created a long poem first published in 1835. During the following years, with the help of the young enthusiast Daniel Europeaus, he expanded the Kalevala; by the final edition, published in 1849, it contained 22,800 verses and more than 50 songs. Recent scholarship holds that Christianity had so far permeated the Finnish world by 1800 that the Kalevala is hopelessly drenched with Christian imagery. But this seems to apply mostly to the male heroes and to the legend of a god-son born to a man-hating virgin named Marja. The sun-goddess material apparently escaped unaffected by the temptation to bring it into the symbolic orbit of the new religion.

In the Kalevala, we are told that the sun was hatched from an egg in the chaos before formation of the earth. Luonnatar, the Daughter of Nature, was in heaven once, but she found it sterile and lonely. So she allowed herself to fall into the ocean, where she floated for seven centuries. Then a little duck appeared, seeking somewhere to build her nest. She located the only dry spot in creation— Luonnatar's knee, protruding from the water. There she nested, there laid her eggs, there sat for three days upon them.

Then, suddenly, Luonnatar—scorched with the heat—became unable to lie still. Her knee twitched slightly, and the eggs rolled off. As they broke, they turned into marvels. The yolks formed the sun, the whites the moon, the bits of shell the countless stars. All this magic spurred Luonnatar into action. She began digging bays, pulling forth peninsulas, forming an earth-surface so that animals and people would have somewhere to live.

From that time onwards, Paivatar the sun goddess kept busy spinning daylight from a rainbow arch. The Kalevala sings of her as "the beautiful virgin of the air, Sun Spirit, competent maid, holding the weaver's battens, lifting up the heddles, with a golden shuttle in her hands, a silver reed in her grasp." Though unmarried, Paivatar was a mother and seems to have been particularly sympathetic to other women with children. When the moon-maid refused to help the mother of the missing hero Lemminkainen, the sun rushed to help. The all-seeing one knew where the woman would find her son: in the Abode of the Dead. When the mother got there, she was forced to call upon Paivatar again, because she could not gain entry. The sun goddess again granted aid. She flew like a hen with its head cut off into a birch branch; she fluttered like a moulting hen into the bend in an alder branch. For an hour she shone hot, then, for a second hour, hotter; then she shone at full strength for a third hour.

The exhausted guards of the Abode of the Dead leaned over sleepily; then they fell fast asleep, young and old. The sun flew back to heaven. Then the mother of Lemminkainen pulled her son out of the Abode of the Dead with a long rake, while the sun-stroked guards slept on.

In the most important Finnish sun myth—one that recalls other myths of the region—the goddess was stolen, and endless night ensued. Her opponent was, of course, a witch; her rescuers were twin gods. It happened this way: The crafty mischief maker, Louhi, gap-toothed mistress of North Farm, sang the sun into a steel mountain. For five years it was night; for ten years there was not even the glimmer of stars.

The poet Vainomaoien and the smith Ilmarinen were called upon to free the sun. They started by forging new luminaries with heat provided by the sun's baby, fire. This child had been lost by Paivatar. "A maiden on the edge of a rainbow, she rocked the fire, sung the fire in a golden cradle on silver cords. The golden cradle rattled as the fire was being rocked. The fire fell from the girl's hands, shot through the nine heavenly spheres, through the six vaults of many colors." The falling spark killed a child. Then it was swallowed by a fish, which was swallowed by another fish, which was swallowed by another fish—which then had to be captured by a magical net made of flax sown and grown and spun within two days.

The net made, the fish was caught by another son of Paivatar, a capable boy who used a pole to flog the fish into the net, then knifed it to death. He removed first one fish, then the next, from the bellies of the fish that had swallowed them, and then the spark jumped out. It leapt across the world to sting the cheeks of craftsman Ilmarinen, who used magical chants to subdue it to usefulness. Then he set about forging a new sun and moon. There was no smith more qualified for the task than Ilmarinen; he had already forged the magical Sampo, an otherwise unidentified tool, that harnessed all riches. In crafting a new sun—an act that echoes that of the Baltic Kalvis—Ilmarinen used all his impressive skills. "He forged the moon of gold, the new sun of silver. These they lifted up eagerly, carried them nicely, up to the heavens, to the six vaults of many colors, to the nine heavenly spheres."

Sweat poured off Ilmarinen's beard from the difficulty of lifting the huge mirror discs of sun and moon, but they managed to hoist the metal plates into the sky at the heavenly pole. But even Ilmarinen's skill was not enough: The sun did not shine, nor did the moon. They lay there against the sky, beautiful flat plates of metal, and the world remained dark. The gods and heroes stood together in the cold darkness.

Then Vainomaoien, the poet, lost his temper. He stormed over to gloomy North Farm, Louhi's home, and pounded on the door, demanding to know where the goddesses were hid. The evil crew that tended Louhi taunted him: "The sun got into the crag, the moon vanished into the rock and they will never get free, never, never at all!" At the words, Vainomaoien lost his temper again, and struck at Louhi's men with his short sun-hilted sword, a mere barleycorn longer than the swords of his opponents. With two strokes, like cutting the tops off turnips, he lopped off the heads of the North Farm lads. Then he went off to collect the sun. There were nine doors, each with three locks, to prevent his entry. Vainomaoien went back to Ilmarinen's smithy, where he ordered his friend to forge a three-tined cultivator hoe, a dozen ice picks, and a bunch of keys. Ilmarinen set immediately to work. Louhi, made nervous by the battle at her farm and by the knowledge that Vainomaoien was planning to return, flew to the window of Ilmarinen's smithy. Disguised as a bird, she flattered him a bit, then asked what he was making. "A neck ring for that dame of North Farm," Ilmarinen answered coolly. Terrified, Louhi flew home at once. She knew she was trapped. Freeing the luminaries, she flew back to the smithy in the shape of a pigeon. There she casually remarked to Ilmarinen that the sun was rising.

He stepped to the door of the smithy and looked carefully at the sky, then went to Vainomaoien's door and called him forth. The poet rushed out to see the sky virgins spinning forth light. A rush of song to the goddess came forth from the poet:

Hail, lovely sun, for dawning, sun for rising!
Beautiful sun, you got free from the crag.
You rose up like a golden cuckoo, like a silver dove.
Always rise mornings from this day forth,
always when you come here, bring complete good health,
make the forest game accessible to us,
good luck to the tip of our fishhook,
bring the prey within reach of our thumb.
Make now your journey safe and sound,
your rounds comfortable, your circuit in fine shape,
attain joy in everything.

In the beautiful poetry of the Kalevala, this story shows the mythic configuration that Ernst Krause argued was shared among northern Europeans in prehistoric times. The sun goddess, captured by a witch, is kept from shining on her land. The hero gods free her and place her back in the sky. The intermediary portion—the forging of the false sun—cannot help but recall the forging of the sun-mirror in Japan; a route across Siberia, home of metal solar mirrors, might be traced, although it is hard to say in which direction this motif may have traveled. Eliminating the mirror, however, one sees the framework of the Trojaburg myth here in the Kalevala. In northern Europe, this is the central story of the spinning sun goddess: a story of the mother who forever dies into winter, and the daughter whom she holds captive but eventually frees into the company of her hero-husband.

But the congeries of images—spindles and stones, frogs and dwarfs, labyrinths and balls of twine—that we can call the Spinster on the Stone is more than a northern European myth. As we shall now see, it appears in a different but still recognizable form in two culture areas in North America: Northern California and the Southeast. There, thousands of miles from Scandinavia and the Baltic, we will again find the light goddess at work, webbing the sky with her rays. We will find her there at the center of a complex of images that aids us in understanding the connections between order and chaos, between creation and production, between life and afterlife. Webbing opposites together, she creates a reality beyond dualism. Let us travel to meet her.

Chapter Seven ✴

CENTRAL CALIFORNIA:
SUN, THE BASKETMAKER

Just as the metal mirror could not become an image of the sun goddess until technology produced it, spinning, too, is a craft that had to be invented before it could symbolize the sun's energy. There is, however, a difference. In the case of the mirror, it's possible that metalsmiths, inspired by the way clear water reflects the sun's light, sought to recreate that reflectiveness. The physical object may have followed, not preceded, its connection with the sun.

In the case of spinning, however, there is little doubt that the craft came first, then was connected with the sun goddess. Unlike the shining mirror, spinning is not obviously solar. True, we talk of the sun spinning through the sky and the year spinning through its seasons. But these are metaphors that have their base in an activity connected to the sun only because women spun and wove, and the sun was a woman. This was so, as we have seen, in northern Europe; it was also so in North America. Debates among mythographers often rage about whether an image was carried—diffused—through the world, or whether it sprang sponta-neously from an archetypal unconsciousness. The sun as spinner of light and weaver of life seems to be the latter, a true archetype, springing forth in unrelated cultures that had no contact. Just as the craft itself was invented in widely separate areas with no evidence of diffusion, the sun goddesses of North America are apparently unconnected to their European sisters despite similar motifs and symbols.

In America, this archetypal image welled forth not once, but twice. The first occurred on the Pacific Coast, particularly in central California, where the sun, a basket-making woman, had to be brought across long distances to warm the earth; the Achomawi, Maidu and Miwok are part of this complex. The other appeared in what is now the southeastern United States, among the Cherokee and nearby tribes, including the Caddo, Biloxi, Chitimacha, Yucchi and Tunica; they saw the sun as a great ancestor brought to earth in the web of Grandmother Spider.

There may have been other sun goddesses—spinners or not—in Native America, but their memory has been obliterated. By the time the myths that survive were recorded, mostly by outsiders, European culture had been under Apollonian influence for the better part of two thousand years. There is no question that some early recorders simply altered facts in order to bring Native American religions into the philosophic orbit of the conquerors. In addition, dramatic linguistic differences between Indo-European and Native American languages encouraged misunderstanding. Some of the latter languages were genderless, so the recorder could assign the sun either sex, as he chose; in others, grammatical gender was based on something other than sex, as among the Lenape, where gender divided the noble from the ignoble; the animate from the inanimate, leaving ample roam for misinterpretation. Some languages lacked pronouns, allowing outsiders to envision gods where goddesses were intended. Or a Native American informant, speaking English, scrambled the new language; even today some Native language speakers, like Germans speaking English, refer to people by opposite-gender pronouns.

Sometimes necessary questions were not asked, as in Gifford's massive research project among the Apache and Pueblo people in the 1930s on culture element distinctions. Methodically, interviewers inquired if the moon was male or female; if the stars were male or female; if the sun was male. They did not ask if the sun was female. One is left to guess whether those who answered "no, not male"—like the Mescalero, Ollero, and Llanero Apache—saw the sun as female, as having no sex, or as being of both sexes. Similarly, one wonders how to interpret to information that the Mescalero and others had a menstrual ritual in which a girl's head was painted with sun symbols. Was this to show her identity with the sun goddess? Such interpretations would be easier had Gifford not biased his questions.

It is almost incredible to discover, in the middle of the twentieth century, an Apollonian vision so strong as to distort anthropological research in this fashion.

Thus, sometimes deliberately and sometimes accidentally, wrong or partial information was taken down. Then whole cultures were wiped out, leaving early inaccuracies to stand as the record of a tradition. Elders died, taking with them the people's knowledge: myths, rituals, entire languages. Young Native American people, raised in white schools and speaking white languages, turned to the writings of white people to discover their heritage. Given these conditions, that we have any record of the sun goddess in North America is testimony to the love her people bore her—to the memories and integrity of three men in particular: Istet Woiche of the Madehsi Achomawi, Seostre Youchiquant of the Tunica, and Maxey Simms of the Yucchi. Each singlehandedly preserved an entire cycle of sun-goddess mythology that would otherwise have been lost. Non–Native American scholars, too, deserve credit for defying tradition to publish the fact of the sun goddess's existence in myth; notable is Mary Haas, who, uncovering a beautiful solar myth among the Tunica, wrote articles and books on the subject despite the academic unpopularity of the material.

The analysis that follows is highly conservative; only cultures in which the sun goddess was or is definitively acknowledged by her people are included, so that in an enthusiastic reclamation of the solar feminine we do not repeat the insults of others who have redefined cultures and mythologies. But, considering the prejudices affecting the type of information gathered on Native American religions, we can speculate that there were other groups whose original mythology included a sun goddess; as Jordan Paper put it, any area where Native Americans differ from European culture is likely to have been correctly transmitted, but that does not mean other myths and images which resemble European material were correctly recorded. There are indications of a feminine sun among some Southwest groups, among the Haida and related Northwest Coast peoples and among a number of Iroquoian and Algonkian peoples. We cannot now accurately measure the extent of the sun goddess's dominion in North America.[1]

The two cultural complexes we shall explore, however, offer no such problems of interpretation; the sun is recorded in all myths of these cultures as a feminine divinity. The first culture is central Californian—the culture of those who lived in the valleys and mountains around what are now Sacramento and Placerville. Little is published on the myths of these nations, despite the beauty of their tales. Part of the reason for contemporary ignorance may be linguistic. Of the 58 language families north of Mexico traced by John Wesley Powell in 1891, 27 were found along the Pacific coast. In addition, there were over one hundred California dialects, three-quarters of them mutually unintelligible; the great majority of California languages have no kindred tongue.

Another problem for the historian is that these groups, always small, were easily eliminated by massacre, disease or assimilation. The fact that the peoples of central California held on to their culture until only 150 years ago did not save it from being destroyed almost without a trace. Unlike the mission Indians to the south, whose culture was mutilated as early as the 1500s by contact with colonizing Spaniards, these central nations retained their historic ways until the great gold rush of the mid-1800's. Unfortunately, when white settlement came, it came in a boom, and the native population of central California was all but destroyed by the explosive goldfield development. The Maidu, for instance—on whose land John Sutter struck gold—began the nineteenth century with four thousand people and ended with two hundred.

This near-extinction meant the end of the area's indigenous culture. Anthropologists divide native California into three zones: the southern, central and northern. It might be better, though, to say that there was one major Californian culture—the central—as well as two smaller zones to the north and south. A. L. Kroeber, the dean of California anthropology, estimated that two-thirds of California's residents were of the central group; those in the southern area were part of what we call the Southwest Culture, while the northern peoples belonged to the Northwest Coast Culture. Central Californian culture, despite dozens of languages, was unified by domestic habit and by ceremony—among women, by the art of basketry and by the rituals of female adolescence—as well as by the predominance of a sun goddess in the mythologies. This unity goes back millennia, apparently to the time of the first migration to the area. The Penutian-speaking people, whose sun myths we will shortly examine, are believed to have come originally from Asia, for Asian-style sinew-backed bows are found among them; as we shall see, their solar myths share motifs with Southeast Asian and Indian tales as well. The Penutians, Kroeber says, were among the earliest entrants into California, they preceded the Algonkians, Athabascans and Shoshoneans, and were preceded only by the Hokans.

Because of the paucity of archaeological finds—much was crafted of organic materials that decompose easily—it is difficult to date exactly the first Native Americans' arrival on the Pacific Coast. Excavations of detritus mounds near San Francisco Bay suggest habitation from around four thousand years ago. But recent finds suggest that California may have been the site of the first wave of Asian immigrants to the area that is now the United States; the clay floor of a mountain camp in the Stanislaus National Forest, 150 miles east of San Francisco, has been dated as ten thousand years old.[2]

Only a little is known about this first period, most prominently that the immigrants brought the craft of basketry with them; the twining weave of their baskets remained consistent for thousands of years. Among Californians, basketry was the only way to create textiles; weaving of cloth was unknown. And among Californians, the Central Culture was the most advanced in basketry. Basketry was also the most characteristic and most highly developed art form throughout California. Every woman made baskets, the way every woman in spinning cultures made thread. Women gathered the reeds and grasses, dried them, then coiled or wove them together in characteristic shapes. Throughout the area, coiled baskets were the rule (twining, the other major basketry technique, is basically a southern California craft, although central Californians used it occasionally). Coils were arranged sunwise (clockwise) only. No baskets were coiled in the opposite direction from the sun's movement, though—unlike in spinning, where a reverse movement will buckle or break the thread—no structural damage could be caused by such a change.

The baskets were made from various reeds and grasses; the Achomawi, for instance, used willow and tule, ornamented with grass and ferns. Once made, the baskets saw heavy use. They stored food through the winter; they stored clothing and personal effects. They protected beads from weather; they carried babies. They were containers for water and pots for cooking. Loose-woven baskets were nets or traps for fishing.

Basketry is the earliest fiber craft. It might seem that the invention of spinning should have preceded that of weaving; it seems necessary to make yarns before one weaves with them. The opposite, in fact, is true: Weaving came before spinning, because plant stalks form a natural "thread" for weaving or plaiting. Similarly, it seems obvious that the spinning of animal hairs should have preceded the spinning of fibers from plants, because animal fiber naturally twists and mats, forming yarns and felts, while plant fiber does not. But, in fact, one need only tear plant stalks to form a thread. Basketry with saplings, then with plant stems, then with fibers from plant stems—this was the order in which fiber craft naturally developed.[3]

This was the case in central California, where, in addition to baskets woven of willow and grass, twine ropes were made using tule reed. Its fibers were stripped, then spun on the thigh using a perforated whorl. This rope—rather like postal twine, the closest we now come to the world's first thread—was used to make bird or fish nets.

It was women who made the baskets, and with their baskets the women's ceremonials were the oldest and most consistent part of this culture. Of all of the women's rituals, the most important had to do with menstruation. Throughout the area, menstruating women were considered to be so charged with energy as to be dangerous, and sacred. During her menses, a woman's behavior was circumscribed. She lived in a menstrual hut outside the village. She had no family chores to do; often she was proscribed even from talking to anyone. When talk was allowed, it was only with other women.

Most sacred of all was menarche—called by a unique word not used of any other flow during a woman's life—when, according to the oldest beliefs of the region, a girl was suffused with power. She was kept in utter confinement and was especially forbidden to have her face uncovered. Local myths of a cannibal-sun suggest that a jealous sun goddess may hide behind this part of the rite—one who would kill the young girl or mar her beauty. The power of such a goddess, resting temporarily in the girl, would likewise allow her to blight with her own sight. We have encountered this idea before; light was the sun's glance; similarly, the sun-like girl's eyes were enormously powerful, so it was important that she refrain from looking at anyone vulnerable to her magic.

As part of her confinement, the girl was forbidden to scratch herself with her fingers, a scratching stick being provided for the purpose. Sometimes she was required to fast; when she was allowed to eat, others fed her, and she was in all cases forbidden meat. In many places, she was required to gather firewood throughout her confinement; sometimes she had to secretly deliver the wood to village families. In almost all villages, a dance was held to celebrate her confinement's conclusion.[4]

These traditions were shared by all the central Californians whose sun-goddess traditions we shall examine. We begin with the Maidu, whose sun-goddess myth is the most widely published of those extant—although Kroeber pointed out that, because of the Maidu's reverent secrecy regarding sacred matters, much of the myth has probably been lost. The Maidu lived on the eastern part of the Sacramento River, near today's town of Chico. Theirs was not an extremely rich land; part was tule swamp, another part the volcanic Marysville Buttes, yet another a major hot springs. But in the foothills were fish-filled streams and on the hills acorn-bearing oaks. It was a land not rich, but rich enough.

The Maidu myth begins at the beginning, when there was no sun, no moon and no stars, when the world was covered with water on which Turtle and Peheipe floated on a raft. Into this dark watery world came the hero Earth-Initiate, brother of the sun. It was his job to form a world out of chaos, and to do so he first called to his companions, "My sister is about to rise!" Then the hero's companion Peheipe, the Father-of-Secret-Societies, shouted loudly. The sun arose at the sound. She was so powerful that the earth crinkled into gullies and mountains from her heat.

"Does she ever rest?" asked the hero's other companion, Turtle.

Almost in answer, the sun set in the west. Then it was dark, pure dark. Peheipe shouted, "Is there no rest from these extremes of light and darkness?" At Earth-Initiate's word, the brother moon arose, bringing the stars with him. Earth-Initiate then told his companions that in this world there would always be good and evil—good the wisdom of life, and evil a drowsiness towards life that leads to eternal sleep. Should good ever begin to turn to evil, he said, the third element would arise to restore the balance: Coyote, who awakens good by acting out evil. This was the first day of the world as we know it.

The Maidu, like other central Californians, did not imagine the sun as a being coexistent with the universe, but as something that had to be called into creation—or stolen, or begged from another group that owned it. Possibly this reflects a long arctic sojourn en route from Asia; the sun's "travels" towards her people could reflect her people's travels south to warmer climes. Further evidence of Asian origin comes in the form of myths that show an exchange of sexes between sun and moon, which we have encountered among the Ainu and in Korea.

One Maidu story relates that the sun was a man who lived with his sister in an ice-covered sweat lodge in Honey-Lake Valley. He was a cannibal who stole children from the earth until attacked by Frog Woman. This Frog Woman was a famous basketmaker who lived in a large winter home; she never dropped a bit of grass from her mouth as she wove. To escape from Frog's attacks the sun traded identities with his sister, saying, "I will be the Night-Sun Man. You must be the Day-Sun Woman."

Because he had been eaten by the Frog Woman, the moon each month is eaten up and then grows again. After he exchanged roles with his sister, they saw each other only as they passed morning and night. "Nothing troubles me any more," the sun says to her brother each day. "Good," he answers.[5]

In this story we have a mixtures of two motifs. One is the exchange of identities between the luminaries. The other is the attack by the frog—a common sun myth, as another Maidu story, one told among the people of today's Butte and Plumas counties, shows. It begins with the sun and moon, brother and sister, living together in a solid stone house. They refused to come out and light the world. Many creatures came to beg them to rise, but the visitors never even got in the door of the stone house. Gopher and Angle Worm set off to see what they could do.

When they reached the stone house, Angle Worm made a hole in the ground, intending to burrow inside the house. Gopher did the same, but he was smart enough to be carrying a bag of fleas. Gopher got in first and released the fleas inside the hut. Sun and Moon started scratching. They scratched and they scratched. But the biting wouldn't stop. So they went out.

The sun told her brother that they would have to separate, because the two of them would be too hot for the world. She tried the night, but the stars accosted her. So she traded places with her brother and moved to the far north, where she built herself a house of ice. It looked like a mountain, it was so big.

From this fortress the sun stole people from the earth and killed them. One day she came upon Frog's house and stole one of her children. The second day she came back again, and stole another one. The third day, she figured Frog would be watching, so she waited. She waited ten days before she went to Frog's house again. Frog was making a basket when Sun arrived. Nonetheless, Sun managed to steal the last child, and then ran away, pursued by the frantic Frog.

As she ran, Sun created a willow patch that distracted Frog; she began to gather basket twigs for a moment, but then remembered her dreadful mission. She ran all the way to Sun's ice house. There she tried to climb it but kept slipping back down, for the ice was like glass. But she was determined to have revenge, so kept trying until she reached the top.

There she challenged Sun to come outside. As soon as Sun did so, Frog swallowed her whole. The revenge seemed complete until Sun began to swell and heat up Frog's belly. Soon she had grown so huge that she burst out of the Frog's skin with a bang. Frog was blown to bits. (There is a moral provided in this version of the story: There will always be people who steal, because Sun conquered Frog.)

There are other familiar solar motifs here in addition to the sex-exchange pattern; there is the slippery Sun's house, here made of ice rather than glass; there is the hint of incest, in the sun's living with her brother, which as we shall soon see is a widespread Asian myth; there is the refusal of the sun to rise. There is also the frog, a curious solar creature. We encountered it as the sun's enemy among the Indian Minyong, in the story of Bong and Bomong. In the Baltic, too, frogs are said to be denied the sight of darling Saule. Yet sometimes the frog seems to be not the sun's enemy but the sun herself, as in Russia where Baba-Yaga and the spinster Vasilisa are conjoined; among the Saami of Scandinavia, the sun-disc painted on the drum was referred to as a "jumping frog," and among the Tunica of Mississippi the ancestral sun goddess was represented by two statues: one of a woman and one of a frog.

Why this connection between frog and sun? The most likely possibility is that the frog is a winter-sun image. Sun-like in the egg stage, the amphibian lives both on land and in the water, like the sun who sinks into the water to travel the night sea to her rising place in the east. But, most importantly, the female frog swells up in the winter with eggs—up to twenty thousand of them. By vernal equinox, when the song of male frogs fills the waxing days, her skin is stretched thin across an almost totally round body. She almost looks as though she has swallowed the sun. And, although she does not burst, the sudden evacuation of all her eggs, in approximately five seconds, leaves her thin and indistinguishable from a male or non pregnant female frog.

This spawning behavior is caused not by increasing temperature but by the frog's response to light. The apparent enmity between frog and sun is reminiscent of the complex connection, in Scandinavia, of dwarfs and the sun goddess: they are the smiths who make her shining necklaces, yet they are turned to stone by her gaze. To be an enemy is to be connected. The fact that we have, in the frog and the dwarf, negative solar images does not change the fact that both are bonded to the sun goddess. There are many cases where Frog Woman undoes the work of Sun Woman, as among the Clackmas Chinook—relatives of the central Californians— among whom Frog and her daughters indulged in sexual and antisocial behavior that noble Sun Woman refused. But in other stories Frog Woman is a double of the sun: weaving baskets, sitting atop a round hut, snaring human children for food. Sometimes she is even related to the Sun Woman, as among the Miwok, for whom Old Lady Frog was the sun goddess's grandmother-in-law.[7]

These fragmentary myths may have traveled from Asia with the Penutian people, together with the shamanic practices that are so marked in central California. As in Korea, a central Californian woman was called to shamanize, rather than consciously selecting the vocation. This happened when the sun provided a dream-visitation that inspired a potential shaman to take up the craft; the sun goddess thereafter was her "personal" or familiar spirit. After the dreamer woke, a public ceremony introduced the new shaman to the tribal group before practice began. At this point, the nascent shaman accepted as tutor an older member of the shamanic society. Exhibitions of magic were not unusual at these gatherings, the purpose of which was multifold: to hail the new shaman as someone able to contribute to tribal life in a special way, and to make sure that the new shaman's spirits—thought to be somewhat undisciplined—were initiated into the society's control.[8]

The shaman's later life was, in the main, devoted to healing. This was done through the extraction of "pains," small, clear quartz-like objects with sharp ends that were inside people and had to be extracted. Upon completion of the extraction ceremony, the shaman ate the stone, kept it for its power, or destroyed it. Like stones in the Baltic and in Scandinavia, the "pains" were themselves sun-goddess symbols. As the Concow Maidu from the Round Valley area related, at the beginning of time the creator blew milkweed cotton into the east to light the sky. This didn't provide enough illumination, so he set a big white rock crystal there. Then he gave his favorite daughter first choice at ruling the sun or the moon; she chose the sun. He sent her to the east to travel in the crystal, accompanied by a friend who would carry the morning star. That is why, the Concow Maidu said, woman is brave in the daylight, because the sun is shining.

There is much to be done in reclaiming the entire sun-goddess cycle of the Maidu. Unfortunately, parts may be forever lost, as seems to be the case with the goddess myths of the largest group, the Nisenan or Southern Maidu. Once among the most numerous of California natives, their numbers declined when gold was discovered near the geographic center of their territory. Within four decades, the Nisenan way of life had all but vanished. It is known, however, that they were deeply religious. Among the Nisenan, natural objects like trees and the sun were seen as sentient beings with will and choice. "It looks to me," one Nisenan said to an anthropologist, "like that tree could kill us, the wind could kill us, if it wanted to." It didn't make sense to the Nisenan that natural phenomena were without consciousness. "Who's tending the sun?" a Nisenan speculated. "There must be somebody." [9]

Near the Nisenan, in the western Sierras, lived Penutian relatives of the Maidu called the Miwok. Among them were the Mokelumne River folk, who told the just-so story that Wittabbah the Robin carried fire from a great distance—burning his breast on it as he traveled. Once he'd reached his goal, he made the sun from the precious fire, besides hiding some in the buckeye tree so that people could get it, in the form of firewood, when they needed it.

The Miwok, like the neighboring Maidu, believed the sun—Hi or Hiema or Hintaku—had to be convinced to light the world. The story begins when the sun shut herself up in her stone house and refused to come out. The sky was dark, and Hawk Chief was very far away. He went to his grandfather and demanded daylight. Coyote, his grandfather, said he'd see what he could do, and went to visit the doves.

"My grandson doesn't like the dark," he said. "Can't you do something about this?" The doves said they'd see what they could do.

They'd been to the sun's house and knew where it was, so they set off. When they got there, they sat down and waited, hoping she'd come out of her own accord. They waited and waited, but nothing happened.

Finally they decided to shoot stones at her house to make her rise. But they couldn't agree on who should do the shooting. "I'll do it," said the older. "You might miss."

"You?" said the younger. "You're too old. Your arm is weak. My arm is strong."

"Okay, okay, so shoot," said the older. The young dove took up a slingshot and whirled it around. The stone, flying from the slingshot, hit the sun's house and went right through the wall. The sun was frightened and rose from her smokehole to check on the damage. But she found that there was only a little hole, so she went back in.

The older dove started shouting. "Strong arm! You don't know what you're talking about!" The old dove took up the slingshot and whirled it round, and round and round. When he let the stone fly, it sailed through the air so fast that it smashed right into the sun's house, right in the center. The sun, frightened out her wits, rose straight up into the air and stood overhead. Coyote and his grandson were very, very happy.

Sometimes it was not that the sun refused to shine; sometimes it was just that her light was too weak and she had to be brought nearer. The Hookooeko Miwok of Tamales Bay said that in the beginning the world was dark, because Hekoolas the Sun-woman lived too far away in the east. Because the people wanted light, Coyote sent two men to bring the sun goddess closer. She lived so far away that it took them a long time to get there. And, when they did, she told them to go away. She did not intend to move.

They came back and told Coyote. He sent an army to capture her and bring her to this world despite her objections. They went to the land of the sun and found her—a woman covered with abalone shells that made her shine so brightly you could not look at her directly. They tied her up with ropes and brought her back. Then they placed her in the sky where she could make light for all the people.

Of the still-extant myths that tell of moving the sun, the most impressive was told by the Achomawi, who lived in the Pit River area near Sacramento but hunted all the way to Mount Shasta. Their homeland was centered on a thermal spring, although we do not know if the spring was used in ritual. There were eleven groups of Achomawi; the sun myths often appear to be lost. However, among the Madehsi Achomawi, a cycle of sun-goddess stories was preserved by the last Speaker of the Laws, Istet Woiche (William Hulsey); he thereby saved his religion from complete extinction. Published in a small volume that has been long out of print, the myth is little known today, although it ranks among the most impressive Native American epics.

The Madehsi told this story cycle each year during the winter months, beginning at winter solstice and continuing until the spring equinox. The tale begins when the Chools—the man in the moon and the beautiful, fat sun woman—lived under the ocean and lit the world very dimly. People on earth wanted more light, so the hero Annikadel told Cloud Woman and her brother Kwahn to bring the Chools closer.

Cloud Woman went to sleep in a tree, waiting for sunrise. When the Chools rose, she sang them this song:

> I am in this world.
> I travel in the air.
> I was not born on the earth.
> I was born in the sky.
> I have come to call you from the ocean.
> You will be needed in this world.
> When trees come, you will quicken them.
> When people come, you will comfort them.
> Don't refuse me; I'm not deceiving you.

After she sang this, she saw the light reach halfway up into the sky but no further. Cloud Woman knew she would have to go to the home of the Chools to tell them the world was not finished until they were in the sky. The next morning, as soon as the Chools were out of the water, she sailed through the air singing to them, "The world is not finished yet. When you are placed where you ought to be, the world will be finished."

The Chools agreed, but they were tired and wanted to rest as they traveled. The first night they rested on top of Mount Shasta. They were so hot that they burned right through the gravel where they camped and left a huge crater. The Cloud Maiden was worried about how slowly they traveled, so the next day she took a deep breath and blew them along.

In three more days they were at the North Pole, where they were placed on the ice so they couldn't burn any more holes in the ground. Then a boy, Edechewe, decided to visit them in their home in the North. Annikadel the hero warned him that the sun woman would try to destroy him with her heat, and he told the boy that he would be tested on his way four times: by Whirlwind—before which he should turn into rock;

by the Thunder Brothers—whom he should shoot with fish eyeballs in a sling shot; by the Lightning Brothers—whom he should fight with green reeds; and by the Wicked Ghosts, who would offer him poison food—and whose house he should burn down.

He passed these tests and gained the company of the Woman Made of the Shadows of Flowers. The left part of her hair was made of the shadows of red flowers; the right was made of the shadows of flowers that blew in the wind. They went together to Choollodeyumche, the place where the Chools lived.

After nightfall, they went to the roundhouse where the Chools lived. There the weaver sun was making a grass basket. She acted as if she didn't see them, but she did. The Moon acted as if he didn't see them either, and he didn't. Two girls came up—the sun's daughter and the moon's daughter—and sat next to Edechewe. They became his brides.

In the morning, the sun woman went out to light the world, and Edechewe woke up to find himself outside the roundhouse, being carried off on the back of the dragon Himnimtsooke. He woke up twenty steps from the ocean, where he was about to be drowned. "Wait! Wait! I have an itch! Let me scratch!" he called to the dragon.

"Really, now! I don't let people stop and scratch," said the dragon.

"You must! I really have to scratch!" The dragon stopped just five steps from the ocean, and Edechewe's brother, Yahtch, who was hiding in his hair, leaped out and stabbed the dragon with an obsidian knife. Then he hid in Edechewe's hair again, and Edechewe went back to the roundhouse.

The next day the sun woman got up to sit on top of the roundhouse. She turned to the east, then to the south, then to the west, and then got down and went into her house for the night. That night the moon man asked his son-in-law to take a sweat bath with him. The daughter of the sun told him not to go, but Edechewe was brave and went with his father-in-law to the little earth house where he smoked people to death.

The moon built a fire and started a blaze of human bones, but his son-in-law opened the fire door and stuffed in real wood. "You can't sweat with this kind of fire," he said. He built a bigger and bigger blaze, dragging in armloads of wood—red fir and cedar—to add to it. "When these smoke, they don't get hot," he explained. "That's why bones are no good. When things blaze, they make heat."

The Chool was almost burned up. He ran out of the sweat lodge towards the ocean, and fell dead. Edechewe went in to dinner calmly. When the family asked him where the old man was, he said be didn't know, but that be wasn't worried. The next day he went to where the moon was lying, took a stick of azalea, and hit him with it five times, while he walked in a circle around him. The Chool sprang up alive. "You're all right, after all, boy," he said.

Then Edechewe went out hunting for deer. When he came back, the moon man was dancing around as he did every night. The next day the Chool said that he wanted to play out on a long pole—which, in Edechewe's absence, he had put over a narrow bay full of monsters. He was going to drop Edechewe off to be eaten alive. But the hero had other plans. He lured the moon man out on the narrow pole and shook the pole gently so that it sprang back under his hands.

The moon man enjoyed this. He called for more. Then Edechewe pushed harder, and harder, and the moon bounced higher and higher, until suddenly the Chool shot off the pole into the air high above the ground. "You have put me where I've always wanted to be," the Chool called down. "Now go get my wife and my daughters and send them up, too."

But when Edechewe returned to the roundhouse the mother and her girls objected. They didn't really want to go into the sky. "This doesn't look right," Edechewe told the sun. "He is up there, and you are down here." The sun thought about it and decided to go up. So Edechewe took her to the middle of the pole and counted. One, two, three, four, five, and he shot her up into the sky.

Then he sent up her daughters, one to stand by the side of the moon, one to stand by her mother's side. After all this, the sun and moon were finally in the right place, but this was not the end of the story. For in the sky the sun and moon were both motionless, getting hotter and hotter and hotter, and people were beginning to die from the heat. Eagle Woman and Condor Man tried to set a meeting to talk about the problem, but found that they couldn't tell what time to meet because there were no days and nights. They became alarmed, and immediately gathered the other beasts.

The beasts argued and argued about what was to be done, and finally Spider Woman volunteered to find Annikadel and ask him for help. She got into a little basket made out of net, put the Whirlwind under it, and whirled herself over to the hero Annikadel. When she got to his home she told him about the heat of the Chools, that they were standing too close in the sky and had to be moved. Annikadel's grandfather said that it was a difficult task—to travel for three days through good air, then ten days through warm air, then twenty days through air so cold no one could live in it, then forty days through hot air, then sixty days through heavy rain, then through ice for another sixty days. Annikadel said he'd try it. His grandfather gave him magic caps to protect him and magic canes to use to cross the ice.

Annikadel stepped into Spider Woman's magic basket, and off they went. The trip took less time than the grandfather said, and very soon they were in the far north, outside the world. There Annikadel left Spider Woman and went on alone. First he reached the daughters of the moon and the sun. To the moon's girl he said, "Look north," and when she looked and saw the land of ice sparkling clean, she was pleased. Then he said to the sun's daughter, "Look south," and she saw flowers, flowers everywhere, and she was pleased. Then he talked to the parents. He flattered the moon. "You will thaw like ice and then become new again, and the people will be amazed." And to the responsible sun he said, "You must travel through the sky, going dawn in the west and coming back up in the east. And I am going to lower the sky in the winter, so you'll have to travel lower then yourself." When they both agreed, he set the girls in the sky and went back to the Spider Woman, who took him back to earth.

This myth-cycle—given here only briefly—deserves to be better known, full as it is of beautiful solar images: the sun as a basketmaker weaving on the roof of her house, the sun's placement on a mountain of ice so she won't melt the earth, the woman made of the shadows of flowers who guards the entrance to the sun's realm. The fact that this story came so near to being lost hints at the treasures now beyond recapturing.[10]

Among the many intriguing features of the Madehsi myth is that Spider Woman appears here as the creature who brought the sun to her present place in the sky (we will see an almost identical story among the unrelated Cherokee). This is the only extant California solar myth in which Spider Woman plays this role, but in other American cultures she is constantly connected to the sun. The Navaho Spider Woman, for instance, taught the tribal women to weave on a loom with a warp of sun rays and a batten formed of the solar corona. Spider Woman, wherever she appears, is a creative seamstress; among the Pima her duty was to sew earth and sky together. Sometimes, when the creative spinning goes awry, the spider becomes evil: the Aztec, according to the Borgia Codex, saw spiders as the malevolent spirits of women who, dying in childbirth, lived in the afternoon sun. Related to the spider is the widely-known solar game called cat's cradle, in which a "spinner" creates figures from a long loop of twine. The Zuni particularly connected the game with the spider; it was invented by Spider Woman to represent her web.

Among the Navaho, too, the game was invented by spiders and could be played by people only in winter, when the originators were hibernating. Breaking this rule would mean falling into Spider Woman's den forever. In South America, too, the spider plays a prominent part in bringing textile crafts as well as light to the world. The Toba of Argentina said that a young and an old woman were sent to discover how Spider wove; they spied upon her and then stole her bag of thread while she slept. Once back in the village, however, the women could not tell if their threads were made of sheep's wool or yucca pods. Unfortunately, guessing the latter, they found they could not spin the fiber so they reversed their decision. But they had no sheep, for the animals were all owned by stingy Partridge. Frog was asked to approach Partridge and ask for some sheep. Frightened of Partridge, Frog swallowed his pool; her body swelled up but she did not burst. Partridge begged and begged to have his water back, then finally agreed to give the whole flock of sheep to humanity. At that, Frog disgorged all of Partridge's water and drove the sheep home. The women learned to weave, and the first thing they made was a poncho for Frog.[11]

The invisible Spider Woman in this story is connected with Frog, as usual a female entity. In Native American myths, the spider too is almost invariably female (although occasionally she has a male spider as companion). The spider is predominantly a female image because the female spider is the one we know: It is she whose webs we see. Round like the sun, she spins spirally out from a center, like light webbing from the solar orb. Spiders spin silk from within themselves—creating "nests" not like a bird collecting twigs but like the all-mother creating the world.

Spiders spin from spinnerets near the abdominal apex; they use silk for webs, for sacs and dens. Spider is the primordial builder, constantly rebuilding and repairing. Her web is more than just a home. It is an extension of the hunting spider: She sits at the hub, waiting for vibrations on the lines. The web itself cannot hold prey; the spider subdues her food with poison or overpowers it. Then she swaths it in silk, which finally subdues the prey. As she spins the shroud for her insect dinner, the spider actually spins her food as well, like a shish kebab on a grill. Once the grill is fully packaged, the spider transports it to storage. Perhaps this methodical trapping and wrapping gave rise to those visions of the sun as a cannibal or thief of children.

But spiders don't spend all their time at home: They can fly through the air, apparently without support—though in fact the spider spins a dragline to ride the winds. Spiders travel in two ways on their gossamer.

They can build a "silk road," flying out a line and traveling to wherever it attaches; or they can attach a line and then sail forth. The most spectacular form of spider travel occurs during that period called "gossamer summer," when baby spiders in balloon-like nets that look like little baskets travel through the sky. The blowing baby spiders catch the sun, sheening the air. Native Americans, noting the way spiders travel the wind and capture the sun's beams, endowed the cosmic spider with the ability to travel to the sun-mother this way.[12]

Today there is a general feeling that spiders may be poisonous or dangerous, but this is not in fact the case. In northern climes no native spider is poisonous; in the south only the tarantula is dangerous. It is possible that with the repression of Native American culture came revulsion against one of its great symbols, as happened to the snake in the Middle East. In America, children tend to be terrified of spiders, even though in the European tradition from which most of their ancestors hail, the house spider is considered an emblem of luck and protection. Spider Woman, who brought the sun to us, is now sprayed with poison, smashed with shoes, clubbed to death with brooms. As our atmosphere thins, bringing the sun's light too close to us for safety, we can ruefully recall her work in placing the sun accurately at time's beginning, and meditate upon the web of life we're endangering.

Chapter Eight

SOUTHEASTERN NORTH AMERICA:
THE STONE ON THE SERPENT

We began this survey of the spinning sun goddess in northern Europe, where we found her concerned with making daily life sacred and the celebrating women's part in the ordinary round of existence. Among Native Californians, we found a similar image in the basket-making sun goddess, whose arrival from afar began life as we know it. The sun spinster thus appears as a force of order in the most everyday sense: Saule trims the forest's treetops, Berchta rewards careful handcrafts, the fat Chool is placed exactly where she can warm but not burn the earth. The sun goddess, regulator of the seasons and of the day's light, embodies the ordering principle of the universe.

Hers is not an Apollonian order, rigid and narrow, excluding darkness and change, admitting only steady brilliance. Rather, her order accepts change as implicit and regular: seasonal flux and tidal flow, menarche and menopause, birth and death. Darkness is as much her domain as is light: The dwarfs whom she turns to stone create her halo-necklace. Even time's end is within her power, for although the Fenris Wolf devours the sun, she yet gives birth at the moment of her destruction. Thus the order that the sun goddess embodies includes apparent opposites: darkness as well as light, change as well as stability, time's end as well as its daily maintenance. We move beyond simple polarities with this image. Light and darkness, viewed from within these myths, become parts of an ordered whole, alternating in periodic change.

But although all things change, they do not necessarily do so predictably. What of random events and occurrences, those that—being beyond the anticipated flux of periodicity—seem to defy the sun goddess's system? What of accidents and storms and eclipses and sudden death? What of chaos?

We have learned in recent years of the subtle system that, in fact, predicts—if it does not regulate—chaos. But the patterns that compose it seem beyond human perception, so vast is the scale on which they are charted. A migration of butterflies in Australia is imperceptible to Americans battered by the storm to which it gives rise. Yet Native Americans of the Southeast, in their mythology, intimated modern knowledge of the connection between chaos and order. To them, the sun goddess served as "the Apportioner," cutting time and life into predictable units. And, in juxtaposition—although perhaps not in opposition—to her, they described another mythic being, one ruling the events that disrupt her order, a divinity of creative and dangerous chaos. In this chapter, we shall examine the myths of the Cherokee, as well as those of their relatives and neighbors. In doing so, we encounter a disturbing but provocative image: a monster serpent, crowned with a crystal, whose power opposes that of the sun. In meditating upon this serpent, we find a new vision of the sun goddess's power—and of her limitations.

The crystal-crowned serpent is found in the mythologies of southeastern North America. There, sun-goddess worship was widespread. Of the region's four main language groups, the speakers of three recognized the solar feminine: These were the Iroquoian peoples, including the Cherokee as well as their Iroquois relatives to the north; the Muskogean, including the Natchez, Tunica and Chitimacha; and the Siouxian, including the Biloxi and Yucchi; all of these are peoples whose sun-goddess myths are preserved. Only those whose languages were in the Caddoan group seem to have lacked a feminine solar divinity.

But the sun goddess may have been even more prominent in southeastern North America than this listing suggests. The mythologies of many groups are apparently lost. In addition, deliberate misrepresentations and wrong transcription was here, as elsewhere, likely. Even Native Americans themselves, attempting to survive under European rulership, occasionally altered their mythologies. In the nineteenth century, for instance, the Shawnee prophet Teenskwaatawa tried to bring his people's religion into the orbit of patriarchal Christianity by changing the sex of Our Grandmother above; his attempt did not succeed, but others may have, whether launched by Native American people themselves or by the non–Native American transcribers of their myths. Happily, however, much sun-goddess material did survive. Extant, for instance, are the myths of the Yucchi and Chitimacha, the rituals of the Natchez, and, from the Cherokee, both a solar myth and the ceremonies based upon it.

The Cherokee were unusual in the Southeast, in that they spoke a northern tongue; they were Iroquoian, their language connected to that of the Seneca and Huron. Cherokee history tells of earlier, more intimate connections with their Iroquoian relatives; it is likely that the groups lived in close proximity during the culture's prehistory. Cherokee is close enough to other Iroquoian languages for linguists to determine that the two groups must have separated some thirty-five hundred years ago; approximately 34.3 percent of the words are similar. In addition, ethnobotanical studies reveal similar names for plants, and similar myths of their origin and uses; the herbalist occupies a similarly prominent position in both cultures.

The Cherokee had more in common with their northern cousins than language alone. Both had traditions of dwarfs or "little people" associated with rocks, stones and cliffs. The groups shared a myth about the creation of food from the body of the first woman; similarly, a version of the Cherokee's so-called Orpheus myth—in which the sun's daughter was almost brought back from the dead—appeared among the Huron, an Iroquoian people. In both cultures, too, masked dancers appeared in ritual: The Iroquois False-Faces and the Cherokee Boogers both spoke gibberish or foreign tongues, pretended to be pregnant, and interrupted community dances to demand to perform their own.[1]

One of the most important connections between the Cherokee and their Iroquois relations is in the sun's feminine gender. As the Seneca tell it, the luminary's history begins with the sky-mother Ataensic falling from heaven. Below her stretched only an unbroken expanse of water, dotted here and there by water birds. These birds, looking down, thought they saw a woman rising from the depths. But, no: It was the falling Ataensic, mirrored in the water and growing larger as she neared splashdown.

The birds watched the pregnant sky-mother descend, shrieking in fear that she would drown. Then one realized that the water would form a mirror only if there was something beneath them to back up the silver surface. And so the waterbirds began to dive, filling their beaks with soil, carrying it up, building an island for the goddess. By the time Ataensic splashed down, a resting place had been built. There on the island earth, the sky-mother gave birth.

And there her daughter Gusts-of-Wind grew up. She grew into a young woman so splendid even the air itself fell in love with her. Conceiving, Gusts-of-Wind grew heavy with twins. One of them was evil; he fought so violently with his brother in the womb that Ataensic's daughter was killed as the evil twin Tawaiscara—"Flint"—broke into daylight from his mother's armpit. When the benevolent twin Yoskeha— "Sapling"—emerged, Tawaiscara blamed him for the death of their mother.

Distraught at losing her daughter, Ataensic believed the evil boy and cast his brother out. Then she cut off the head of her daughter. "Even

155

though you are dead, you shall still serve," she said. "You shall give light to this earth." Ataensic fashioned the sun from the head of her murdered daughter and the moon from the shredded remains of her body. But she did not have the strength to raise the luminaries to heaven. She hid them in a place where only she and Tawaiscara could see them.

Yoskeha, banished from his home but undeterred in his intention to do good, wandered the world performing heroic acts. One was to place the sun in the sky. Gathering animals from the world's four corners, he sneaked into the place where the sun was hid and rolled out his mother's head. Ataensic and Tawaiscara gave chase. Passing the sun among themselves like a ball in a relay-race, the animals succeeded in getting her to heaven, from which she could light the sky. The evil twin was unmasked, Ataensic forgave Yoskeha, and, together, they watched as the head of Gusts-of-Wind illuminated the morning sky.

So goes the Seneca version of the creation of the sun, Enedeka Dakwa. The myth was repeated among other Iroquoian peoples. There were slight variations: Sometimes it was the goddess's body that became the sun while her head became the moon; sometimes sky-mother Ataensic herself gave birth to the twins and was torn apart to form the luminaries. Some variants include those solar creatures, the frogs: They, not water birds, brought earth up from the water's bottom; or all the water in the world hid under a frog's armpit until set free by one of the twins; or frogs swallowing the sun caused an eclipse.

The myth of the sun's birth from the head of Gusts-of-Wind is not the only information we have about the Iroquoian sun goddess. We also have record of the ritual that honored the goddess. Even after the arrival of Christianity, Iroquoian peoples celebrated the Sun Thanksgiving. There was no special time of the year for the dance, which was called whenever anyone dreamed that it was necessary for the people to remind the sun of her people's affection. Starting at noon, arrows were shot up at the sun while people danced around in celebration of her importance to the people.

Iroquoians lived under what early male observers called "petticoat government," but which Paula Gunn Allen characterizes as "gynocracy," rule by women. Women, especially mothers, held primary power, both political and social; in recognition of their vital role in the nation, the penalty for killing a woman was set at twice that of killing a man. In the codification of Iroquois law, called the White Roots of Peace, women—defined as "progenitors of the nation and owners of the land and the soil"—were acknowledged to be the only ones with power to begin and end wars. It was also up to the women to select tribal leaders. The matriarch of each of the nation's forty-nine families chose the sachem, or chief, of that family line. This was not necessarily the oldest child; whomever the mother determined was best suited took the post. Once the chief had been installed, the mother watched his behavior carefully and could depose him at will.

Socially, too, women were the center of the culture and arbiters of family law. They conveyed their family status to their descendants, settled domestic and family disputes in a kind of court, determined when daughters could divorce, and took care of daughters' needs before and after marriage. Women managed the funerals, determined what foods would be served at festivals, and kept safe the historic chief-wampum belts. Iroquois religious rituals, too, had a feminine orientation: As Martha Champion Randle has pointed out, men's lives found no reflection in religion, which was based in the cycle of women's lives: War was not celebrated, whereas birth was; hunting was not honored as farming was.[2]

This Native American matriarchy was among the first to be affected by Christianity, which virtually destroyed it. But the Iroquois's relatives, the Cherokee—Tslagi, in their own language—had greater success in holding onto their national heritage. Cherokee history is a mixture of tenacious, resolute clinging to old ways, and pragmatic adoption of European—later American—ways to assure tribal survival. The Cherokee were among the Five Civilized Nations who converted to Christianity; they regularly sent delegations to Washington; they maintained non–Native American legal counsel to negotiate treaties. Their brilliant Sequoia designed an alphabet to transcribe their religious beliefs; and the Cherokee diligently kept alive their traditions, including a great number of sun-goddess myths. Some of these were recorded in the early nineteenth century by the Cherokee themselves, others by non–Native Americans close to the people, so that we have virtually a description of a living tradition—a rarity in the Americas, where the religion of the people was most often recorded by those seeking to kill or convert them.

The sun was the primary object of worship to the Cherokee. She was the only deity to whom prayers were addressed. Each morning the people prayed to her by bowing towards the dawn—if possible over water—and saying *A ke yu ku gu-squa ne lo ne hi*, "hail, Sun, my creator." The sun's name was Unelanuhi, "The Apportioner," a reference to her division of the year into seasons and perhaps of her control over lifespan. She was also called Aag:hu Gu:gu, "Beautiful Woman," a word also used of the glow of the dawn, and Sutalidihi, "Six-Killer," a name whose interpretation is lost.

The story of how the sun came to warm the earth recalls other Native American stories in which the luminary was brought from afar. Early in creation, the Cherokee said, there was no light here on earth, because the sun lived on the other side of the world. Everyone was always bumping into things and stubbing their toes, so a council was called to determine a remedy. The fox said there was plenty of light around the end of the world. The possum volunteered to bring it to this side. He tried, but when he'd stolen part of the sun's fire, it burned off his tail and fell away. Then the Buzzard tried, but the fire burned off the feathers on his claws before, again, it fell away.

It was Grandmother Spider, Kanene ski Amai yehi, who figured out what to do. She wove herself a little basket, then spun a web to the other side of the world. In this basket, on this web, she traveled across the sky to the greedy ones who kept the sun for themselves. She wove and wove until she reached the sun. Then she reached out, grabbed the sun, roped it into her basket, and fled back across her waiting web.

But the new sun sat too low in the sky for comfort. People were burning up, dying from the heat. So, handbreadth by handbreadth, the animal elders moved the sun upwards. One handbreadth was not enough; two, not enough. Up and up she went, until she stood seven hands high in the air. There the sun was just right, and there she has stayed to this day.

The idea of the too-hot sun appears as well in the Cherokee story that the north went traveling and fell in love with the daughter of the south. When they were married, he carried her to his country, where all the people lived in ice houses. The next day, when she got up, the houses started to leak. As she climbed higher and higher, the walls began to collapse. People begged the young man to divorce his wife so that their houses would not be ruined. Because he loved her, he held out against them for a time, but finally he had to let her go. She went back south, far enough away not to burn down the villages.

Another story says that Unelanuhi had a daughter, whom she visited every day in her little house on the high point of noon. Every day, as the sun looked down, she saw people squinting up at her, faces contorted in an attempt to gaze upon her brilliance. This made her think them ugly, so she decided to kill them all. Every day she scorched the earth from her daughter's house, until everyone on earth was perishing from the heat.

The spirit people, the Little Men, told their human kin that, in order to survive, the Little Men would have to kill the sun. They transformed two people into snakes—one into a copperhead, the other into a spreading adder. They traveled to heaven and hid near the sun's daughter's house to wait the arrival of the goddess.

As she stopped there, the adder got ready to strike. But the sun's brilliance blinded him, and he just spit some yellow slime, which is all his species can do to this day. Angered, the sun-mother called the snakes foul names, and they slunk off in disgrace.

Below on earth, people were still suffocating from the intensity of the heat. So the Little Men turned two more people into snakes—this time, into a rattlesnake and into the monster called Uktena, whom we shall meet again later. They traveled to the sky to kill the sun.

But the overeager rattlesnake rushed at the sun's daughter rather than wait for the sun herself. He struck, he bit her, he killed her—and then, terrified, ran away with Uktena back to earth.

The sun-mother, finding her daughter dead, shut herself up in the house and refused to come out. Darkness descended on the earth; people began to freeze. The Little Men told the humans that now it was necessary to bring back the sun's daughter from the ghost country Tsusgina'i, in the Darkening Western Land of Usunhiyi. Seven men were outfitted for the journey, with sourwood rods and a box for carrying the daughter's soul. When they arrived in the land of ghosts, the Little Men said, the travelers would find all the spirits dancing in a circle. Every time the sun's daughter passed in this circle dance, they must strike her with a sourwood rod until she fell to the ground helpless. Her soul was then to be placed in the box for return to the land of the living. Under no circumstance, the people were warned, should they even peek into the box.

Was ever such a warning heeded? Seven times the men struck the sun's daughter as she passed in the ghostly circle dance. She fell down, their helpless captive. They squeezed her into the box and began the journey home. But soon the girl awoke and pleaded to be let out. She was hungry, she said, she was suffocating. Please, she cried—and finally they listened. They didn't open the box, really; they just pulled the lid back a hair's breadth to allow the girl to breathe. Something flew past. Then they heard, from a nearby tree, the call of a cardinal.

When they returned to the land of life, the box was empty, for that red bird had been the daughter of the sun. Since that time, because of that failure, no one who dies can be brought back from the land of ghosts.

The sun, all her hope vanished, dissolved into tears that threatened to flood the world. A council was held. It was decided that the prettiest girls, the most handsome men, should be sent to entertain the weeping sun.

This was done. But there was no change. They danced, they sang, they waved their arms telling fascinating stories, but the sun never even glanced at them. Then the drummer suddenly changed the beat. Surprised, the sun-mother looked up. A dazzling array of human beauty surrounded her. She smiled—and so it was, the Cherokee say, the sun returned to us. But now we must die, because only the bringing back of the redbird would have banished death forever.

The story immediately recalls the great thanksgiving festival of the Iroquois, during which arrows were shot at the sun while dancers cele-brated her. The ritual enacts what the story describes: an attack on the sun followed by a dance necessary to renew her. It is possible that both derive from the time of contact between Iroquois and Cherokee. Similarly, we can find connections in the Cherokee understanding of the sun as a face or an eye in the sky, looking down at her earthly children; this vision recalls the Iroquois idea of the sun as the severed head of a goddess-mother. After she had been reconciled to humanity, Unelanuhi, watching from above, ceased to see us as ugly and became a helpful, watchful goddess.

Myths tell of how she offered assistance to those on earth who needed it, as she did when the world's first couple had the world's first argument. The woman, this legend tells us, became furious at her hus-band. Leaving him, she began to wander over the empty earth. The man, not willing to part with her, followed at a distance, but she took no notice of him.

The sun goddess, however, could see everything that had happened. She took pity on the lonely beings. "Do you still desire her?" she asked the man. When he nodded, she decided to help his cause.

First, she created huckleberries, bright purple bits that sparkled tan-talizingly before the woman's eyes. The woman took no notice, squash-ing them with her feet as she walked over them. Then the sun goddess created the service tree, dangling its red fruit into the woman's face. Again she passed by.

Finally, the sun created tender red strawberries. The woman, tempted at last by this new food, stopped. She stooped. She filled her hands, then her mouth, with the berries.

The moment she tasted them she thought about sex. She kept eating and eating, thinking about having sex—with her husband, the only man on earth. She ate and ate, not moving from the patch. Then she stood up and waited. Soon he came up behind her. She did not move. He moved closer to her; she did not run. He embraced her, and she embraced him back. And the sun goddess left the strawberries behind to remind women of pleasure.[3]

These tales and myths are appropriate to a matrilineal, matrilocal culture. The Cherokee, like their cousins the Iroquois, functioned gynocratically. Cherokee women met in their own council; only they could decide when or if to wage war and what would be the fate of any war captives. Members of the council were called Beloved Women; they included those designated as Peace Women and others designated as War Women, the chief of the latter being titled Pretty Woman.

Power in the household as well as in the state rested with women. A Cherokee woman passed her life in the same household, with little drastic change. She was a girl, she grew up, she married—all within her mother's house. The possessions her mother gave her were hers to keep; in case of divorce there was no hardship to her or her children. Conversely, a young man moved upon marriage into the household of his wife; there her mother and aunts controlled all property. His role in the family was often quite marginal; he was, in fact, away from home hunting as much as five months of the year. In later life—around a man's forties and fifties—he began to stay home more and was recognized as having some authority within the family.

The myths of such a mother-centered culture perhaps naturally assume the centrality of the goddess. This is especially true of the sun goddess, mother of all. She was pictured as a woman whose hearth-fire above us kept us all warm and healthy. As such, she was a magnified version of the household mother, represented by her own hearth fire. But the fire was more than simply the mother's servant and familiar. Each household fire was believed iteself to be a sacred woman; it had to be fed a portion of each meal and, if neglected, would torment the offender in the form of an owl or a whippoorwill. It was forbidden to spit into the fire or throw anything into it that had been touched with saliva. Worse than that would be urinating into fire—an incredible sacrilege.

As the hearth was the center of each home, so was the center of the village an ever-blazing fire. It was housed in a seven-sided temple building, representing the seven matrilineal Cherokee clans. A massive timber structure that held up to five hundred persons at one time, the temple served both as a sort of city hall for concerns of the people and as a church for the celebration of ritual. The equidistant pillars of the outer wall surrounded two inner walls of seven pillars each, around a single central pillar. Around these walls stretched rows of tiered seats. The entrance faced the rising sun, but a series of baffles formed a maze to prevent anyone from looking directly within. At the west, opposite the door, were costumes and sacred objects. There, during ritual, chiefs sat on clay-whitened seats, directly before the altar.

In the center, a round hearth held a fire, which—like the fires of Sul and Bridget—was never allowed to die out. Neither was anyone allowed to take fire out of the temple; the Carolina trader, Long, lit his pipe at the temple fire only to have it snatched from his mouth as he thoughtlessly walked out puffing. The priest told him the sacred fire was not to be "mixed with common fire." Even the ashes were honored. They were buried annually by a designated priest; should a child wander near the *skeona*, the sacred ash-burial zone, the priest had him punished by scratching him all over. The sacred fire was rarely discussed by Cherokees, who kept its secrets as well as the *mystai* of ancient Eleusis kept theirs, but it is believed that the fire mediated with the creator for humans.

As such, the fire played a part in the important Ripe Corn Ceremony, when it devoured the first fruits of a new harvest. This was one of seven feasts—seven being the Cherokee sacred number, reflecting both the number of matriarchal clans and the world's seven directions (north, south, east, west, above, below and the center); it is possible that the related Iroquois derived the number of their clans magically, by multiplying seven times seven. Seasonal ceremonies emphasized the sacredness of the number seven; six took place every year, with the seventh celebrated every seventh year. These seasonal ceremonies included the First New Moon of Spring, when the Friendship Dance was performed, the chief told the future using quartz crystals, and the sacred fire was relit; the Green Corn Ceremony in August, when the sacred fire was extinguished and rekindled after the chief had acknowledged its connection with the sun; the Ripe Corn Ceremony in late September, celebrating the harvest; the October Great New Moon Ceremony, held in honor of the creation of the world, when women danced to the moon and each person looked into the crystal to see if he or she would die that winter; the Atahuna or "Finds Made" Ceremony ten days later, when a black purgative brew was drunk by all; and finally the Burning Bush Ceremony, a great midwinter dance. The seventh ceremony, performed only every seventh year, was the Uku or chief ritual. Occupying the calendrical position of the Great New Moon, it required the chief to appear in a bright yellow costume. For more than a day his feet were not permitted to touch the ground. When they finally did, it was in the center of the village square, where he danced the slow Uku dance.

In addition to these calendrical rituals, the Cherokee held the sun goddess's ceremonial game, called *dats ela nuni*, or "things transformed." The ritual, shared by many peoples of the Southeast, developed out of a prehistoric game called chunkey, which used a polished stone in a mixture of bowling and pole-throwing; a player cast the smooth stone, then he and his opponent threw poles at it, with the one who hit nearest the landing place of the stone declared the winner. The Cherokee version of this game was dedicated to the sun as the all-seeing Apportioner; the referee, beginning the game, reminded the players that they were in her gaze. After fasting and purging themselves, the players painted the sun at the center of their chests, often surrounded by serpents. The game was a rough sport in which the players deliberately tried to hurt each other. During the game—which could last as long as eight hours—players could drink no water, but only the juice of wild fruits.

The ritual game of the Cherokee is related to that of the Iroquois, whose ceremonial ballgame is the ancestor of modern lacrosse, a game which mimics the action of the benevolent twin Yoskeha and his animals in attempting to raise the sun into the sky. Armed with racket-like sticks, players used an egg-shaped wooden ball that could not be touched with the hands. Huge numbers of players engaged in the game; La Potherie witnessed one match where the number of contestants was estimated at one thousand, although companies of three hundred to four hundred were more common. The ball game was played only in the summer, beginning when the ice broke up and continuing until harvest time; sometimes the game was specially played when famine or epidemic threatened. The game was violent; some players were crippled for life, others killed in the contest; a player's death that occurred while he was impersonating an evil spirit was held to be a good omen. Everyone was required to attend the games, young and old, male and female.[4]

Of the Southeast's solar games, the most sensational was that of the Cherokee's neighbors the Yucchi, a mysterious group whose language has no close relation in America. Their full name, Tsoya'ha Yucchi, meant "children of the sun from far away;" ironically—given that they were ancient in their lands—only the last part was used by their neighbors to refer to them. Their sign-language gesture for themselves was simple: a finger pointing upwards to the luminary. They were a small nation, numbering only five hundred at the turn of the century; their descendants live in Oklahoma today.

In the 1930s, Maxey Simms, a Yucci elder, single-handedly preserved the mythology of his people. Their creation story begins with the earth covered with water and populated only by a few animals, a few birds, and the sun goddess, Tso. They all met together to hold council, Maxey Simms related, "about what they should do to find the earth. The sun took the lead at their meetings." The animals tried searching for earth: the beaver first, but he failed; then the fish-otter, who also failed. Finally the crawfish said, "If I dive into the water, the following signs will show: If I cannot come back to the surface of the water, blood will rise up. If, however, I come back with earth, some dirty yellow water will rise to the surface."

The crawfish dove and dove, and the animals waited at the surface. After a long time, dirty yellow water appeared. Then the crawfish emerged, carrying a miniscule bit of earth. The animals took that dirt and hit it against something sticking out of the water, and so the earth was made. Then other animals were created and life began.

But there was no light yet. So all met again under the leadership of the sun. "They expected the glow worm to do it; it flew around, but it only made faint gleams of light," Simms said. They asked the moon, too; she gave light, but it was still too dark.

The world's last chance for light was the sun goddess. She said, "You are all my children, I am your mother, I will make the light. I will shine for you."

"Up she went," Maxey Simms said. "Just as she went up, the earth was flooded with light; all the creatures and earth were glad and sang aloud. Right at noon the sun stopped on her way. When they saw it, they said the sun should light the earth that way."

In this first daylight the animals rejoiced. But soon the council had another problem: Some of the animals loved the new light so much that they wanted it to be daylight all the time, while others felt it should sometimes be night. It was the ground squirrel who broke the council's tie by saying, "The night also should be, for the people to have intercourse so that they can increase." And that was that.

The sun goddess of the Yucchi was the ancestor of all humanity. It happened, Maxey Simms said, because the sun was menstruating. Her blood fell on the ground and formed a baby. (Perhaps because of this, menstruating women were held to be enormously powerful. They spent their periods in seclusion to the east of the village, did no housework, and did not talk to their husbands.) The sun goddess then took up the baby boy and made a warrior out of him. He was named Tsoya'ha, or Son of the Sun.

The Yucchi, his descendants, were thus direct descendants of the sun goddess. Her people learned all necessary skills from their great foremother, including how to hunt and what to eat. She was such a fond mother, Simms said, that should all the Yucchi die, the sun would go into permanent mourning, covering her face and weeping until death took her.

The sun goddess also gave the Yucchi food. A mainstay of the people's cooking was corn soup—called *tso-ci*, or "sun fluid"—prepared by pounding dry corn and cooking with wood ash for flavor. Sometimes hickory nuts were added to make a sort of gruel. How did the Yucchi learn to make such soup? Their myth tells us that a woman one day slashed open the sky, and out from it poured the tasty soup. The sun stopped in her path, repaired the sky, then called a meeting with humanity to explain how *tso-ci* was correctly made without damage to the sky's fabric. Corn flour—*tsukha*—was also named for the goddess.

The spectacular Yucchi ball game was part of a New Fire Rite, through which tribal life was renewed. First, a new blaze was ceremonially kindled in the town square; then all took purgatives from pots rimmed with sun symbols. After an all-night dance, women gathered on the field and sang loudly to start the main event. The game began with conjuring and chanting by the referee, who was also in charge of keeping score. Using red-stained hickory rackets, the players ran between two goals set 250 feet apart and marked by the originals of our football goals; they hit the ball towards the goal. This round ball was formed of deerhide around a magical object—perhaps a crystal, perhaps a bit of red cloth. There was only one rule—the ball must never be touched with the hand. Other than that, anything was allowed.

When the ball was in play, all the players rushed at it and at each other. The onlookers added verbal ridicule and insult to the process. When a goal was made, the player gave the Yucchi version of the football spike: He strutted like a turkey, flapping his elbows with his hands in his armpits, giving the taunting gobble yell. Frequently he was clubbed by the other team for doing this. The first side to score 20 took the game; no credit was given for emerging unscathed, or even alive. Players were sometimes fatally injured, as in the Creek vs. Yucchi match of the late 1800s when four men died.

These games were connected with myths, like that of the Iroquois, in which animals help the sun find its correct place in the sky. The Yucchi's explanatory myth said that the sun was once stolen from the sky and put in an earthen pot by an old woman. Rabbit came to her house to recover it, and found a group of people there. He asked them to sing while he danced. "Sing 'Rabbit, Rabbit, Rabbit,'" he instructed them.

They did so. "Rabbit, Rabbit, Rabbit," they sang, and he danced. As they did so, be muttered to the people to move the earthen pot towards him, and they did so. "Move it again," he said, "I am dancing like a crazy person." And so they moved it again, and he was able to grab the sun. They chased him, but he got away.

Running, he bashed the pot into bushes and trees, but it wouldn't break. Finally, he reached a hornbeam tree and broke the pot to pieces, and the sun popped out onto the ground. All the creatures of the earth assembled and decided to put the sun up into the sky. But the smaller birds couldn't get it hoisted up all by themselves; when they tried, it fell back down. When their larger relatives, Buzzard and Wren, tried grasping it on each side, they made better progress. It worked; the sun mounted into the sky.[5]

The myths make much of the effort to place the sun in the sky, because to move between worlds is difficult. To rise from the earth, the sun goddess must be able to make the transition between worlds. Although she lives in the sky, she cannot remain there only, but must descend into the sea to travel beneath the earth. She must become a boundary being. So she appears in the mythology of the Tunica, who, like the Yucchi, were neighbors of the Cherokee and whose mythology might similarly have been lost save for the memory and devotion of a single man. The Tunica—their name means "people"—lived in the extreme northeast of Louisiana and in the Mississippi county now named for them. They were a nation of weavers; their mulberry cloth was famous throughout the area. Always a small group, their numbers fell drastically with white settlement. By the middle of this century, their language— one unrelated to any other—had entirely died out, as had most of the people.

The last surviving speaker of Tunica, Seostrie Youchiquant of Louisiana, told the story of her people's sun goddess in 1933 to anthropologist Mary Haas, who recognized the story as the Tunica's myth of their central divinity. A kingfisher, the story begins, was able to turn himself into a man. So off he went, courting women. Once night he took a girl back to his house, telling her he lived in an upstairs room. When she woke up, however, she was out on the limb of a hackberry tree. The girl was perplexed and ashamed at finding herself in a bird's nest. She was also hungry, but was not delighted when the kingfisher—now back in his bird shape—brought her a plateful of minnows for breakfast.

"I think you should just stay out on the water all the time," she said. "As for me, I'm going to sing a song." She sang a song. Then she said, "Now I'm going to go up to the sky, and be the sun." And she did so, radiating light as she rose. Now she shines above us, and is called Tahc-i; in her honor the Tunica danced the Sun Dance.

Kingfisher and girl are here both boundary beings, able to move between earth and sky. Another embodiment of the Tunica sun goddess permitted her to move between water and air. One of the earliest surviving descriptions of the Tunica, by La Harpe, says that among "their household gods are a frog and a figure of a woman which they worship, thinking that they represent the sun." Mary Haas, in writing of this fragment, laments the fact that the Tunica myth that revealed the connection between frog and sun has been lost, although perhaps a remnant remains in the figure of Old Toad Woman, a man-eating monster; stories about her could be told only in winter after sundown, when presumably toads would be sleeping peaceably in their ponds and would not hear the gossip people told about them. The Tunica also had a taboo about killing frogs, for fear that this would bring on a drought; Youchiquant blamed the dustbowl of the 1930s on white people's eating frogs' legs.

The sun goddess was the most adaptable, most powerful of boundary beings; she was able to live on land, in the air or in water. Her ability to dive into the water as she sets, and to rise again in flames the next day, is evidence of her power to pass through the barriers between worlds. This power especially impressed the Chitimacha, neighbors of the Tunica. Their Chief Benjamin Paul recorded a solar myth in which God told the sun and the moon to bathe often in order to stay beautiful. The sun had no compunction about descending into water, so she obeyed, keeping herself bright and shining. For this reason, the Chitimacha honored her, and she in turn honored their requests; she held still overhead during their battles or when their harvest needed to be completed. The moon, however, had less confidence, and refused to bathe. As a result, the sun shunned the dirty moon, although, enamored, he still chases her across the sky.[6]

In addition to the frog and the kingfisher, there are other transformative boundary beings in Southeastern mythology, but only one approaches the sun in power: the monster serpent crowned with crystals. We have already met this snake as Uktena, in the Cherokee myth of the death of the sun's daughter; its image surrounded that of the sun on the chests of ball-playing men. We will see it again in the art of the Death Cult and in the Great Serpent Mound of Adams County, Ohio. In this complex mythic system, snake and sun are connected; it would be easy to say that they were opposites, but this philosophy is more complex than such simple dualism allows. The serpent of chaos exists outside the domain of the apportioning sun, for it breaks up the patterns that the Apportioner creates. The snake of chaos is not evil, in a dualistic sense, but simply utterly different from the ordered solar energy.

To better understand the serpent of chaos, we must first understand the role of the sun as the Apportioner. The Cherokee goddess's name means "allotting," "dividing into equal parts," "separating"; the same word-stem was used to express division of tribal territory into allotments. She was the divinity whose duty it was to bring order—"the one word (that) epitomizes the Southeastern belief system" to this world. Ours was a realm of dark chaos until the sun was brought across in the little basket of Grandmother Spider. Thereafter, the world was "structure, expectableness"— not unchanging, but ordered within its changeableness. In addition to dividing night from day, the sun was also the divider of life from death. Death was thus not a form of disaster or chaos; it was part of that natural order epitomized—and controlled—by the Apportioner. Just as the town fire became polluted by the year's sins and had to be extinguished and relit, life became exhausted in a body and was snuffed out. Presumably there was some belief that, like the new fire, life would start afresh.

But there remained the unexpected—disasters of various sorts, starvation that occurred in no discernible cycle, sudden healing and even creation—what the Cherokee's Iroquois relatives called *utgon*. Only the fact of these events, these energies can be predicted—not the timing of their occurrence. And so *utgon* was the domain of Uktena. No spirit, but a being as real as the sun was real, Uktena had a ringed serpentine body as big as a huge tree trunk. Like other snakes, it slept with its eyes open, the sun's rays always penetrating them. The monster had bird wings and deer horns—and, most importantly, it had a diamond set in the middle of its forehead, called *ulstitlu* ("it is on its head"), *ulunsuti* ("transparent") and *igaguit* ("daylight"). The force of the serpent was crystalized in that diamond.

The crystal-crowned snake is found frequently in folklore throughout the world. Among the Dravidians in India's Tamil Nadu, it is believed that a snake that lives for a century without biting a human grows an inner gem. Vomited out by the snake, the gem glows sufficiently that the serpent can see its prey in the dark; a human who captures it will be rich. In Africa, too, it is believed that a python has within it a fiery jewel, which, as among the Dravidians, it uses to capture its prey. Covered by a black cloth, the jewel can be captured for riches, but the serpent will attempt to kill the seeker. Like the Uktena, these serpents are dangerous, but promise great wealth. The sun never offers such sudden changes of fortune—either for good or for ill.[7]

Uktena's opposition to the sun is revealed in the Cherokee's primary solar myth. In this story, Uktena was sent to kill the sun, but before it had a chance to do so, Rattlesnake sprang at the sun's daughter and killed her, causing the sun to retreat. Because of this, simply looking at a rattlesnake was believed to cause ultra sensitivity to sunlight; dreaming of a rattler demanded the same precautions against such blindness as an actual bite.

However powerful and effective Rattlesnake was in his attack on the sun's daughter, it was the sun itself who was the snakes' intended victim. Such incompetence made Uktena angry, so it departed to seek out deep parts of rivers and lonely parts of mountains, called by the Cherokee "where the Uktena stays." There it hid, far away from the ordering light that Unelanuhi showers on the earth. And there it might have rested undisturbed, except for the ambition of people to have its power.

That power rested in its crystaline forehead jewel. Any white crystal, the Cherokee said, had the force of the serpent in it. But the most magical crystal came from the forehead of Uktena itself. It was small, only a few inches long, and triangular. Its convex sides tapered to a point. Inside it, a single red streak ran directly through it from top to bottom. It did not, like other jewels, simply reflect Unelanuhi's light. The *ulunsuti* shone with its own special light. So powerful was it that someone happening upon the sleeping snake would run, confused, towards rather than away from the monster. The snake would then eat up the bedazzled victim.

Being devoured, however, was the least of the victim's woes. To cast eyes on Uktena meant death to the viewer's entire family. Nonetheless, the stone was sought after by those greedy for its power. For the Uktena's crystal and ones like it brought with it all sorts of luck—in love, in hunting, in farming. Its most important use, however, was in conjuring and prophecy. At the Great New Moon Ceremony, the Cherokee shaman used such a crystal to predict who would live through the year: At dawn, all submerged themselves in river water seven times, then emerged and, one at a time, stared into the stone. Those who saw themselves standing upright would survive the winter; those who saw themselves prone would die. These latter tried magic to escape their fate, but what the crystal predicted usually came true. According to the Cherokee Uguwlyuak, members of the East Cherokee band would not enlist in the Civil War until consulting the *ulunsuti* to determine their fate. In one case, three men went to consult a white crystal. The shaman held the stone out and, within it, they saw their images flowing along the red line. Two men's images stopped half way, but the other's spread all the way to the top. From this the shaman predicted—accurately, as time showed—that two would die halfway through the war while the last would return home.

Only the stone in the forehead of Uktena could permit one to see beyond the patterns set up by the Apportioner. Because the snake had the power to disturb order, it also, paradoxically, could predict such disturbances. To find this magical stone was therefore a heroic feat. Only one among the East Cherokee was successful in bringing back the transparent stone from the head of Uktena—Agna-unitsi, "the groundhog's mother," a great magician, whose trophy was the great treasure of the people. The red-streaked stone had to be fed blood each day. That of small animals would do for ordinary times, but deer blood was demanded for extraordinary occasions. If a conjurer forgot to feed it, it would devour her when next she appeared.

Although the Uktena is best documented through Cherokee sources, the serpent was known to the neighboring Yucchi as well; they danced in its honor as late as 1900. Swanton records the belief that the head of this man-eating snake was once cut off, but grew again onto its body. The head was then put at the top of a tall tree, but the tree was dead the next morning and the snake monster whole again. Finally, when the medicinal cedar tree was used to hold the snake's head, the snake died.[8]

Acknowledgment of the serpent's power may have been even more widespread in the Southeast before the historic period, for the region's impressive prehistoric culture emphasized the serpent in its art. Long before the Cherokee and their neighbors appeared in the area, emblems of a Uktena-like monster were created there. Connections between this earlier culture and those that followed have not been definitively established, yet the Uktena suggests that there was indeed a link. On a snake-decorated pot found in prehistoric Moundville, for instance, the serpent's wings and horns are noticeable parts of the pattern, as are its rattle-like tail and the rows of scales around the jewel on its forehead. Other pre-Cherokee artifacts show dancers wearing wings and antlers; Hudson contends that these represent Uktena-dancers like those known to the Yucchi. Yet other prehistoric designs seem to foreshadow Cherokee solar myths, notably the water spider bearing the sun on her back, which, though found on pre-Cherokee Mississippian artifacts, could serve as an illustration for the story of Kanene ski Amai yehi, the sun-stealing Grandmother Spider.

Archeologists prefer not to speculate on whether—much less how much—Cherokee mythology and ritual can be linked with those of the pre-Cherokee people of the area. Even less are they eager to consider a possible connection between the Cherokee and the prehistoric people whose burial and effigy mounds are such a magnificent, mysterious part of the Ohio and Mississippi River valleys. Yet the artifacts portraying Uktena suggest that there was, indeed, a link. And if the mythology of the Cherokee Uktena is a vestige of prehistoric Mississippean beliefs, then one of America's great mysteries may be unraveled: the meaning of the Great Serpent Mound in Ohio.

The Serpent Mound is only one of hundreds of effigy and burial mounds erected in prehistory through the river valleys of the Midwest and Southeast. Those responsible for these impressive earthworks were fourth in a series of Southeastern peoples. First had come the Paleo-Indians of 8000 to 1000 B.C.E., about whom little is known; next came the Archaic Indians, similarly little known. In approximately 1200 B.C.E., however, the Woodland Cultures emerged along the Ohio and Mississippi Rivers. Pottery finds from this era are decorated with frogs and Uktena-like serpents; the famous Tremper boatstone shows a horned snake monster. This serpent image survived into the next phase, the Mississippian Culture, which created America's great mounds; if the Uktena is indeed the descendant of this serpent, then it can be said to have survived into historic times as well.

During the Middle Mississippean Period—the period of the Temple Mound civilization, only a few hundred years earlier than the first known Cherokee lived—there emerged in the Southeast a religion known as the Death Cult. In its art we find an Uktena-like serpent with bird or animal features—wings, talons, horns. Antonio Waring has teased out several important strands of the Death Cult's fabric: an annual new fire ceremony with an agricultural orientation; an emphasis on peace and weather control; the chunkey game; use of an earth lodge and dance ground; and a chief related to the fire-sun deity. Most of these, as we have seen, are found among later, historic peoples of the area.

Death Cult art shows a strong solar orientation. Solar symbols are manifold and frequently employed. The cross and sun circle were used to represent a sacred fire fed by four logs; the open eye, a familiar sun image, was also employed by the cult. Antonio Waring summarizes Death Cult motifs as "a rather extreme form of sun symbolism." Although, once again, those who have written on this culture imply that the divinity so honored was male, there is no proof of a male solar divinity; in fact evidence indicates the divinity was female. All but one of the historical groups that employed Death Cult ceremonials and symbolism depicted the sun as female; the exception is the Creek. In general there is less evidence for a male than for a female sun divinity among the Death Cultists.

Many Death Cult artifacts have been found in American mounds. Those who built the mounds are called the Hopewell people; the name comes from a rich archeological site in Ohio. The Hopewellians thrived from the early part of the Christian era until approximately 400 A.D., across the Midwest and as far south as Louisiana. A hundred years ago, these "Mound Builders"—the term is considered outdated by archaeologists—were declared a distinct people killed off by later Native Americans (who apparently suffered the same fate at the hands of even later immigrants); fifty years ago archeologists were certain that the Hopewellians were the ancestors of the Cherokee; today conventional wisdom once again tells us that we can trace no links between the Hopewellians and historic Native American groups.[8]

Perhaps we can't—at least, we can't trace any unarguable links. But suggestive connections appear in the most famous solar culture of the Americas, that of the Natchez, whose land was located just east of the Mississippi. This nation is considered the most likely descendant of that people who erected Pimson Mound in Georgia—members of the Hopewellian Woodland Culture, whose religious symbols informed all of the Southeast. Not only are the Natchez likely descendants of Hopewellian peoples, but their rites and traditions follow Waring's delineation of those who participated in the Death Cult. Among the Natchez, as among the Cherokee, we find both a female sun deity and a crystalline snake.

The Natchez encountered European colonists in 1682. Two members of La Salle's exploration party—Henri de Tonty and Zenobe Membre—were the first Europeans to write of the Natchez; from de Tonty's and Membre's notes we can gain an idea of what Natchez life was like at that time. Tonty and Membre, arriving by canoe at a Natchez town, were astonished at the large, square adobe buildings roofed with arches of cane, which stood in neat rows around a rectangular common ground. Two buildings were especially impressive: the chief's house and the Sun Temple, both built on high mounds, forty feet square with a fifteen-foot high dome. Membre recorded the details of the temple: "Over it were rude wooden figures, representing three eagles turned to the east.... The interior was rude as a barn, dimly lighted from the doorway, and full of smoke." Before a central altar burned a perpetual fire guarded by two old men.

The day after Tonty and Membre's expedition, the Sun Chief called upon La Salle, who was ill. An impressive procession preceded him: two men bearing white plumes, then a warrior carrying a highly polished copper mirror representing the sun, then a group of tambourine players and adoring admirers of the king. This story, although the only proof that the solar mirror was known in North America, cannot help but recall Japanese Shinto. Like the ancient Japanese, the Natchez saw themselves as descendants of the sun goddess.

The Natchez based their worship upon a complex class system, which was based, in turn, on a theory of descent from the sun divinity. This sun deity was assumed by European recorders to have been a god; much has been written by those delighted to find a rich—indeed, florid—solar culture in the Americas, which, assuming a universally male sun, seemed another example of patriarchal solarity. But a male sun god among the Natchez is entirely impossible, considering the nation's kinship structure. A matrilineal people, the Natchez divided themselves into four status levels—Suns, Nobles, Honored People and Commoners—according to their closeness of relationship to the sun. Membership in the three noble classes passed through the mother only. Thus, Noble women had Noble children; Honored men's children had the status of their mother, whether she be Sun or Noble. Sun men could marry only Commoners; their children were Nobles, having a status ranking below the father but higher than the mother.

As for Sun Women, they alone could pass on the status of Sun to their children; Sun fathers could never sire Sun children. The chief, known as the Great Sun, claimed to be the child of the luminary. This parent must have been a sun-mother, as he could not otherwise have inherited the title of Sun; a male sun would not have passed the sun title to his child. Therefore, the great sun divinity of the Natchez, so happily embraced by those looking for an American Ra, could only have been female, and the nation's Sun women must have been her earthly incarnations.

Sun women—also called White women—married and divorced at will. Should a man be unfaithful, his wife had him decapitated. She herself, however, was not bound by such rules and could have as many lovers as she wished. The men were little more than sexual servants. According to Thomas Nuttall, a white botanist who visited the Natchez from 1818 to 1820, a man married to a Sun woman acted thusly: "In the presence of his wife he acts with the most profound respect, never eats with her, and salutes her with howls, as is done by her servants." In howling at the Sun woman, her husband was acting just as the Natchez chief did each morning in greeting the sun, for the chief was required to howl three times to her as she rose.

The Great Sun Woman was the most powerful of her class; she did what she willed. In 1700 Gravier recorded that the Great Sun Woman who had just died was a warrior who, dressed and coiffed like a man, personally led her people in battle. When she died, massive ceremonies, complete with human sacrifice by men who volunteered for the honor of accompanying her to the afterlife, were held for many days. The Great Sun Woman was regarded as the direct descendant of the sun; her son was charged with maintaining the sacred fire. During her lifetime, this Great Sun Woman was auxiliary chief and wielded substantial power. Should a chief die, the next Sun Chief was chosen from among his sister's sons; if she had none, rulership passed to the son of his nearest female relative, never to his own sons. Clearer evidence of matrilineality would be harder to find.

The Natchez called the sun goddess Wah Sil or Great Fire. In her honor, the Natchez kept a perpetual fire burning on the hearth of their solar temple, with three logs alight; as each log burned out, another replaced it. Should the fire go out, the nation would be endangered, and the chief would be put to death. In this windowless fire temple, visiting Jesuits related, were carvings of "some extraordinary snakes" together with pieces of crystal; these were the most sacred objects in the temple. Their connection with crystals shows that these mysterious Natchez snakes were relatives of the Uktena.[9]

The Uktena and its crystal, therefore, seem to have roots in prehistoric Southeastern culture, conveyed from the Middle Mississippeans to their historic descendants. Did these Mississippeans build the Ohio River Mounds? And were they ancestors of the Cherokee? This subject has been greatly argued, but there is no archeological evidence that proto-Cherokees built the Ohio Valley mounds. Of course, absence of evidence is not evidence of absence. The Cherokee themselves traditionally believe that their people built the Great Serpent Mound and the other famous Ohio mounds; they also say that around the fourteenth century they lived in the Ohio Valley and built earthworks there until driven southwards by war.

Perhaps, as archeologists contend, the Cherokee did not build the mounds themselves. It is, however, likely that the Cherokee were in the vicinity when the giant creations were erected. Scholars agree that the

Cherokee passed through the Alleghenies; it is thought that the split from the main Iroquois stream took place there. Similarly, in a history of the Delaware, called the Walum Olem, it is said that that nation fought the Cherokee for a generation before turning them southwards, beyond the Ohio River. Thus, contact with the Temple Mound civilization of the Middle Mississippian could have influenced what would become Cherokee culture. The likelihood of this proposal is suggested by the discovery of mounds, complete with Cherokee-like pipes and other artifacts embedded in them, along the route the Cherokee were said by the Delaware to have taken southwards.

If the Cherokee are related to the Temple Mound builders, whether as racial descendants or as a people influenced by the great culture, then perhaps we can find in Cherokee mythology a way to interpret one of America's mysteries. In Ohio, Hopewell earthworks—geometric sculptures set in beautiful river valleys—are among the treasures of ancient North America. There is Fort Ancient, with its now-buried sun-serpent laid out in white stone as a solstice marker; there are the magnificent mounds near Columbus, huge embankments looping in circles and marching in squares. There is the mound complex near Chillicothe, the giant single mound nearby and, most memorably, there is the Great Serpent Mound, as magnificent an ancient monument as Stonehenge, though far less well known.

The Great Serpent Mound is a vast, enigmatic effigy that snakes down a hillside in the rolling countryside of Adams County. It is in south central Ohio, near nothing in particular. Dayton and Cincinnati and Columbus are all possible points of reference for this earth sculpture, but it's not really near any of them. Rather, the Serpent Mound is an hour to ninety minutes' drive, through working farmlands, from any urban area. Now a national park, it is often virtually empty of tourists, located as it is near nothing else scenic. Sometimes there's no one there at all, and the visitor has the Great Serpent Mound to herself.

There are two ways to view the Serpent Mound. One is from above, from the viewing stand provided by the National Park Service. Looking down, you see a green mound writhing down the hill. It's almost 1,000 feet long, tail to head; it's 20 feet wide and 5 feet tall. At the left you see the tail, curled in upon itself, then four deep snakey U's. Finally comes the curious head: two long mounds on either side of a shape like cupped hands, which surrounds an oval-shaped mound, then a semicircular mound connected to a misshapen circle. It does not look much like a serpent's head. Since the Great Serpent Mound's discovery in the mid-

1880s, this part of the mound has inspired various interpretations. Some have seen the serpent as spitting out an egg; others, as devouring one. Some have seen the serpent as devouring a frog—or spitting one out. It's not at all clear, from above the mound, what the builders intended.

But there is another way to see the mound, one currently forbidden by the U. S. National Park Service but apparently practiced nonetheless: from the back of the beast itself. You start by mounting the tiny coiled tail; from there you can't see the head, because the sculpture is so subtly curved into the hillside. What seems, from beneath the mound, to be a short walk is astonishingly long, and oddly precipitous, from this new perspective. Worse, the twisting of the snake's body is sharp enough to induce vertigo; the snake seems to writhe under your feet.

Then you approach the head.

At this point the hill seems to sweep downwards, and vertigo increases. You must climb over one mound, then up another to enter the round space—the egg, the frog, whatever it is. The entire walk may have taken seven minutes or so, but what walkers report takes place in a time-less plane. Almost invariably, they report a sensation of fear or fright. Robert W. Harner, a sociologist, reports that he felt oppressed by a sense of dread: "the coldest, most abject, hopeless terror I have ever experi-enced. I felt the hair rising on the nape of my neck. I could neither move nor speak. I knew that even though I was completely alone, I was not completely alone." Others report similar feelings: Martha Graham chore-ographed a ballet on the theme of human sacrifice after visiting the mound; Susan Gitlin-Emmer, a Los Angeles artist, has painted the mound with a nuclear-danger symbol at its head.

Although such subjective reactions are discarded as evidence by most academic researchers, it is notable that a common thread connects the experiences people report at the mound. Since a connection between the Great Serpent Mound and Uktena has not previously been posited, it is unlikely that visitors could have been predisposed to these feelings by the myths of the sun's snake-enemy. Yet they describe their experi-ences similarly: Walking the serpent's back was almost inexpressibly ter-rifying, they say, like an encounter with chaos.[10]

What if the Great Serpent Mound represents the being that the Cherokee, centuries after the mound's erection, called the Uktena? If so, the experience reported by visitors to the Mound is certainly appropriate. Chaos is frightening in a different way than death is, for death remains in the domain of the Apportioner. On the back of the Uktena, walking down a green hill under a calm blue sky, visitors report feeling cold winds rise, hearing vibrations like ancient drums, falling down dizzy after only a few steps. Few express interest in returning. They do not eagerly plan for another encounter with snake.

Beyond this subjective evidence, what indication do we have that the Serpent Mound could represent the Uktena or its ancestor? The most convincing is the sculpture's as-yet-unexplained shape. Let us imagine that the odd-shaped head does not, as has been argued, represent a serpent eating or disgorging its food at all. What, then, could the shape indicate? The head seems divided in two, which is what gave rise to the idea of another creature, which, would only be near the mouth if its life were in danger. But if one assumes the apparently divided head is bisected, a single eye or a jewel is possible.

Certainly a jewel in the forehead of the serpent is as likely as a frog or an egg in the mouth. If the serpent of the mound is, indeed, the one who reemerges as the Uktena, then the myths told of that later serpent have relevance to the great one sculpted in the Ohio earth. And, over and over, the later myths point to a distinct energy that the Uktena embodies, one that cannot coexist with the energies of the sun goddess. But that goddess rules everything—light and dark, life and death. She spins forth the light by which we perceive the ordinary, albeit still miraculous, world in which we breathe our first and our last. She sees our mistakes as well as our victories, our losses as well as our harvests. Our ancestral mother, she knows us down to our mitochondria.

What, then, is left for the serpent to control—save that which cannot be apportioned, which cannot be divided and neatly labeled, which cannot be predicted? The paradoxical opposite of the sun goddess, whose energy makes order out of our world, the snake frees everything from order and—in creating disorder—allows for the possibility of a new, perhaps better, order to follow. Recent scientific theory tells us that wherever we find randomness there is, in fact, a larger pattern, one so immense we cannot comprehend it. Wherever we think we see chaos, there is in fact a great arching sweep of fractals with their majestic and coherent and imperceptibly vast order. The stone on the serpent, similarly, alerts us to the wild power that lies beyond even the Apportioner's range. It is an unthinkably dangerous power, but one vital with possibilities. It could bring us incomprehensible riches, or it could bring us unspeakable pain. Not everyone will search out the jeweled snake, but those who do—if they do not die—can read the future.

Within the round space—the jewel—in the head of the Great Serpent Mound, a bush is growing. Despite governmental warnings to the contrary, people are clearly walking on the mound—because in that bush are coins, buttons, bits of cloth, shoelaces. The diversity of offerings suggests that it is no cult that has come here, but individuals who, moved by the intensity of their feelings, leave a token behind. Bits of torn shirt-sleeve flutter in the wind; the sun glints off a pile of nickels and dimes. Encountering the chaos that precedes the sun's dawn, even modern tourists bribe the serpent, hoping to be transformed rather than destroyed.

Part Three

THE WAY DOWN IS THE WAY UP

Day breaks: the first rays of the rising Sun,
stretching her arms.
Day breaks, as the Sun rises to her feet.
Sun rising, scattering the darkness, lighting the land.
With disc shining, bringing daylight,
as birds whistle and call.
People are moving about, talking, feeling the warmth.
Burning through the Gorge, she rises, walking westward,
Wearing her waistband of human hair.
She shines on the blossoming coolibah tree,
with sprawling roots,
Shady branches spreading.

—Sacred song, from Dulngulg cycle of Australia's Mudbara tribe

≈≈≈≈≈≈≈≈≈≈≈≈≈≈≈≈≈≈≈≈≈≈≈≈≈≈≈≈≈≈≈≈≈≈≈≈≈≈

Chapter Nine

THE PACIFIC RIM:
A ONE-BREASTED WOMAN,
HER BROTHER'S LOVER

There is a story told in the Arctic. It is that the sun was once the girl Malina, who lived with her brother Aningak near the great ice-fjord Iloulissat. Although she was quite young, Malina's menarche had passed. Her face had been tatooed with radiating lines formed from sewing through her skin with a bone needle dipped in soot from the seal-oil lamp. Her sun-rayed face proclaimed her readiness to receive lovers and to bear children.

One time, Malina and her brother were playing together where all young people amused themselves in winter: in the dance house, a hut of snow with a roof of leather, badly lit and windowless. There they played the game of snuffing out the light. Aroused by his sister, Aningak sought her among the sweaty bodies and had sex with her each night when the lights were doused.

Willing enough to enjoy the intercourse, Malina became curious about who her lover was. So she darkened her fingers with soot and, the next time Aningak seized her, covered his back and his face with stains. Then Malina took a handful of dry moss and lit it. In the light, she saw her soot-stained lover: her brother. He also lit a tuft of moss, but the flame was not strong, only a glimmer of embers.

Still aroused, the moon began to chase the sun around the hill. When he had almost caught her, she cut off a breast with her ulu—her woman's knife—and threw it at his feet. "Eat that, since you want me so much," she screamed. Then the sun rose into the air.

The moon continued to pursue her, but the sun always rose higher than he could reach. Now, Malina races through the sky dressed in white reindeer leather, chasing seals on the Arctic Sea. Aningak endlessly runs after the sun, making himself thin from exertion in the process. Once a month he disappears entirely, for he has to travel down from the sky with his team of spotted dogs to hunt enough seals to grow fat again. Malina shares a house with her brother at mid-sky, but because summer is always full of light and winter without it, she never has to see him. From the earth, however, we can see them both, and the sooty mark on the moon's face.[1]

This story was told from Greenland—whence came this particular version—across the North American Arctic, wherever Inuit peoples were found. It is truly pan-Inuit, with only one other myth—that of the food-mother Sedna, a myth structurally parallel to the Malina myth—found as frequently. The sun goddess must have been an important divinity, else why would every single village tell her myth, varying a few details, but keeping the whole recognizable? Yet little is known of rituals addressed to her. That such rituals did, in fact, exist is indicated by the sun and moon masks that predominate in the culture; similar masks were used in evoking other divinities during religious events.

The arctic sun goddess's myth is a powerful one, full of primal force and excruciatingly vivid details. And it is a mysterious myth as well, for the same tale is found in Southeastern North America, in South America, and in India. Brother-sister incest, marking of the lover's face, shame and self-mutilation, transformation into luminaries—these are constants throughout the myth's hemisphere-wide range. It is arguably the preeminent myth of the Pacific Rim, extending literally from the North Pole to the South, from Alaska to Argentina. Yet the various stories of the "sun sister," as folklorists call the tale, have never been studied together.

It is possible that this complex, widespread story has been so long ignored simply because scholars generally refuse to devote attention to a feminine sun divinity. But even academic bias can fade when an exciting research subject presents itself. It is also possible that the myth has not yet been studied because of the methodological questions that would plague any researcher on the sun-sister myth; cross-cultural studies are notoriously difficult. Yet a third possibility is that the strong suggestion of cultural diffusion—the transmission of mythic material from one people to another—contained in the myth disquiets today's scholars. Discussion of diffusion is currently out of favor among American anthropologists.[2] Yet the possibility cannot help but occur in the context of this myth. For although the sun as mirror and spinner are images that could spontaneously occur to people regardless of contact, that of the sun as a mutilated girl who slept with her brother is vividly unusual enough to suggest a single original source.

However tantalizing the question of diffusion may be, it can be dealt with only sparingly here. Our interest lies, instead, in the tale itself and in its spiritual meaning. For this myth is utterly unlike the West's Apollonian vision; its meaning is not accessible to those unwilling to abandon cultural presuppositions. Self-mutilation and incest are not as pleasant, to Western psyches, as are mirror-goddesses and sun-spinsters. To understand the meanings of the sun-sister myth, we must lay aside fear of invasion of the body's boundaries, remembering that in many cultures ritual demands the cutting off of a body part (a finger, for instance) to attain sanctity. Similarly, we must move beyond interpretation of the sun-woman's relationship to her brother as necessarily odious and exploitative, unless the myth indicates it is; incest, as it appears here, is necessarily different from that occurring in twentieth century America. The knowledge contained in this tale cannot be gained without forgoing prejudice.

We begin our exploration of this powerful myth among the Inuit people—the so-called Eskimo, although they did not refer to themselves by that Algonkian word for "raw-flesh eater." They descended from Paleo-Indians who migrated during the fourth Pleistocene glaciation, some thirty thousand to forty thousand years ago, east across Beringia, the land bridge between their homeland and the American continents; they were the last North American people to do so. The Inuit now live across Greenland and Canada, through coastal Alaska, into eastern Siberia; some seven thousand miles separate the most distant of these related peoples.[3]

Their language and culture vary slightly over the vast reaches of the arctic and subarctic regions, but all agree on the sun as a once-human girl who, after discovering her incestuous relationship to her brother, rose into the sky to light the day. In this arctic land, where the sun retreats for as much as three months and leaves the world in cold and darkness, the sun goddess's myth is fiercer, more violent, than in more temperate lands. The fullest version on record was told early this century by the Inuit elder Ivaluardjuk to the explorer Knud Rasmussen along Hudson's Bay. It begins with an old grandmother who lived with her grandchildren, the boy Aningat (a name only one letter different from that of Malina's brother) and the girl Seqineq. The boy was healthy—but blind, unable to hunt, so the family was starving. One day a bear began to gnaw at their window frame. The old woman aimed the boy's bow while Aningat drew it, and the beast was hit. "It sounded," said the boy, "as if my arrow struck a beast."

"No," said the grandmother, "just the frame of the window."

Seqineq went outside with her grandmother and found the bear lying dead on the ice. Then the grandmother built a little hut for the boy and forced him to live alone on dog's meat, while she and the girl feasted on bear. Seqineq, however, took pity on her brother and brought him juicy bear meat in her sleeves.

One day Aningat said to Seqineq, "Did you ever see a loon close at hand?"

"Yes," said Seqineq.

"Will you take me to the lakes where they are?" he asked.

"Yes," she said.

"Will you build stone landmarks for me so I can find my way home?" the brother asked.

"Yes," she answered.

She took him to the lake and left him there. He sat until he heard water splashing from the oars of a kayak. Someone spoke to him and called him to the kayak, and someone took him into the boat, and then someone took him down under the water and asked him if he felt dizzy there. "No," said Aningat. He was taken underwater several times, and each time held under a longer time. Finally the stranger asked, "Can you see anything?"

"No," said Aningat, although he could see dimly by this time. He was put under water a few more times, and then the stranger asked, "Can you see now?" And the boy could see. The loon rowed the boy back to land, and he followed the landmarks left by his sister. When he got home he saw the skin of the bear stretched out, drying.

"Where did that come from?" he asked his grandmother.

"Oh, it was left behind by people who came here in an umiak boat," said the grandmother. "They've left already."

It was spring, and the whales were moving along the ice edge. The boy went hunting with Seqineq. His task was to throw the harpoon, hers to hold the end of the line. One day they took grandmother fishing with them. She said she would hold the line, and so the children went down very close to the edge of the ice. Just then the whales came swimming in and the grandmother called out, "Strike! Strike!" And they made a feint as if to strike at a small whale, but deliberately struck the largest. As the huge whale began to sound, it pulled the grandmother completely off the ice and into the water.

For a moment she seemed to be running atop the water, and then she was gone. After a while the head of the grandmother appeared above the water, and she sang a song that said, "Grandchildren, grandchildren, why do you leash me like a dog?"

The boy sang back. "Grandmother, grandmother, why was I given none of the meat from the first bear I ever shot?" The grandmother had no answer, and she disappeared under the water.

The children left the place where they had been born and wandered around the world. In their wanderings they met the imps, the *kikiliqaciait*, with their long claws. They built a snow hut among them, not knowing how dangerous that was. One day Seqineq went out for water. The imps told her there was some in their hut, "but you must pull your clothes aside over the hips and come in backwards."

She did what they told her, and they began to claw her to bits. The girl called for help, and her brother struck down the imps one after another. As the battle was raging, an old man lay on his cot picking his nails. "I told you not to start a fight with them that way," the old man said. Aningat picked up a tent pole and brained him.

The couple set out again looking for people like themselves. But instead they found people with no holes in their bottoms. They lived surrounded by huge lumps of caribou meat, but could only suck the juices because, having no anuses, they could not defecate. Strange as these people were, Seqineq found a husband among them and Aningat a wife.

But Aningat's wife had no vagina, because these people also lacked that opening. One day he took a knife and cut one into her, and she began to sing with joy, "Oh, my husband slit my lap, and it will never close up again!"

Seqineq became pregnant. When her labor began, her mother-in-law sharpened knives to cut the baby out of her, for that was the way it was done among those people. Aningat stopped her. Seqineq gave birth normally, to a normal girl child. At this, the women of the rumpless folk became very excited, and began to stick themselves with meat forks, trying to make openings so they would not have to be cut apart to have babies. Some of them succeeded, but some of them cut themselves so badly they died on the spot.

It was as Seqineq was lying in the birth hut, while the feasting house was filled with people dancing in celebration of the birth, that Aningat began to lie with his sister. He always made sure he put out the lamp first, so she could not see who was doing this. To find out, she blackened him with soot from the lamp and then followed him to the dance hut. And there, of course, she saw her brother being teased. "Look," they were all saying, "Aningat has soot all over his face." Humiliated, Seqineq ran back to the house to get her ulu, then went back to the feasting house, where she hacked off one of her breasts and threw it at Aningat. "You are so fond of my body—eat that!" She ran out, grabbing a torch as she went; he fell over a block of snow and put his own torch out. Thus they ran in a circle around the village until they rose into the sky.

This lengthy version of the story ends just as the earlier one had, with the transmutation of the siblings into luminaries, but it is filled as well with additional solar motifs: the boy's blindness and its miraculous cure by sun-lit water; the hostage-holding grandmother; the dwarfish imps. But incest is the centerpiece in this version of the story, as in its other variations. In Canada, the incest was deliberate and the couple fled out of shame only when discovered; along Alaska's Kobuk River, the sun maiden was seduced while secluded with her first menstrual blood, which together with the blood from her amputated breast still colors the red sun today; in Point Barrow, the sun-woman cut off *both* her breasts before rising to the sky to warm orphans, appearing occasionally on earth as a beautiful woman with a skeletal back; among the Ten'a—an Athabaskan people of Anvik, near Inupiat territory—the sun-woman stirred her bloody breasts into blubber-and-berry "ice-cream" before escaping into the sky and cursing humanity with sickness.

There are a few divergent tales, such as one in which intercourse occurs between foster mother and son rather than brother and sister, but the commonalities are greater than the differences. Primary to the stories is a taboo sexual relationship. In some instances, both partners know the identity of the other but keep it secret from the village. In these tales, sun and moon choose to move skywards to live there free of human morality; or else the discovery of their scandalous relationship causes them to flee to the heavens. Along the Bering Strait, where the sun's retreat is of the former variety, the sister rises to the sky in order to nurse her brother from her breasts. There above, she sings happy songs to her brother, like the one which begins:

My brother up there, the moon up there begins to shine;
He will be bright.
My brother up there, he is coming up there.

But in the greater number of versions, the relationship is based on ignorance on the one hand, deceit on the other. The sun-maiden enjoys her partner while ignorant of his identity, but the moon-man knows exactly what he's doing. The sex act itself is non-problematic: Enjoyment of sex with unidentified partners was part of arctic life, especially during the long winter, when days and nights ran together in darkness; clever ruses to discover the partner's identity were not unusual. There is no indication that the woman was displeased; she was only curious. This curiosity further suggests that she enjoyed the sexual events sufficiently to be interested in a longer-term bond with the man—little knowing how deep their bond truly was.

It must be said at this point that there is no proof that the stories have been recorded accurately. They may have been bowdlerized in translation; there are many Greek myths of Apollo's "loves," for instance, that disguise rape stories; it is possible that here, too, the events insinuate rape. In fact, a few Inuit tales say that the sun was forced to have intercourse against her will. Most often, however, the sun enjoys sex with her lover, and even welcomes him; the problem arises when she discovers that her lover is taboo to her. Following Jordan Paper's rule that whatever differs from European tradition or morality is probably correctly recorded, while what agrees is suspect, we can conclude that in the original myth, violence is not the operative factor.

In the Greenland version of the tale, there is evidence that not only argues against violent rape, but suggests complicity on the part of Malina. For the sun-maiden was tempting fate, at the very least, by engaging in anonymous sex games while her brother was present. In general, siblings did not remain in a lodge with each other when sex play began. If the sun-maid had been intent upon keeping to the spirit as well as the letter of the taboo against sibling incest, she would have left the lodge, or demanded her brother leave, before beginning her sexual encounters. It is difficult to argue, from the details of that story, that the sun goddess was a mere innocent preyed upon by her lustful brother.

Yet little is recorded of the personality of the Inuit sun goddess. More is known of the general temperament and the powers of the moon-man. He was not, in general, a friendly character. A troll-like being, he constantly threatened to tear down the pillars that supported the sky-dome. Epidemics were said to come from his eclipses, which also were held to predict attacks by enemies. Although not altogether an unsavory character—he did protect orphans on Baffin Island—the moon-man was not a trustworthy fellow, either.

Despite his apparent duplicity and evident enmity for humankind, the Moon-Man was the one to whom shamans, called *angakoks*, journeyed in their enchanted flights in search of healing and knowledge; best go in pairs, a shaman from Kotzebue warned in 1899, because of the evil power of the moon. Like the Siberians and Koreans and Japanese, whose indigenous religious tradition they shared, the Inuit relied upon those talented with shamanic powers to intercede with spirits through visionary travel. "We do not all understand the hidden things," one elder told Rasmussen, "but we have the people who say they do. We believe our *angakoks*.... If we did not believe the magicians, the animals we hunt would make themselves invisible to us; if we did not follow their advice, we should fall ill and die."[4]

The same religious idea, Mircea Eliade reminds us, is encountered throughout Asia. Although not identical in detail—the Inuit *angakok* does not use a solar mirror to shamanize—the religion of the Arctic is nonetheless continuous with that of Siberia. So is the initiation procedure: The shaman, whether male or female, is called to the profession by "Arctic hysteria" and its attendant magical symptoms. These might include illness, hallucinations, or trances. Most emphatic of these symptoms is the appearance of light inside the body, which causes it to shine like a lamp. Only shamans had such a light, which drew *inua*, or spirits to them; ordinary people looked to the spirits "like houses with extinguished lamps" by comparison. Thus, to a spirit, a shaman looked as the sun or moon does to humans.

The transmutation of Malina and Aningak into luminaries was thus equivalent to a transmutation into shamans. And the event that caused them to shine was their apparently deliberate incest. Similarly, other forms of unconventional or lawless sexuality could be a prelude to shamanic initiation. Homosexuality or transvestitism was often part of the lives of male shamans in the Arctic; the moon was marked on the face like a marriageable, tattooed woman, suggesting that he was a transvestite shaman as well.

To visit this sky-shaman, the *angakok* ascended on a thread or a tree; less frequently, the shaman simply sprouted wings. The shaman's sky-climb is an important motif in myths connected with the sun goddess and her multi-leveled universe. Such a journey was not made simply for pleasure or adventure; it was a dangerous trip, taken in order to cure diseases or to solve other human problems. And these diseases, these problems, were in turn caused by the violation of taboos, or what Eliade calls "disorder in the sacred." In the classic way of sympathetic magic, the shaman mounted to the taboo-breaking moon in order to cure ailments brought on by the breaking of taboos.

These shamanic ascents were often dangerous, as were the descents to the underworld the shaman also attempted. In the cosmology of these people, the universe was multi-leveled: sky, earth and underwater. To pass between these levels, great skill and daring was necessary; the shaman had to become the sort of boundary being we have encountered in southeastern North American mythology, one able to traverse the space between the levels of reality. In addition to the thread or tree, a mountain or a ladder could be used by the shaman as a means of mounting or descending to another level. Once having affected this change in levels and performed whatever magical duties were necessary, the shaman still had to have strength and courage enough to dare the journey back.

A thinly disguised shamanic story involves a girl who traveled to the moon-man's abode. After refusing to marry any of the village boys, she fell in love with a bodiless head. But her parents were furious at the affair and threw the lover into the rubbish heap after skewering him through one eye. The head, rolling out into the sea, rejected the girl. She ran around in anguished circles until a sky-road opened. Not heeding the warnings called out—too late—by her head-lover, she followed it to the moon-man's house.

There she found an old woman and a child, who told the girl that she had entered the moon's house and that she should immediately escape. They helped her by plaiting a rope of animal sinews on which she could swing to earth. Warned by her hostesses that she had to keep her eyes tightly shut until she hit the ground, then open them immediately, the unfortunate girl miscalculated. Arriving on earth with a sudden thud, she didn't open her eyes quickly enough and was changed into a spider—the ancestor to all spiders in the world.[5]

This reads like a cautionary tale about failed psychic journeys. And, indeed, there was never a guarantee the *angakok* would return to normal consciousness after a trip above or below the earth. To be sure, there were less dangerous ways to shamanize: Movement could be confined to the earth plane, such lateral movement being useful for spying on enemies or finding game. But true magic involved more. And true magic was dangerous. It required visits to distant spiritual lands where the *inua* were encountered in all their force. To reach these regions, the shaman could travel up, to the realm of the luminaries. But sometimes the same results could be gained by traveling down, to the undersea realm of Sedna.

This food-provider, the pan-Inuit goddess Sedna, is parallel in Inuit myth to the sun. This is her tale: Born a woman on earth, she married a bird but was fiercely unhappy on his island. When her father came to rescue her, he killed her lover. In retaliation, the bird-people caused a storm to blow up. Knowing he would otherwise not escape, her father threw Sedna from his kayak. She grabbed the boat with her hands; he cut them off. Desperate, she threw her bleeding stumps over the side of the boat; he sliced them off. Finally he stabbed out one eye and let her sink into the ocean. There her fingers became fishes, and her arms became seals—the food for humanity.

Inuit cosmology was thus parallel: a one-eyed woman below earth, wounded by her father; a one-breasted woman above, wounded by her brother. Given the absence of the sun from the arctic sky for as much as three months each year, times when the food provided by Sedna was most important, it appears that Sedna substituted for the sun in the latter's absence. The fact that the sun goddess ruled land animals, and Sedna sea animals, the meat of which were not to be eaten at the same meal, is also complementary.

The two goddesses had much in common. To each of them, shamans traveled over narrow roads—a tree, a mountain path, a thread, or the edge of a bone knife. Going to the sun entailed passing the woman named Wide Crutch, who attempted to make the shaman laugh and then tore out his entrails to feed her dogs. Shamanic journeys to Sedna—more fully recorded among the Inuit than those to the upper world—were undertaken whenever *agdlerutit*, lice-like parasites, bothered Sedna so much that she refused to send forth game. Then the *angakok* climbed an ice-covered slippery wheel, ran past a kettle full of boiling seals and a pack of mad dogs, and finally crossed a thin bridge across an abyss to remove the lice.

And what caused the lice to grow? The breaking of taboos, especially those concerned with birth, like the taboo against concealing the conception of a child. Were no taboos ever broken, no shamanic journeys need be undertaken. Sedna was concerned with taboos concerning birth; the sun with taboos about sex. Both taboo systems revolved around concealment or deceit. Considering that the Inuit lived in tiny groups in a harsh environment, how anything could be concealed for long is difficult to imagine. To set oneself so far apart, to be so antisocial as to keep a secret—that was the source of the disorder that, transmitted throughout the group, destroyed the integrity of the Inuit's relationship to the food-providing land.

The most famous European parallel to the myth is that of Oedipus; incestuous love, kept secret, reduced the land to poverty until the taboo breaker mutilated himself. As eyes offer a visual pun for breasts, it is possible that the Oedipus story is a faint and distant recollection of an arctic original remembered more fully by the Inuit. The incest involved in the sun-sister tales, however, is of a different order than that in the

Oedipus cycle. With virtually no exceptions it is between brother and sister, a relationship so horrifying to the Inuit that they believed it could end the world. This type of incest Sally Falk Moore posits as referring invariably to a creation myth. If we imagine a primordial couple, we imagine as well their first children mating in order to continue the race. Descent of any kind, Moore avers, "postulates divine ancestry.... If all men are descended from one couple, then every marriage is distantly and vaguely incestuous." Wendy Doniger O'Flaherty has posited incest as one of the three major methods of creation, the others being fire and dismemberment; the Inuit myth, with the incestuous sun goddess, mistress of fire, dismembering herself, encompasses all three.[6]

If the myth refers to creation, it is possible that the ancestral mother is the sun, the ancestral father the moon. But only in this oblique way do the Inuit suggest the sun as the ancestral mother of humanity. Far to the south, however, we find a group that declares themselves descended from the sun, and who tell the same myth of incest between the sun and her brother. We have already examined most of their sun-goddess legends, for it is the Cherokee who tell a simplified version of the Inuit myth, in which the sun marks her brother's face but does not amputate a breast before rising into the sky.

How did this arctic story find its way to southeast America? Perhaps it came directly from the Arctic to Cherokee lands; perhaps it took a roundabout route. The proto-Cherokee may have traveled to the Southeast from the north, carrying the myth learned in the subarctic region with them, or they may have originated in South America and somehow learned the myth there. This latter possibility is supported by basketry traditions. The distinctive Cherokee basket, which has as its rim a thin oak hoop bound with hickory fiber, is otherwise made only by natives of the Orinoco and Amazon basins in South America; in addition, both Cherokee and South Americans used unusual double-weave and chain-and-diagonal basket-weaves.

If the story reached Cherokee territory via South America, we have yet to learn whether it traveled there from the North American Arctic by land, or from Asia by sea. Sea travel is more likely than the distances might, at first, suggest, for there are prevailing east winds on which early navigators could have depended; the current from Japan to America is strong enough for boats to have drifted the entire distance in historic times. Given the excellent navigational skills of early Asians, circum-Pacific routes are plausible. Such transoceanic contact would explain the corded-ware pottery, called Valdivia and dating from approximately 3600

B.C.E., that has been found along the coast of Ecuador; it dramatically resembles early Japanese Jomon-ware.

There are other connections: Ritual destruction and rebuilding of temples occurred in Central America as well as in Japan. And a vestige of a connection between Japanese myth and the sun-sister myth occurs in the first part of the Kojiki, where we are given the odd but apparently important detail that the weaving maiden Wakahirume died from puncturing her vagina; in the Nihongi it is Amaterasu herself who is wounded thus. David Kinsley sees in this an encoded incest story, with the sun's brother, Susano-o, guilty of violent sexual assault on his sister. Like Sedna with an eye put out, Malina with an amputated breast, Wakahirume/Amaterasu suffered an assault on the body's integrity: eye, breast, vulva are all punningly connected.

Japan, then, could have been a source of the myth or a station on its route of transmission. But, as we have pointed out, diffusion of the story is less important here than its meaning. However the sun-sister story traveled to South America, the tale made a home there, among at least a dozen South American Native groups. The Taulipang, Cuna, Okairu, Cunibo, Witto, Zaparo, Shipaya and Guarani, as well as the Yamunda and Tumapasa—tell some version of it. Among other tribes its motifs — brother-sister incest, marks on the moon's face, and one-breasted women—occur separately. The myth's appearances cluster in Greater Brazil, around the Amazon River—so named because early European explorers heard tales of one-breasted warriors, which they associated with the Greek vision of Amazonia—and far south of there, on the highland called the Gran Chaco.

In the first area, a classic form of the tale is told among the Mbya: The moon visited his sister Inga Woman's hammock nightly; one night she painted his face with black dye, which he saw the next morning in the mirror. Try as he might, he could not scrub it off. Meanwhile, his sister, pregnant, wandered away and was dismembered by jaguars, who doubtless tore off her breasts in their blood orgy. Just north of Amazonia, in Colombia and eastern Venezuela, the same story was told. There we hear as well of the goddess Maneca, whose single teat gave as much milk as a normal mother's pair. It is not said how she came to have only a single breast.

Myths evocative of the shamanistic world view occur throughout South American; similarly, sun goddess myths are widespread there. In the far south, the Argentine Toba—a matrilineal people, like most in the Gran Chaco—have the best-recorded South American mythology of the sun goddess. Their solar creation myth is a particularly charming one. Once, they said, the sky was full of women, each of them a sun-being, smooth and fat and round. Although life in the blue sky was lovely, they were curious about the hairy creatures they saw beneath them, and so, one day, they decided to visit the earth. One sun-maiden plaited a long twine rope, and they swung down to the earth's surface—all but one maiden, who stayed at home.

On earth, the sun-maidens discovered that the hairy creatures were men—ugly, but interesting in their own peculiar way. After a day of playing with these new creatures, the sun-women started home. Alas! One of the rude beasts had eaten the sky-rope! Trapped below, the women could henceforth only look up to their beautiful sister above, watching as she grew old each summer, becoming a slow-walking woman whose tired stride lengthened the days till solstice; watching her grow young again in winter, striding quickly so that the days ended fast; cheering her as she fought with iron weapons against the jaguar that tried to eat her.

The idea of a rope to the sky-mother—an umbilical cord, some would have it—links this tale with the shamanic vision of a narrow path to the realm of the sun goddess. Female shamanism was common in the sun-goddess cultures of South America. The layered cosmos, its upper and lower worlds sandwiching our everyday one, was traversed by shamans in South America, as in the Arctic; the shamans often tied themselves into trees or stood on stakes, the better to ascend to her realm. As in the Arctic, too, the transformative power of taboo-breaking is part of the South American myth complex. Jean-Paul Dumont has used the solar-incest motif to argue that the sun and moon, by behaving like animals (one Panare term for incest is "to have sex like monkeys"), remove themselves from the human plane, becoming both "too natural but at the same time too supernatural." The bestial brother and sister transubstantiate easily to the superhuman. The way down, as in shamanic journeys, turns out to be the way up.[7]

Native Americans of both continents, then, shared a sun-goddess myth, whether it traveled south by land after Beringia sank, or by land to Alaska and by sea to South America. But this does not end the mystery of the sun-sister, for the same story appears as well in India. How did this vivid tale of incest and dismemberment come to that subcontinent? Did it travel south from a Siberian original—or did it travel from the east, like the wind, with early navigators? This is a fertile ground for further study. But even without knowing how the myth reached Sri Lanka and southern India, we can ascertain that it did so early. For it was told by the oldest of the subcontinent's people, the Dravidians and the Tamils, indigenous people who kept their beliefs alive for millennia after the Indo-European invasion in 2000 B.C.E.

The invader's divinities became primary in Hinduism, but Dravidian influence continued in powerful figures like Kali and Durga, while aboriginal myths were told still, as folktales, in the hills. Knowledge of a sun goddess thus held on in Tamil and Dravidian areas, even where Vedic tradition emphasized a male sun god. Most of what we know of the pre-Indo-European sun goddess was collected a century ago, when colonization by England coincided with the popularity of antiquarian pursuits back home. Oral histories and mythologies, taken down in massive volume from storytellers and elders, capture the old sun goddess of the subcontinent.

The same incestuous myth is told of her as along the Pacific Rim, although Indian myth posits an aggressive, rather than a deceitful, moon-brother. Among the Khasis, we find the girl Ka Sngi (her name means sun), and her two sisters—Ka Um (water) and Ka Ding (fire)—living with their brother U Bynai, the moon. In the beginning, the Khasis say, the moon was as bright as the sun. But he was a spoiled and self-centered young man. He wandered around aimlessly, consorting with bad companions. He spent many nights away from home, without telling anyone where he was going. He drank, he gambled, he pursued whatever pleasure caught his fancy.

Then be began to desire his sister. When she realized what he was planning, she grew furious. Scorching his face with hot ashes, she said, "How dare you think such thoughts of me, your elder sister, who has taken care of you and held you in her arms, carried you on her back as a mother does?" U Bynai was so ashamed of himself that he left home to wander through the heavens. His sisters, however, stayed home with their mother until she died. Then they formed the earth from her body.

Another Khasi version of the story says that the civet cat, U Kui, cut the line that held earth and heaven together, eliminating communication between the spheres. Those below were plunged into darkness because the sun had hidden herself in shame over the propositions made to her by her brother, the moon. Many animals went in search of the sun—the elephant, the horse, the rhinocerous, the buffalo—but none could find her. Finally, the cock saved the day, by convincing U Bleisang, the divinity who removes the curse of incestuous love, to do so for the sun goddess. Then he crowed three times, and she reappeared.

The first of these tales is interesting because of its narrative similarity to the Eskimo, Cherokee and Mbya myths. Like them, the marks seen on the moon's face are explained as made by the sun in her anger at his treachery. The second myth bears the additional motifs of the cut sky-ladder and the hidden sun, both of which we have seen in Asian shamanic sun lore. Incest, of course, figures as well in both stories, connecting them to the Pacific Rim sun-goddess complex.

And then there is the appearance of the wild cat, U Kui, reminiscent not only of the panther that dismembered Inga Woman, but of Grand-Aunt Tiger as well. In Dravidian myth, the tiger is often a doublet of the incestuous brother himself. The Naga tell of a boy who developed the nasty habit of scratching his sister's legs with his sharp nails. Though she objected, he continued until their mother played a trick on him: She pierced his water buckets and sent the boy off to draw water. He spent a day trying to fill the buckets before realizing what was the matter—then, furious at the trick, he sprang upon his mother and tore one of her breasts off before disappearing into the forest in the form of a tiger.

This mythic tiger married a human girl whose parents gave her up for dead when she went into the forest with the cat. When she bore her first child, the girl noticed the tiger hitting its head on the ground in order to lick the baby's blood. Terrified, the girl ran away, the tiger in pursuit. Reaching her mother's house, she begged to be let in. But the mother did not believe her pleas until it was too late. Half in, half out the door, the girl was torn apart by mother and tiger-husband. After mourning for a time, the two decided to eat the girl's flesh—and, after that, tigers were always man-eaters.

These tales are reminiscent of the Inuit sun goddess's demand that her brother eat her flesh; perhaps we can find clues here to the primal version of the myth, in which a violent communion takes place. Such mythic cannibalism, by mother or brother or both, occurs elsewhere in the region as well. In Mahokoshal a brother, noting the sweet taste of his sister's blood when her cut hand bled into his curry, decided to kill her and eat her. This he did, but she returned to life by being reborn as a flower. In the Indian mountains, among the Koraput, the woman Uyu-sum cut her own daughter's throat in order to have something to eat. But the child's soul blazed out through the wound and threatened the world with a holocaust. To avoid the world's destruction, Uyugsum swallowed her daughter, lighting up from within and rising to the sky to became the sun.

A Khasi tale of the ravening tiger-brother goes like this: Ka Nam, a beautiful girl, was born on the borders of the great forest. Her mother feared constantly that someone would kidnap her for her beauty, so she kept the child almost imprisoned in a secluded part of the village. The girl's father, however, finally convinced her that the child should lead a more normal life. This was to be her undoing.

One day, as the girl was drawing water from a well, a huge tiger dragged her off to its lair. The tiger, U Khla, was very hungry. When he realized what a tiny morsel the girl was, he decided to keep her for a while and fatten her up. He brought her little candies and made her feel at home. Ka Nam forgot to be afraid and grew into a young woman with perfect trust in tigers.

Her host, however, had not lost sight of the ultimate objective in rearing the girl. When she had reached full growth, he invited all his tiger friends for a feast. A little mouse, however, overheard the tiger inviting his friends and reported it to Ka Nam. She ran away and, as the mouse had told her to do, went right to the cave of the magician toad U Hynroh. He said he would protect her, but in fact he only intended to make her a slave. Telling her he was going to make sure she would be safe from the tiger, he turned her into a truly hideous toad.

The tiger, returning to his den, found his captive had escaped. He grew furiously angry and called down curses on whomever had stolen his prey. The other tigers, when they realized they wouldn't get anything to eat, turned on U Khla and tore him to death.

Meanwhile, back at U Hynroh's, the little mouse had witnessed Ka Nam's transformation. Taking pity on the girl, she secretly led Ka Nam to a magical tree that led to the sky. The maiden climbed into the tree and spoke the mouse's magic words: "Grow tall, dear tree, the sky is near, expand and grow." The tree grew and grew until it reached the sky, and there the maiden entered the Blue Realm. And immediately the tree shrank again to the size of a bush.

Ka Nam, up in the sky looking like a hideous toad, went from palace to palace begging for help, but the heavenly folk were so repulsed by her ugliness that they threw her out. Finally she approached the palace of Ka Sgni, the sun-mother, who gave her a latrine to live in.

There she sat one day, with her toadskin off, combing her hair. And there the son of Ka Sgni saw her and fell in love with her. He ran to his mother and asked her to move the maiden indoors so he could be near her. Ka Sgni, a wise mother, waited to see if the infatuation would pass. She also went out to spy on the toad in the latrine and, sure enough, saw the maiden without her toad disguise, shining with loveliness.

Realizing that the maiden had been bewitched, Ka Sgni knew she would have to find the maiden asleep, and then burn the toadskin. She did so, releasing the maiden but incurring the fury of the magician toad.

For days he tried to devour Ka Sgni, causing the world's first eclipse. Below on earth, the people stood in fear, watching the goddess fighting for her life. They screamed and they cried, they beat on drums and cymbals. When he heard the commotion, U Hynroh thought an army was about to advance on him. He released the sun goddess, but continues to attack her periodically, hoping humans will be too busy to help. For this reason, the Khasi say, it is important always to make a lot of noise during an eclipse.

We could recognize the sun goddess in this story even if her name did not reveal her identity. Solar motifs abound: the sun's well, from which the maiden was kidnapped; the tree of heaven, through which she reached the sky realm; the ravenous tiger deity; the evil sun-eating toad. Like Grand-Aunt Tiger, this just-so story includes, as well as hides, its original cosmology. In the same way that Amaterasu's myth both disguises and suggests an incestuous relationship to Susano-o, the attack on the sun maiden's bodily integrity—shown in these tiger myths as an attempt to devour her—can be read as a disguised incest myth; remember Malina's demanding that her lustful brother eat her breast.

David Shulman goes so far as to say that the incest motif is latent in all Tamil mythology. Incest is part of many myths, and particularly attaches itself to sun goddesses like Mysore's Bisal Mariamna, whose solar mirror we encountered in Chapter Two. In Mysore, where Tamil influence is high, Bisal Mariamna was described as both the wife and the sister of Shiva. And that's not the only incestuous relation in this goddess's mythology. There is a famous tale that Bisal Mariamna and her six sisters stole a young woman's husband for their sexual pleasure. One night, they decided to let him return to spend the night with his wife, although they hypnotized the woman, Kantarupi, so that she was ignorant of what occurred. A few months later Kantarupi realized she was pregnant, but knew not why; her father cast her out into the woods, certain that she'd been unfaithful with a secret lover. There she was adopted by a prostitute who exposed the baby, a boy, in a snake temple, where his own grandfather found him and raised him.

Years later, the now-grown man passed through the prostitute's quarters and, seeing Kantarupi, fell in love and arranged a meeting—en route to which he stumbled over a calf whose mother soothed him by saying, "What can you expect of someone about to sleep with his own mother?" The young man was baffled at that. Imagine, then, his surprise when, approaching Kantarupi, all the mother's milk she had never given him to drink exploded from her breasts at him. All ended happily, however, with the stolen husband reunited with woman and child. The likely incest that Bisal Mariamna's theft had set into motion was thus averted.

Even further south, we find another version of the pre-Indo-European sun goddess of the area. She appears in Sri Lanka as Pattini, the one-breasted patron of the island, who is still served today by transvestite priests who enter shamanic trances. One of the major goddesses of the area, she is honored in long poems like the *Shilipatikarum*, the epic of the silver anklet, as well as in rituals and folkways. Her myth centers on self-amputation of her breast, but within her rituals are telling references to incest.

In myth, Pattini appears not as an incestuous sister but as an exemplary, indeed impossibly pure, wife. Born miraculously from a mango, Pattini married a prince with whom, for some unexplained reason, she could not have intercourse. He left her for a prostitute, on whom he squandered his fortune, returning home penniless to Pattini, who was herself mired in poverty as an abandoned wife. But she, ever-loving, gave him her priceless silver anklet—her last possession—to sell in the marketplace. Unbeknownst to him, the queen had once had an identical bracelet, which had been stolen. When Pattini's luckless husband appeared with the apparently incriminating evidence, he was captured and executed for theft.

Pattini herself went to the marketplace; then she went to the king himself. But too late—her husband was already dead. Enraged, Pattini tore off her left breast and threatened the king with it. But he, scoffing, merely invited her to eat it. She threw it instead at the city. It burst into flame, destroying everything but the body of her husband, whom Pattini lovingly resurrected.

The resonance between this myth and that of the Inuit Malina is clear in these last details: The goddess cuts off her breast, and someone (not, this time, the goddess herself) suggests eating it. In these myths, no one actually eats the breast, however often the suggestion is reiterated. Then why this insistence on eating human flesh, particularly the bloody, just-amputated breast of a goddess? The repetition suggests that, in fact, the breast was devoured in some versions of the myth, just as it is in the stories that substitute tiger for brother. What meaning this cannibal communion could have is examined in Chapter Eleven.

The connection between the circum-Pacific sun goddess and Pattini is suggested by the motifs in Pattini's myth, but Pattini's solar identity is indicated even more directly in liturgies directed to her. She is born "of the pure dynasty of the sun," her ritual songs say, and "she banishes darkness," she "arrives like the sun in your midst in great beauty." Hers is the fire of the sun; summer's heat and drought are said to be caused by her fury at her husband's death. Pattini's fire can be dangerous, threatening to life. Thus cooling ceremonies are necessary; these include drinking sacred water in which an anklet has been dipped. Its circular shape connects the silver anklet both to the goddess's breast and to the sun itself; some versions of the epic, making the connection more plain, describe Pattini as throwing her anklet, not her breast, at the murderous king.

Amputation of a goddess's breast occurs elsewhere in Dravidian India; the Gond of Bilaspur say that the primordial goddess was torn apart at creation: Her breasts, flying up, became the sun and moon, while her sparkling clitoris became the lightning. As in the Sedna-Malina pairing, we find in these myths the breast doubling for the eye, just as in petroglyphs that make a visual pun on eyes and nipples, or Greek Baubo figures that form a bearded face of the torso—nipples for eyes, navel for nose, vulva for hairy mouth. The sun-as-breast is the sun-as-eye in what Michael Dames calls "both/and" logic. Thus the myths that focus on the goddess's single breast are radically connected to those in which the sun is envisioned as the sky's eye.

Pattini's connection to the other one-breasted goddesses of this Pacific Rim cycle is obvious, but less obvious is the incestuous content of her myth, for it continually stresses Pattini's wifely dignity. Though the incest motif has been severed from Pattini's myth, no ritual can be performed in her honor that does not mention the crime continually. In rituals to Pattini, a prominent part is played by a creature named Gara Natuma. This Gorgon-like, snake-haired creature dances wildly through the sacred precincts, intent on banishing evil that might disrupt the proceedings. And what evil is it that must be banished from Pattini's presence? Sibling incest.

Although the goddess is said to be pure, her dancing demon is an incestuous brother. Born Dala Kumara ("Tusk Prince"), he was the beautiful Giri Devi's brother. At her wedding, be went crazy, ate all the food, then kidnapped her. Taking her to the forest, he lived with her there until she committed suicide by hanging herself from a tree. He never recovered from his loss. Unless rituals honoring him are held regularly, his terrible fury at losing his sister-lover will devastate the world. Should the rituals be correctly danced, however, Pattini will restrict Gara's influence only to homes where twin rat snakes, lizards or scorpions had been seen copulating—a sign of sibling incest in the household. Therefore, although her myth omits the sibling incest found in other versions of the sun-sister myth, Pattini cannot be worshiped without the unlawful love of brother and sister being given prominence.[8]

The one-breasted woman, her brother's lover, is thus a major form of the sun goddess, found from Sri Lanka and India through Japan, across the Arctic and down into South America. There are, as we have seen, two major parts to the story. Firstly, there is incest, which, we have seen, probably indicates that the story is a disguised origin myth. Secondly, there is the amputated breast. But why this odd detail? What reason could the originators of this myth have had for such a terrifying, awful action?

It's possible that the goddess's self-mutilation could have begun as a just-so story. The sun, a storyteller could have said, is a goddess. But she isn't shaped like a woman, a listener might demur. That's because, the storyteller could say, that all we see is a breast in the sky, giving off light like milk. But where's the rest of the body, this listener demands. It's just a breast, because it was cut off. Who cut it off? Why, the goddess herself. But why? Because...

But given the myth's wide range, it seems highly unlikely that a simple just-so story was deemed so worthy of repetition and transmittal that it traveled throughout the Pacific Rim. There must have been another, more spiritual, more profound explanation for the action of the goddess. And clues to that explanation can be found on the island continent of Australia, where the bright black sun goddess smiles at us from her home in the Dreaming.

Chapter Ten ✸

~~~~~~

AUSTRALIA:
THE SUN IN DREAMTIME

This story was told for millennia on the island continent of Australia, always in secret, for it was a sacred story: Once, in the Dreaming, Walu the sun-woman slept soundly in an underground cave. Her arms covered her bright black face. Finally, she woke and stretched—raising her arms, stretching her fingers wide—and the first light streamed into the sky.

Walu climbed over the world's edge, beaming. She stroked the soil; trees and plants burst forth, fragrant and singing softly. Spirits emerged to help shape the rest of creation. They dug rivers, piled up earth into hills, sculpted animals and birds, while Walu watched with pleasure.

When she grew tired, Walu sought a place where she could gather her cloud-cloak around, bury her face in her arms, and sleep. Off on the western horizon she saw the Island of Bralgu. There she traveled and there she rested.

The next morning, when she rose and saw the lovely new-green land, she was pleased with herself. The plants grew, nurtured by her rays, and the animals feasted on their fruit. Spirit people, observing the land's beauty, made it their home. They came from the underworld, they came from the sky, and they came in peace.

Three came together, paddling a bark canoe. Two were the daughters of the sun goddess. The elder was named Bildjiwuraroiju; her younger sister was Miralaidj. From their vulvas poured the sun's own rays; they were, in fact, the sun herself embodied. The young women traveled with their brother, Gandjudinju.

Bildjiwuraroiju carried sacred carvings of the parrot, the goanna, the porpoise and the ant, together with a uterus-shaped mat. The little dilly-bag in which she stored these totems was also sacred, with lengths of feathered string representing sun's rays dangling from it. The sisters summoned power with the totems and the sacred songs that only they—and not their brother—knew.

These three were so close they were called by one name, the Djanggawul. But the sisters would not share power with their brother; if he came near, they fell silent and hid their treasures. Gandjudinju begged to be taught the songs, to be given totems. But he was told, "Men will beat us and take everything we own if we do not control them with this power." Impressed with this possibility, Gandjudinju decided to steal the totems, but Bildjiwuraroiju kept them under constant watch. Miralaidj did not like men and spent her time in the company of girls her own age, digging yams and lily bulbs. Barnambir, the morning star, was her special friend; together they walked the beaches looking for shellfish and climbed the trees looking for nuts.

Walu, the sun-woman, watched them. And the Djanggawul brother watched the sun, with mounting lust. Every time he saw her walking brightly across the sky, he got an erection so long his penis reached the ground. One day he and Bildjiwuraroiju hunted for wallaby in a far valley, walking a great distance before they found plentiful game. Late that day, covered with mountain dust, hot and thirsty from hauling their heavy catch, they came to the sea and plunged in like children.

Above, Walu warmed them. Her beams aroused the Djanggawul brother until he turned to his sister in desire. Though returning his lust, she hesitated because she knew Walu would see. But she did not hesitate long.

All-seeing Walu saw indeed. She also saw that Bildjiwuraroiju conceived. She confronted Gandjudinju. "You cannot stay here any longer," she said. "Take the mother of your child and find a land that will feed her. Bildjiwuraroiju should take her totems, so that her children will have spirits to call on for help."

As brother and sister gathered up their belongings, Miralaidj demanded to go with them, but the pair refused. Afraid of abandonment, the younger sister crept to her brother's side that night and made love with him in the darkness. Because she knew she had conceived, Miralaidj won the right to travel to the new land.

The Djanggawul cast off from shore and traveled for a long time, guided by Walu's rays, until they reached a dry, dusty land that seemed an unlikely new home. But they disembarked and began to walk, the sisters drawing water from the land with their *mawalan,* their digging sticks, and creating plants from their *djuga* poles as they went. From place to place the Djanggawul sisters and their brother went, making waterholes and planting trees, sanctifying the land with sacred songs and the display of totems. The women grew heavier and heavier as their pregnancies advanced, but they kept traveling to make fertile their new world.

Bildjiwuraroiju was the first to bear, beside a waterhole her sister had made, under a tree her sister had planted. A boy child came first, then several more boys, then girls. The boys were laid in rough grass, the girls on soft grass, from which men got wiry hair, women wavy. After those first children there were others, and the children began to have children.

Soon the land was populated. The children fought. The Djanggawul invented laws so that they would live in peace; they set forth rituals, with the women passing along sacred songs that brought fertility and rain. But men grew envious of women's power. Gandjudinju never stopped envying his sisters; even in the new land he plotted to steal their totems. Day by day he grew more obsessed.

One night he tried to steal the totems while his sisters slept, but they sprang up instantly, as if the totems had called to them. "Only women have totems," said Bildjiwuraroiju, beating her brother with her digging stick. The sacred objects were safe once more.

It was not, finally, their brother who stole the women's totems. One day as the sisters gathered food, they were followed by three little men. Bildjiwuraroiju and Miralaidj left their totems on a tree while they climbed another nearby for honey. When the women descended, the precious dilly-bag was gone. They searched until they found footprints and, horrified, realized their loss.

Back at camp, the Djangguwul saw their own brother performing rituals with the stolen totems. In resignation, they told themselves they would have to be content with the power of the womb. "We know everything. We have really lost nothing, because we remember it all. Aren't we still sacred, even though we have lost the treasures?" they asked each other. "Do we not still each have a uterus, and the power to give birth?"[1]

The question that concludes this creation myth of northern Arnhem Land is piercingly ironic. There in Australia—where five hundred distinct peoples have maintained an ancient culture for as long as forty thousand years and where the sun is almost invariably female—Western observers stripped sacredness from women just as thoroughly as have the dwarfish men of myth. For almost a century, non-Aboriginal interpreters divided Australian society into "the sacred" and "the profane"—a division popularized by Emile Durkheim, and confined women to the latter. "Profane" women were assumed to have no spiritual content to their lives, while "sacred" men were imagined devoting themselves utterly to spiritual endeavors that affected the entire tribe. When Aboriginal women treated men without recognition of their natural holiness, male scholars faulted them for not acting in accordance with theory.

Academic male bias was not the only reason for this misconception about Aboriginal women's real spiritual authority. Aboriginal women share their spiritual lives with other women, keeping rituals secret from tribal men. The first anthropologists to study Aborigines were men; these men, knowing little of women's religious life, implied to male questioners that they had none. Of course, men's ritual was similarly secret from women; such ritual secrecy was broken only when non-Aborigines recorded myths, mostly from men, that theretofore had been as carefully guarded as the Djanggawul sisters' totems. (Myths in this chapter have all been previously published; although this does not exonerate writer and reader from occupying sacred space reserved for Aborigines, I hope it does not lead to further sacrilege.)

Women's myths and rituals remain to this day less recorded. Even married female anthropologists in the early 1900s gathered little information, for Aboriginal women quickly surmised that their female secrets might be shared with the male spouse and would thus be jeopardized. Men, left to study men's institutions, invented theories that claimed the sacred for men only.

At mid-century, however, the anthropological vision of Aboriginal women as mere beasts of burden for their menfolk began to change. Phyllis Kaberry, in the 1930s, arguing against "misogynistic stereotypes of Aboriginal women," claimed Aboriginal women were "not only profane but also sacred." That only fifty years ago it could be presumed that *any* woman lived with no knowledge of, or interest in, spirituality should not be surprising, given that only twenty-five years ago scientists finally reached unanimity on the question of whether Australian Aboriginals were indeed *Homo sapiens.*[2]

Kaberry suggested that, rather than being excluded from religion, women had a separate-but-equal religious sphere that echoed daytime economic divisions of the sexes. Certainly there was such a daytime division, for men and women traditionally led parallel lives. Men hunted kangaroo and wallaby while women gathered yams, honey, and small game, the latter task providing far more than 50 percent of the daily food supply; men spent their lives away from camp, while women passed theirs within it. But all, as children, lived the same life—in camp, where they observed everything that was not ritually secret. Adulthood, conversely, was full of secrets. A dramatic break, then, occurred for both men and women at initiation.

Early non-Aboriginal observers, ignorant of female initiation, claimed that lack of it left women permanently profane. But girls were,

indeed, initiated into the splendor and responsibilities of full woman-
hood. Unlike Aboriginal boys, initiated in groups at regular intervals,
girls were initiated singularly, as their menses began. Although the
numerous peoples had different ways, a typical ceremony had the girl
secluded for several days during her first flow. She camped outside the
settlement with older women who taught her songs and myths, then she
reemerged painted with rich designs in red ochre. The new woman was
led to a stream or lagoon and ceremoniously bathed. A procession to the
main camp and exhibition of the girl to the community as a full initiate
ended the ceremony.

In some places, a girl's initiation took the form of ritual intercourse
with a group of men; since she had probably been sexually active already,
this was often a purely ritual defloration. Afterwards, the girl took part in
women's secret corroborees, singing *daragu* (sacred) songs that were
gunbu (taboo) to men. Meanwhile, her ritual education continued, for
she learned sacred songs throughout her life, until as a wise old woman
she instructed young initiates in proper ritual ways.

These women's rituals were predominantly personal, including love
magic, while those of the men dealt with matters pertaining to the seasonal cycle and tribal events. This division of spiritual labors apparently
supports those who argue that men commanded the superior ritual role.
Sharon Tiffany and Kathleen Adams, however, have shown that mating
controls geneological decisions—which are vital because they determine
kinship. Sex determines which totems shall endure, which shall became
connected, which grow less populous and powerful. Aboriginal women of
high degree, then, created the human future through their love magic.

Similarly, Diane Bell has described the way in which Aboriginal
women "grow up" children, relationships, and even the land itself as part
of women's responsibility for the maintence of harmony between and
among humans, and between humans and the land. Women's rituals,
though focused on the personal, were vitally important to the continued
sustenance of life.

Myths like those of the Djanggawul cycle give evidence of women's
importance in Aboriginal mythic life. They also hint at an earlier social
organization in which women were sole possessors of community rituals
later stolen by men. They tell of a time when men, in the words of one
of them, "had nothing—no sacred objects, no sacred ceremonies; the
women had everything." Not only do myths recount a theft of women's
sacred objects and ceremonies; they also, as Stehlow points out, provide
evidence of the female ancestors' overwhelming strength and authority;

the women in the myths are clearly more powerful than their male companions and seem to scare the latter. This is consistent with myths that say women not only invented and owned ceremonies; they also owned totemic objects, *churingas*, which were either stolen or given up willingly to the men. Even the sacred bullroarer was, in a Wiknatara myth, owned by two girls who said as they twirled it, "This belongs to us women, really we have found it. But we leave it for the men. It is they who will always use it."[3]

Was the sun goddess part of this earlier realm? Her myths have been recorded mainly from men's ritual material. It is unclear, however, whether the stories were also ritually told by women, and, therefore, whether they properly fall into the categories of men's, women's, or communal myths. Were these myths created by and for men, to show from how powerful a source men's ritual power had been wrested? Were they created by women, to show that however difficult their life may be, women are related to the divine? Or do they serve a community purpose, supporting the separation of men's and women's ritual worlds?

Cosmology suggests the latter. Men and women did not only occupy different economic and ritual worlds, they came from different places: men from the earth, women from the sky. One story, for instance, says that only women lived in the sky world; men had a little world of their own nearby, but it was a cold place without food. The sun-woman, taking pity on the poor men, gave them light and food so that they might survive.

In our hierarchically ordered universe, we interpret the sky as "above" and superior, the underearth realm as "below" and inferior, but this need not be the case in a multilayered universe. Instead, "the way down is the way up," as Heraclitus said. There is no ascent or descent, except from our limited, mundane point of view. This simple truth has been obscured in the West by millennia of Apollonian thinking. In the sun god's realm, dark and light are opposed, as are up and down, life and death, heaven and hell. But in the realm of the goddess, as we have seen, such simplistic dualism breaks down. Day's luminary, the lifegiver, travels each night to death's realm under the earth; doing so, she dies daily, but daily is reborn. Dark is thus an aspect of light, as day is an aspect of night. The cosmological point is division and differentiation.

Passage between separate worlds, however difficult, can occur. Woman most powerfully embodies the ability to move from level to level, through her power to give birth. Thus the maternity of the sun goddess is frequently emphasized. Among the Wotjobaluk of southeastern Australia, the sun-mother's name was Gnowee; she lived on earth where, because there was no light, she always carried a torch. One day she went too far in her search for yams and lost her infant son. So she rose into the air, where she still travels, carrying her torch, hopelessly searching. The Bandicoot traced their sun totem to two women who came bearing it; the Wurunjerri said the sun is "the sister of us all"; and the Tiwi saw the sun, Wurnipranala, as the intermediary to the blind mother-creator.

The Arnhem Land Gilegu said their ancestral mothers, the Junkgowaa, created the sun with innumerable legs—rays—to travel on. Afterwards the Junkgowaa plied their canoes westwards, expecting the sun to follow them. She did not, so they sang magic songs that brought her out of the eastern sea. They commanded her to light the way to food for all people. Once she was up, the sun explained that she had been slow to rise because she had just had a baby son, whom she was loathe to leave. He remains to this day, like a stone, waiting for his mother to return each night and breastfeed him. Thus, when the Yulegor are awaiting sunrise, they say to each other of the sun's tardiness that "The baby cries often."[4]

Most Aborigines tell stories of foremothers who, like the Junkgowaa or the Djanggawul, came across a body of water and civilized the wild terrain. These ancestors lived in the Dreaming, that parallel space and time where spiritual powers reside. The *alchera* songs and sacred objects that evoke the Dreaming are *churingas*—both words from the central Aranda, whose language is frequently used by scholars to name concepts unique to Aboriginal religion. In their wanderings, the foremothers made and sanctified places known to the tribal group. Aboriginal religion is thus more completely tied to the land than perhaps any other on earth and, through the ancestral mothers, women are especially connected to the land; it is the duty of today's women to maintain the Dreamings of their mothers. So closely does woman relate to land in Australia that the Pitjantjatjara woman interviewed by Nancy Munn described her own moles and warts as forming the pattern on an ancestral rock in her birthplace.

Individual women have individual land-responsibilities; in turn, there is a unique myth to express that responsibility. It is not just any waterhole that appears in the foremother's creation story; it is a specific waterhole, from which drinking water can be drawn each day. Beyond that waterhole is the Dreaming reality, where mythic forces and entities still live in an ongoing creation. Women's land-rituals both reflect and reinforce this Dreaming reality. In this way the Aboriginals learned not only to be at home upon the land but to treasure it.[5]

The connection between a woman and her land is beautifully depicted in one Karraur myth of the sun goddess. It begins with Yhi, goddess of light, asleep in the dark Dreaming. Nothing moved there. It was a world of bone-bare, windless mountains. But this world was not dead. Beings lay in slumber, waiting to be awakened to life.

Suddenly, a whistle startled the goddess. She took a deep breath. Creation vibrated, then filled with light flooding from her eyes. The earth stirred under her warm rays. Yhi drifted down to it, walking north, south, east, west. As she did, plants sprang up from her footprints. She walked the world's surface until she had stepped everywhere, until every inch was covered with green. Then the sun goddess sat to rest on the treeless Nullarbor Plain.

As she glanced around, she realized that the new plants could not move from their rooted flowering. And she desired to see something dance. Seeking that dancing life, she descended to beneath the earth, where she found evil spirits who tried to sing her to death. But they were not as powerful as Yhi. Her warmth melted the darkness, and tiny forms began to move there. The forms turned into butterflies and bees and other insects, which swarmed around her in a dancing mass. She led then forth into the sunny world. There they set to work, buzzing and flitting amid the world's new flowers.

But there were still caves of ice, high in the mountains, in which other beings rested. Yhi spread her light into the caves, one at a time. She stared into the caves' black interiors until water formed. Then she saw something move—something, and another thing, and another. Fishes and lizards swam forth.

Deeper into the caves the sun goddess peered. Other silent forms were there, dark and furry. Cave after cave she freed from its darkness, and birds and animals poured forth onto the face of the earth. Soon the entire world was dancing with life. Then, in her golden voice, Yhi spoke. She told her creatures she would return to her own world. She blessed them with changing seasons and with the knowledge that when they died they would join her in the sky. Then, turning herself into a ball of light, she sank below the horizon.

As she disappeared, darkness fell upon the earth's surface. The new creatures were afraid. There was sorrow and mourning, and finally there was sleep. And, soon, there was the first dawn, for Yhi had never intended to abandon her creation. One by one the sleepy creatures woke to see light breaking in the east. A bird chorus greeted their mistress, and the lake and ocean waters that had been rising in mists, trying to reach her, sank down calmly.

For eons of Dreaming the animals lived in peace on Yhi's earth, but then a vague sadness began to fill them. They ceased to delight in what they were. She had planned never to return to earth, but she felt so sorry for her creatures that she said, "Just once. Just this once." So she slid down to the earth's surface and asked the creatures what was wrong.

Wombat spoke first. He wanted to be able to wiggle along the ground. Then Kangaroo said she wanted to fly into the sky. Bat wanted wings like a bird. Lizard, tired of being snaky, wanted legs. Seal wanted to swim like a fish. And the confused Platypus wanted something of every other animal.

Yhi gave them what they wanted. From the beautiful regular forms of the early creation came the strange creatures that now walk the earth. Yhi then swept herself up to the sky again.

She had one other task yet to complete: the creation of woman. She had already embodied Thought in male form and set him wandering the earth. But nothing—not the plants, not the insects, not the birds or beasts or fish—seemed like him. He was lonely.

Yhi went to him one morning as he slept near a grass tree. He slept fitfully, full of strange dreams. As he emerged from his dreaming he saw the flower stalk on the grass tree shining with sunlight. He was drawn to the tree, as were all the earth's other creatures.

Reverent and astonished, they watched as the power of Yhi, the sun-woman, concentrated itself on the flower stalk. The flower stalk began to move rhythmically—to breathe. Then it changed form, softened, became a woman. Slowly emerging into the light from which she was formed, the first woman gave her hand to the first man. All the animals, delerious with delight, formed circles and danced.[6]

There are aspects of this poetic myth that suggest Western, if not Christian, influence in the transcription, especially the creation of man before woman. Nonetheless, it shows the sun mother in her role as boundary being, able not only to move between levels but to transfer other beings, too. Creation, the conveyance of beings from nonbeing to life was not her only role: She also conveyed them in the opposite direction. Like sun goddesses in many lands, the Aboriginal sun ruled death. The Aboriginals of Encounter Bay say that the sun-woman's lover lived in the world of the dead, where she visited him each night. Similarly, near sacred Uluru (Ayers Rock), the Aranda said that the sun, in the form of the spirit woman Alinga (or Ochirka), rose from the underworld each day; each night she sank back into it. Shamans looking down the hole could see her still there, but ordinary people could not.

Perhaps it is because of her connection with the world of death that the Aboriginal sun goddess is often seen as a cannibal; her duty, this image reminds us, is to gobble up life so it can be reborn. In the south-central Flinders Range, Bila was such a cannibal; sunlight came from the big fire she built each day to cook her victim. She was such an unpleasant neighbor that the goanna lizard Kudnu decided she had to be killed.

Attacking her with a boomerang, he cut a huge gash into her body. With that, she turned herself into a ball of fire and sprang from the earth. As she disappeared over the horizon, the earth was plunged into darkness. Terrified by what he had done, Kudnu threw his boomerang north. Nothing happened. He threw it south; nothing. He threw it west; nothing, again.

But when he threw his boomerang to the east, it caught the sun and brought her back to earth. This, the Flinders Range Aborigines said, created night and day, and this is why goannas are sacred and not to be killed.

The cannibal sun sometimes killed her own young, as in the tale told among the Murray River tribes that, in Dreaming, the now-flightless emu had enormous long wings that allowed her to sail through the sky and never touch earth. One day—if it can be said that timeless Dreamtime had days—a female emu flew close to the earth's surface to see what was going on there. She saw birds by a reedy lagoon, dancing and singing a piercingly sweet melody.

She soared down and landed among them. They were surprised, these wild turkeys. The heavenly emu begged their permission to stay with them and learn their ways, especially dancing.

One of the turkeys was wicked. Hiding her wings behind her, she told the emu that she must amputate her long, graceful wings, which would otherwise be in the way when she tried to dance and run, catch fish and eat frogs. The unsuspecting emu agreed, and so her long wings were chopped off. Immediately, the wicked turkey unfolded her own wings and shrieked with laughter at the poor emu. In a nearby tree a kookaburra laughed and laughed. This is why the emu cannot fly today, and why the kookaburra, remembering the trick, laughs to this day.

The emu, bleeding and in shock, recovered slowly. She began to explore her new earthly home, to taste its new fruits. She built a nice nest and laid her eggs, dozens of them. Then she sat happily to hatch them. As she sat there, the wicked turkey came by. Seeing the vast number of emu eggs the turkey decided to play another trick on the poor emu. Hiding all but one of her own offspring, she began to sing the praises of few children: how much less bother they were, how much more freedom she had. She expressed concern for the short, hard life the emu would have, eaten out of house and home by so many children.

The turkey convinced the emu to break all her eggs but one. Then, chortling *Geralka Beralka, Geralka Beralka,* she brought out her own substantial brood and flaunted them before the unhappy emu.

A year passed—if years can be said to divide the Dreaming. The next breeding season, the wild turkey came back to the emu, where she sat proudly on a nestful of eggs. Remembering the tricks that had been played upon her, the emu told the turkey to leave. But the wicked bird just taunted the emu with nasty names. At last the emu left her nest and lunged for her tormenter. But the wicked turkey sprang for the emu's nest, where she smashed the eggs with her beak.

Panicked, the emu ran for her nest. But it was too late. All but one of the eggs had been crushed, and that egg was in the claws of her enemy. The wild turkey flapped her wings hard and rose into the air, carrying the last emu egg. Then she threw the egg as hard as she could into the sky, hoping it would strike something and break. It struck something, indeed: a huge pile of wood in the sky, which caught on fire. That burning woodpile, say the people of southeastern Australia, is the sun of today.[7]

This myth tells us how vital bodily transformation is, if one is to change levels; notice that the heavenly emu must mutilate her body to live on earth. Death, of course, also alters the body so that a change in level—from this world to the realm of the dead—is possible. And, without dying, women change through pregnancy, bringing forth creatures from nonbeing into life. According to this world view, men are handicapped—unless they can find some other way to transform themselves. And this Aboriginal men have done, through an initiatory event called subincision. In this ritual, a stone knife slashes the underside of the penis, making an opening approximately one inch long at initiation, but enlarged periodically throughout life until it reaches almost from tip to testicles.

The revised penis is wider, and marked with a clear line down its length. This line is important, for it is the route from non-Dreaming to Dreaming, from this world to others. Through bodily transformation, the Aboriginal man creates upon himself a sky-rope, a tool for changing levels of being. This subincision scar, like the arctic shaman's ladder and Grand-Aunt Tiger's rotten straw rope, is a line to the Dreaming.

It should be no surprise, after what we have learned of other Pacific Rim and Asian stories with this motif, that in Australia the sky-rope appears primarily in myths concerning incest. In the Djangawul cycle, brother-sister incest recalls that of other sun goddesses and moon gods. But we also find father-daughter incest in Aboriginal myths. In a Ngulugwongga legend, for instance, the crocodile, Bindagbindag, and the whistle duck, Balmad, had two daughters. Crocodile, each day as he returned home, had intercourse with them in the water when they ran out to greet him.

The mother, watching silently, grew very angry. One day she plaited a long grass rope and hid it in the bushes near the water. Then, when Crocodile was away, she and the girls climbed up a banyan tree into the sky.

Crocodile, coming home to an empty camp, called out for his daughters. The eldest answered from the sky. "Look up here," she said, and he did so. "We're in the sky! Look for the rope to come up!" The mother dropped the rope down to him. As he started to climb, the younger sister cut the rope and Crocodile fell to earth. The rope, still in the sky, can be seen at night as the Milky Way.

The Nguluwongga told a similar story: The moon-man had intercourse with his eldest daughter by sending his penis underground to penetrate her; she was thrown a rope from the sky and ascended to safety. And the Bunga Bunga told a story like that of Grand-Aunt Tiger: A woman, escaping in this case not a tiger but an incestuous father, lured him onto the sky rope and cut it.

Aboriginal incest taboos and the punishment for breaking them are extremely fierce—"escape" from incest was often effected by dying, as the myths imply. Like daughters of incestuous fathers, the dead ascend a sky-rope to the sun's world. Among the Wiradjuri, spirits climbed to the moon-man, whose long penis was wound around his waist, and to the sun-woman, whose long clitoris covered the daylight in her vulva. In determining the fate of the newly dead, they were the first of many interrogators. Later, lewd dancers tried to make the deceased laugh, although to do so would end the soul's life; the same threatening dancers, so like the violent arctic joker Wide Crutch, appeared when shamans attempted to enter the sun goddess's world.[8]

The sky-cord, then, connects us to death just as our umbilical cord connects us to our mother before birth. Only a few can travel that pathway without dying; in Australia, as in Alaska and Siberia, the sky-cord is the regular path of the shaman for changing levels of reality. Initiation into the shamanic arts includes learning to negotiate such passages, in what Eliade defines as "a descent to the lower regions followed by an ascent to the sky." A candidate for shamanic power, Alfred Howitt explains, uses a cord to enter a cave of glittering crystals—clearly a solar place. Eliade stresses that the crystals are celestial in origin, even calling them "solidified light, a uranian sacrality on earth." In some traditions the crystals are linked with the vast Rainbow Serpent, whom we shall soon meet, a combination of images that cannot help but recall the Uktena of the Cherokee.

The initiate is given some of these magical crystals, with instructions for their use, before being freed into the embraces of a treetop. This tree—or pole or post—is an alternative form of the sky-cord, one found also in the Americas and in Siberia. Even the sun herself sometimes has to use it as a route to the sky: According to the Dieri, the sun climbs a tree to her position overhead, then retreats each day into a cave. In Arnhem Land, the sun is actually embodied in a tree, which holds the spirit of the Yulegor ancestral goddess Num u Moiyak; she causes a solar eclipse should anyone wound her tree.[9]

By synecdoche—a part's standing for the whole—the tree can appear as a twig or stick, especially one of those used by women for digging or making fire. Digging sticks are found in sun-goddess myths, as in Arnhem Land, where the Djangguwul sisters create boiling wells by placing their digging sticks in the ground and then pulling them out; the bark-cloth design for these wells is like that of the sun itself, concentric circles. The connection of fire sticks with the sun is more common, and stresses the importance of women in a land where fire was the single most powerful tool. In one myth, the femininity of the sun is explained by the fact that women carry fire sticks as the sun carries beams. In other myths the converse is true: The sun carries fire sticks because she is a woman. These sticks cause the sun's heat and light; during the day they blaze up, whereas at night the sun-woman hides them under the arm of another woman as darkness falls.

A simple stick, then, becomes a powerful solar symbol. In the Ilpalinja ceremony of the Aranda, held when the weather was very cold and spring late, a stick was used to represent Snaninja Ararreka, the sun. In the Quabana Alinga rite of the same people, a bundle of twigs decorated with white and red down represented the sun. Sticks were used by other groups, as well, as sun-*churingas*. In a ceremony of the northern coastal tribes, men stuck carved wooden shafts into the ground just as the sun rose; then they knelt and bowed to the sun-woman.[10]

Not only do the tree, the twig and the fire stick appear as images for the sun goddess. There is also the snake, the most powerful form of the shamanic sky-road or tree of life. In Australia, as among the peoples of southeastern North America, the snake often appears as the sun's enemy. A Worora child's song tells of Daughter Sun, who, walking through a pine forest with her walking sticks—sunbeams—encountered a rattler and fought with him, hitting him with her sticks. Bitten, she walked into the sky in pain and died into darkness. Day after day, the Worora believe, the rattlesnake kills our sun; the sun is therefore thought to be an endless number of identical round women.

There are other stories in which snakes, fire sticks and the sun are connected. In Victoria, for instance, the mythic Karakarok discovered the earth full of snakes; she killed them one at a time until her staff broke, flashing forth into the first fire. An important myth from Arnhem Land is a compendium of such images. In this myth, the Wawalag Sisters—corollaries of the Djanggawuls, sometimes called their daughters—came with their dogs to the earth. There the elder sister gave birth next to a waterhole, and the bloody afterbirth attracted a vast snake who lived there.

The sisters did not realize their plight until the meat they were cooking leaped, alive, right out of the fire and jumped into the waterhole. Then the snake, Junguwull, created a huge storm. The girls took turns dancing to calm the winds, finally dropping with exhaustion. The snake struck, swallowing them and the elder sister's newborn child. It vomited them out, then swallowed them again, leaving the child behind the last time.

This snake appears as male in some stories, female in others; where female, its name means "subincised penis." Even when male, it becomes female through its actions: It makes itself "pregnant" with the Wawalag Sisters and then rebirths their children, by vomiting. Although it is a Western commonplace that the snake is a phallic symbol, this Australian serpent is ambiguously gendered at best. The Dalabon use the term *bolung* to mean both "rainbow" and "snake" as well as "the all-mother." The clitoris of the Djanggawul sister Miralaidj is specifically described as snake-like. The snake is connected with menstruation, perhaps even with menstrual synchrony, the tendency of women living together to menstruate at the same time.

Therefore, although either-or logic invites us to divide the Australian Aboriginal cosmos as Hallan has, into an opposition of phallic snake-water-male and breast-fire-female, in fact this opposition does not hold. That vital part of the dichotomy, the Rainbow Serpent, turns

out to be both male and female. Graphically, we can portray this supposed division of Aboriginal reality as circles and lines—which translate
all too easily into eggs and sperm—with male referents on one side,
female on the other. But in Aboriginal mythology the opposition is not
so clear-cut. Circles, it seems obvious, are female. They include the sun's
orb and the woman's breast, the well and the campfire; space itself is
sometimes conceived as a circle, because the camp is arranged thus. The
vagina is drawn as a circle or disc, and the midday sun is called by a word
that means vulva.

Lines (sky-rope, tree, stick) would seem by juxtaposition to be male,
linear phallic symbols; yet they are connected with women's safety and
with women's tools. The sky-rope pulls women to safety, away from incestuous relatives. The tree, so obviously a phallic symbol, is identified not
only with women but with the sun goddess herself. The fire stick is a
woman's tool; the twig is an emblem of the female sun's rays. [11]

There is one line left as clearly masculine: the one that runs down the
penis. But even this line is connected, in myth, with women. In a myth
related by Geza Roheim, an old man put his penis in the ground at a place
called Kuna-tari ("with vagina"), where he became empowered to wind it
up like a piece of rope. He put it into a little kangaroo-like pouch, but
then couldn't get it out until a woman cut it into little pieces with her
hatchet. And, on the Great Victoria Desert, it was said that a divine
woman invented subincision, but because she used a fire stick many
novices died; an emu-woman finally showed the people how to use a stone
instead.

In addition to these metaphoric connections with women's realm,
the line down the subincised penis had a specific use that even more
clearly points to its femininity: It permitted men to release blood during
rituals. In these events, the subincised area was stabbed to create a flow
that both Ashley Montague and Rita Gross suggest was a mimic menstruation; if, as Knight has argued, the serpent represents menstrual synchrony, then the letting-down of blood by groups of men in ritual would
certainly mimic the group bleeding of women.

But it is not only menstrual blood that the vulva produces; there is
also the blood of birth, often interchangeable with menstrual blood in
Australian myths like that of the Wawalag Sisters. In a barren land where
food is scarce, menstruation may have been irregular and may have
seemed as miraculous as birth itself; at the very least, it would have been
a visible reminder of fertility. And such fertility is continually connected
with the sun, whose color is blood-red: She wears a belt with red parrot

feathers given her by the Djanggawul or a coat of red kangaroo skins given her by her lover among the dead; she dusts herself with powered ochre when she rises and sets, reddening the clouds. Whether the sun is menstruating or giving birth, her redness is a sign of her continued fertility. [12]

The Aboriginal social construct of masculinity found the unmutilated male organ immature; real men, initiates, had the sky-rope emblazoned on their penises. By transforming the body, men made themselves ready to travel between worlds, to mount to the sun through her tree. Thereafter, in intercourse the penis became a rope to the uterine sky world, and the penis's occasional ritual bleeding mimicked the sun's fertile shedding. Blood released at subincision and later rituals created a communion with the sun's maternal fertility; it made the men like mothers, endowed with creative viability. Like the moon-man transformed into a shaman in the Americas, the Aboriginal man was given access to sanctity through his transformation.

~~~~~~

Chapter Eleven

ANATOLIA:

AMAZONS AND ARCHIGALLI

A sunny spring day in Emperor Claudius's Rome: Young men, decked in bright robes, dance in the streets behind a sanctified pine tree. It is the height of the festival—A god's rebirth after his death three days earlier. Crowned with violets and bearing a young man's statue, the evergreen had been buried as though dead. And now, the resurrection!

Bronze cymbals clash and flutes pipe as the *archigalli*, high priests of Cybele, lead the male mysteries, tossing their bleached dreadlocks as they dance. Imagine the men as they cavort through the sun-drenched streets. The women lean down, laughing, from the rooftops where, just last week, they'd watched little gardens of herbs grow quickly and die. Such was life, they knew: so beautiful, so quick to leap into the sunlight, so quick to die.

Below them, the singing young men fling their arms upwards, dancing wildly to the insistent drum. Some of them, before the day is out, will dedicate themselves wholly to the goddess whose black meteoric image moves in stately fashion before them. That dedication will be painful at first, and lifelong.

They will castrate themselves.

They did so, these men of Rome, to imitate a god. The pine tree they carried was the emblem of Attis, the young god they imitated in ritual, a god born of a miracle. There was once—so the myth that guided their self-sacrifice said—a hermaphrodite named Agdistis. Because he was more than simply man or woman, the gods castrated him, burying his severed male genitals near a river's bank. These grew into an almond tree from which the river god's daughter plucked a nut. Placing it upon her breast, she conceived a child. When he was born, his mother named the charming boy Attis.

Attis grew to be as charming a youth as he had been a child. He was so handsome that Agdistis, now a woman, fell in love with him—never suspecting Attis to be the son of her own dead flesh. But the mutilated hermaphrodite's love was unavailing: Attis was sent to Pessinus to wed a king's daughter. Agdistis followed and, in a jealous rage, caused both Attis and the king to castrate themselves.

And so, in honoring their god, Roman men did the same.

There were many variations of Attis's myth—which, despite what Roman youths thought, antedated and explained the ritual, rather than the reverse. Arnobius tells us Agdistis was born when Zeus, unable to seduce the goddess Cybele, masturbated onto her sacred rock. His spilled semen impregnated the earth with the hermaphrodite. Then Dionysus castrated Agdistis by tying his male genitals to a tree while he slept; Agdistis, when he moved to wake, tore them off.

From Agdistis's blood, this version said, a pomegranate tree sprang up. Nana, a king's daughter, ate its fruit, became pregnant, and gave birth to Attis. Although both Cyble and Agdistis—his mother and his father, one might say, albeit indirectly—lusted after him, Attis was ordered by the Phrygian king Midas to marry Phrygia's princess. In a rage, Agdistis drove the wedding party crazy. The princess cut off her breasts, Attis his genitals. From the blood, violets sprang up, and an almond tree.

Ovid tells a quite a different story: Cybele took Attis as her lover, demanding a vow of perpetual fidelity, then discovered him making love with a river nymph; ashamed, he castrated himself with a stone and was transformed into a tree. Diodorus told yet another tale: Cybele, abandoned by her royal family, grew up in poverty and fell in love with the shepherd Attis. Pregnant, she learned her true heritage and returned to her palace home, where her father, furious that Attis was so uncouth and lowly, killed him. The bereaved woman roamed the countryside weeping, causing it to become sterile, as it remained until an oracle demanded the people worship Cybele and Attis as the price for the land's fertility.

These myths are as un-Roman as they sound, for the religion of the goddess Cybele and her youthful companion was an import to Rome from Phrygia, in Asia Minor. How the goddess came to Rome is well-established: In 204 B.C.E., as Hannibal's elephants trumpeted threateningly from the north, the Romans sought the advice of the Sibyl. The fact that the prophetess's original homeland was near Mount Ida, Cybele's sacred terrain, may account for the Sibyl's announcement that only the Phrygian goddess could save the city.

And so the King of Pergamon sent the black meteorite statue of Cybele through the Bosphorus, across the Mediterranan, and up the Tiber. Erected on the Palatine Hill, it was dedicated to the *Mater Deum Magna Idaea*, the "Great Mother of the Gods of Ida." Hannibal turned away, proving the goddess's power; a temple was quickly erected, and dedicated in 191 B.C.E.

Along with the imported goddess came the priests of Cybele. And with them came excessive, ecstatic and, to the Roman, lurid rites—especially that of self-castration and burial of amputated testicles under a tree. Citizens were immediately forbidden to enter the transvestite priesthood; this did not, however, keep them from subscribing to Cybeline beliefs. So popular did the religion become that Emperor Claudius rescinded the earlier order and allowed Roman citizens to become *galli*, named either after the cock who welcomed the sun each day, or after the Gallos River in the goddess's homeland, where Attis had emasculated himself.

After Claudius's decision, Romans served even as *archigalli*, high priests of the goddess. For scores of years, Cybele's worship held sway in Rome, but then lost out to a similar cult centered upon another dying and reviving god. Some of Cybele's attributes were assimilated to the new figure of Mary, Mother of God, and Attis's springtime celebration was converted into another festival, complete with a god's death and resurrection three days later. No longer were spring flowers tied to trees, but the body of a youth still hung upon the Christian Tree of Life; no longer did *archigalli* castrate themselves to honor their god, but priests instead vowed perpetual celibacy.[1]

This was not the first time that Cybele had changed to suit new worshipers. For behind the historical figure of the goddess—crowned with a fortified city, seated between heraldic lions, carrying her round drum—is an old solar divinity from the plains of Anatolia. Although Rome called her Phrygian, Cybele did not originally belong to that patriarchal tribe, which arrived in her homeland in 900 B.C.E., long after her worship began; the Phrygians adopted her from earlier dwellers. Her home was the region dubbed Asia Minor because of a fancy that the peninsula imitated in miniature the shape of the entire continent. There on the high dry plains of today's Turkey, a sun goddess was worshiped for thousands of years, surviving the invasions and deaths of several societies. Although we do not know her original name, we can have no doubt of her power, for her people reinvented her each time they were conquered.

These goddess-worshipers lived in a land that was accessible from several continents. It was a rich land, attractive to invaders for its minerals as well as its soil. Now an arid steppe, Anatolia was, until 2500 B.C.E., a land of oak forests and pastures. There was little rainfall, but ground water—provided by runoff from the nearby mountains—was all the water the Anatolians needed. The limestone karst landscape was full of springs, many of them thermal, which shot out of fountains, bubbled up as pools and burst from mountains. It was a pleasant, productive land. It was also, in myth, the land of one-breasted women. And it was, in reality, the land of castrated men.[2]

The Amazons and *archigalli* of the region from which Cybele derives are parallel figures. Not only are both sexually self-mutilated, but the mutilated organs themselves are parallel. Shirley Ardener has argued that, while penis and vagina are complementary opposites, penis and breasts are coordinates: Both are "external and easily visible on the unclothed body," and "both produce (different) life-giving flows." In India, similarly, breast and lingam-phallus are identified. The male and female figures who appear in the mythology and ritual of this goddess, thus, are fundamentally similar.[3]

Amazons and *archigalli* appear together on a cylinder seal where men in skirts and one-breasted women worship a goddess. She was variously called Cybele, Upis, Artemis of Ephesus and "lady of Ephesus, Light Bearer." At Ephesus her massive statue was said, like the black meteoric one moved from Pessinus to Rome, to have fallen from heaven. One of the splendors of the ancient world, it was covered with globes, which are interpreted as breasts or amputated testicles—an instructive pair of possibilities in light of her Amazon priestesses and castrated priests.

Interpreted as breasts, these sculptural proturbances recall the old Greek tales of Amazons from the goddess's country. Reputedly, these man-hating female warriors amputated one breast, the better to draw the bow in battle; a spurious and impossible etymology derived their name from Greek *a-mazon*, supposedly meaning "breastless." But Greek art never showed Amazons with a single breast; nor is there, in fact, any reason that a two-breasted woman should be more impeded than a man in bow-drawing unless she were using a crossbow; yet crossbows were invented centuries after the Amazons reputedly lived and fought. But, despite such implausibility, the story persisted.[4]

Where, then, did the Greeks derive their tales of one-breasted women? Perhaps the Amazons were distant recollections of a religion in which breasts—separated from the body, if not actually amputated—were a prime religious symbol. And, indeed, such images appeared in ancient Phrygia and elsewhere in Anatolia several millennia before Amazonian legends were told by anxious Greeks fearful of a female-led power on their northern borders. Although it may seem on the surface unlikely that beliefs and symbols of such a remote past could have survived as cultures came and went in the area, religion can be, as archeologist James Mellaart says, "notoriously tenacious when left undisturbed." Anatolia, the plain of Turkey, was a mountainous place where old beliefs could survive in relative isolation. Indeed, today's Turkish kilim rugs use patterns traceable to goddess religions of nine thousand years ago, perhaps the longest documented case of such survival.[5]

The goddess in question dates from the New Stone Age. She was worshiped in a Neolithic city-state on Anatolia's south-central Konya Plain—a city-state that thrived for two thousand years and that was rediscovered in an astonishing state of preservation in the middle of this century. Her name has been lost, as have the myths told of her. Usually interpreted in the conventional way, as an "earth mother," the goddess of Catal Huyuk was, her iconography shows, more cosmic than that label allows. She was as much, if not more, a goddess of the sun than of the earth.

This nameless goddess was shown both as a full-bodied woman and simply as a breast. All around her sanctuaries were women's breasts modeled in clay: often a single breast, sometimes a breast with teeth in its nipples, occasionally one with a bird's beak at its tip. When painted, the breasts were blood-red. Mellaart has argued that the breasts offer a visual pun on the beehive, representing queen-bee cells; indeed, the goddess in human form sometimes wears a beehive crown, and bees and their hives appear in some religious paintings. As we shall see, this connection of breast and beehive survived to classical times. During those later times, bees were believed "begotten of bulls," as Porphyry recorded; in Catal Huyuk paintings, too, we see goddesses removing swarms of bees from the nostrils of bulls. Around the breast images were horns, usually of bulls; some statues showed the goddess with legs spread out directly above these horns, suggesting that she was in the act of birthing animal life.

These ancient sanctuaries echo even more ancient religious art. W. I. Thompson sees Catal Huyuk as an uninterrupted development of Paleolithic cave art: the womb-cave at Lascaux, with its painted animals, transformed into a cave-like building with explicit statuary. Mellaart himself sees "undoubted links" between Catal Huyuk and such Upper Paleolithic sites as Beldibi, Kurtun and the Palali caves. Despite similarities, though, there is a major difference. The earlier caves—Lascaux and others—were painted nearly thirty thousand years ago, during the endless ages when we gathered wild plants and hunted the vast wild herds. Catal Huyuk flourished at that pivotal point when the new crafts of farming and husbandry permitted a more settled life.

This Neolithic revolution may have begun so that nearby herds would provide assured sacrifices for the goddess; the convenience of herding meat rather than hunting it was realized later. Complete domestication of herd animals, however, ran counter to the animals' biological tendencies—in particular, to the tendency of male animals to fight for access to females in estrus. Early herdsmen must have been in frequent danger during the rutting season. Perhaps male calves were, at first, simply killed to avoid trouble. But, however tasty veal might be, such a practice resulted in wasted meat in a marginal economy. Productive husbandry, then, relied upon an important discovery: castration.

We now take for granted the knowledge that testosterone is responsible for both aggressive mating behavior and sperm production, and that sperm provides genetic material. But these facts are far from obvious to the naked eye; we cannot cut open a testicle to see hormones, or even sperm, within. Some early genius may have noticed that a calf accidentally injured in the testicles behaved more calmly than other male cattle thereafter, and grew into a larger, fattier specimen. This herder then, to cut losses caused by hormone-plagued bulls while providing the greatest amount of meat, extended the clipping service to other young males in the herd. Later it may have become clear that calves inherited characteristics of unaltered bulls rather than steers, so that selective breading was undertaken.

There is no evidence that human castration rituals occurred prior to the Neolithic agricultural revolution ; these rituals were, we may assume, derived from husbandry techniques rather than the other way round. Castrates, by one bold action, made themselves into steers in the goddess's herd. Therefore, the meaning of the horns that deck the sanctuaries at Catal Huyuk is more ambiguous than has been supposed by those who interpret them simply as symbols of virility. They are not shown as part of complete animals, so there is no way of knowing whether steers or bulls are intended. If they belonged to steers, they would be symbols not of reproductive strength but of food; the sculptured breasts would be parallel symbols, for women's mammaries provide nourishment but have no reproductive function. Just as the goddess-mother made food out of herself, castrated steer-men made themselves into her food. Their identity with the goddess is more complex than simply that both lack testicles.

Though we do not know whether ritual castration was practiced at Catal Huyuk, the goddess there and in Rome was the same. That she was a sun goddess is suggested by the solar discs found in Alaca-Huyuk, a Neolithic site near Catal Huyuk. In the Neolithic city itself, Mellaart found sculptures of a heavy-set woman seated between two lionesses: the very image of Cybele seven millennia later, as Mellaart himself has argued. These "bull-killing lions," as a Roman prayer calls them, are the familiar emblems of the solar goddess.[6]

The route of transmission from Catal Huyuk to Rome was through the Hittites, in whose legends we find the Amazon mythologem of the queen who had sixty children, thirty boys and thirty girls; the boys she left to die on a riverbank, while keeping the girls near her. These Hittites built an empire in Anatolia two millennia after the fall of the Neolithic cities of the plain. They called the goddess Khipa or Khebe at first, then Kubabas, and finally, in late Hittite times, Kubaba, the closest ancestor to Cybele. The Hittite goddess mounted on two lions both harkens back to the great mother of Catal Huyuk and foreshadows the Romanized Cybele.

Who were these Hittites, transporters of an ancient sun goddess through vast ages? A century ago they were known only from a single Biblical reference, and were thought to have been a minor tribe. But such was far from the case. It is one of the fascinations of prehistory that vast empires can be erased for millennia. The empire of the Hittites began to be reclaimed after almost four thousand years, when, early this century, excavators located the royal archives of the Hittite capital of Hattusus, now Boghazkoy. Dating from 1400 to 1200 B.C.E., most of the writings in this treasure trove are religious texts; many of them were found in a single temple. Although only a fraction of the texts have been translated and published, they clearly deal with a religion centered on a sun goddess.

The Hittites called her by many names, using titles adopted from other languages as well as names in their own language. She was Gasania, "My Lady." Or Estan, later a sun god's name. Or Wurusemu, a name inherited from earlier people. Or Hepat, from "the far country, that which you made the land of cedars," as a prayer addressed her. Most commonly, she was "the Sun Goddess of Arinna, my Queen, Queen of all countries" or Arinitti, the name derived from her city. The location of Arinna is not known, but it is thought by Garstang to have been the center of a sacred territory whose queen was priestess of a famous solar shrine.

Shrines to the Hittite sun goddess were carved on rock outcroppings; upright stones, called *huwasi* in Hittite, were engraved with sun signs in her honor. At Yazilikaya, near Boghazkoy, an especially impressive shrine shows a parade of divinities headed by the sun goddess. Standing on a lioness, she has a high crown of rays; she is followed by two identical but smaller female figures, perhaps her daughter, Mezullas, and granddaughter, Zuntehis. Few statues of any material but stone have been found, presumably because those made of precious metals were later melted down. Those few, however, show the goddess in a gracious open posture, a bird-like winged sun as her headdress. She also appears emblematically on Hittite "standards," or staff-heads, which are topped with a rayed disc, and, in the disc-shaped idols, covered with concentric circles, found at Kultepe.

She was called the land's father and mother; she was the judge who allotted to each person exactly what he or she deserved. Even the gods received their power from her, in return for which they opened and closed the door of heaven as she passed into the sky. Her servants were the fortune-tellers Istustaya and Papaya, who divined the length of a king's reign or a worker's hard life by their magic mirrors and spindles.

As goddess of fate, the sun was naturally queen of the dead. It was to her that funeral services were offered. Otten has reconstructed, from Hittite fragments, a funeral that apparently took two full weeks. Conducted by an old woman, the funeral started with sacrifices of oxen and goats; the fiery offerings went on overnight. Then, at dawn, women quenched the fires and ate and drank to the soul of the dead. A human figure made of fruits—figs, raisins, and olives—was placed on the pyre and filled with food and drink. The priestess balanced gold and silver on a scale with mud, calling out to the judge of souls, the Sun Goddess of the Underworld, to offer salvation to the deceased. Thus the deceased were seen off to their next lives.

The sun goddess was ruler of the heavens; reflecting her status, the early Hittite queens were often powerful rulers. The seal of the Hittite-Egyptian treaty in 1271 B.C.E. showed the goddess embracing the queen, with the words "seal of the sun goddess of Arinna, seal of Putukhipi, great queen of Khatti, daughter of the land of Kizawaden, mistress of the city of Arinna, mistress of the land, mistress of the goddess." Not just the sun's chief priestess, the queen was considered identical with the goddess; her title was Tawanannas, "Mother Goddess." Later, however, the queen lost power to a king-consort. The transfer of power is reflected in the Apology of Hattusilis, in which the goddess appears to queen Puduhepa in a dream, telling her, "I will make your husband priest of the sun goddess of Arinna," thus making him closer to divinity than even the dreamer was.

Similarly, whereas in early times the consort of the sun goddess was subject to her, over centuries he became more prominent. This god controlled storms, rainfall and other weather. He appears iconographically as a bull or steer, although no Hittite bull-myth has yet been unearthed. In myth, he was an Attis-figure, a damaged or impaired god. In one important myth, he was attacked by a snake that stole his heart and eyes—possibly in proxy for his genitals. A mortal, enlisted by the goddess, tied up the serpent, whereupon the Weather God killed it. The tale of the snake's killing was recited during Purulluyas, the Hittites' greatest festival —so important an event that King Mursilis II once stopped a war to celebrate it.

In the Weather God's other important myth, he appears as what Hans Gustav Guterbock calls the Vanished God, for the story concerns his disappearance from earth. At Nerik, in central Anatolia, the Weather God withdrew from earth, either in fright or in anger, by hiding in a hole or cave; his departure took away life and fertility, which were restored only when another weather god banished him forever. In another version of the story the god, here called Telipinu, took all the growing grain with him when he disappeared. All the gods ate and drank, but could neither fill their stomachs nor quench their thirst. At last the goddess sent a bee to find the god; he was located beneath a tree and stung awake. Telipinu woke in a rage, but the goddess Kamrusepas healed him of his anger. His feast, we are told, was celebrated by setting up an evergreen in a temple and hanging a sheep's fleece on it.[7]

The bee sent to raise the Weather God appeared again in Anatolian Ephesus, where priestesses were known as *Melissae* (bees), and castrated priests as *Essenes* (drones), in a hive led by the Queen Bee Goddess herself. This goddess, known as Artemis or Ephesia, was sculpted as a strong matronly woman covered with globes, which, as we've seen, are usually interpreted as breasts or testicles—apparently amputated ones, so unnatural is their position on the goddess's body. But Mellaart has argued that the nippleless so-called breasts are, in fact, bee-cells, pointing out that the queen of the area was named in classical sources as Omphale, which means "beehive." There are many other Ephesian bee connections: Porphyry explained that souls were born, in the form of bees, from Artemis; the bee was said to have been domesticated by an Attis-like boy, Aristaeas ("the noble one" or "the best boy"), lover of the goddess; rosettes formed of headless bee bodies were found in the ruins of the Artemisium.

Tombs shaped like beehives were common in the area. Perhaps it was known that honey preserved the body against decay; priestesses surrounding the drones, sexual slaves of the goddess, would make the honey of immortality for him. The tree, in this symbolic system, could become a home for bees only after it died or fell; castration was therefore connected with a yearning for immortality, the organ providing a "fallen tree" for the honey of life. Honey is also, obviously, sweetly edible; the motif of provision of food from flesh here recurs.[8]

The bee-stung Vanishing God was ancestor to Attis, as were other Hittite divinities to Phrygian descendants. Attis's story appears elsewhere in the eastern Mediterranean, most prominently in Ugarit of the fourteenth century B.C.E., during the Hittite empire's height. In the Ras Shamra texts, the goddess is named Anat, called as Cybele was the "Lady of the Mountain." She was the lover of her brother, the weather god Baal, who bested a threatening serpent, Lothan, in a contest reminiscent of the Hittite Purulluyus.

But the god had to vanish, and so Baal did. After a fight with Mot, god of sterility, Baal disappeared, taking with him all the world's vegetation. His sister-lover begged the help of the sun goddess, Shapash, to free Baal. Together they hunted through the mountains. Weeping and sorrowing, Anat "desired (her brother) as doth a cow her calf or a ewe her lamb." At length, Anat and Shapesh found the body of Baal on the plain of Shlmmt. Anat sat down and cried, "Baal is dead! Baal is dead!"

She took his body to the heavenly mountain Sapan, then descended to search for his murderer. It did not take long. Finding Mot, she seized him, ripped off his clothes, and demanded her brother's soul. He admitted he had devoured it—that he was guilty of "making him like a lamb in his mouth and crushing him in his jaw like a kid." In revenge, Anat killed Mot with a sickle and ground him in a mill, then scattered his flesh over the fields like grain for the birds to eat.

This performed the miracle: Baal was released into life again. But Mot was not, as it turned out, dead. As soon as Baal was alive again, sterile Mot revived. Baal, paralyzed with fear, refused to fight, but Shapash, the sun goddess, urged Baal on until he attacked Mot like a serpent. They fought furiously, until Shapash intervened. She demanded that Mot return to the underworld, for it was Baal's time to reign on the earth. And so the god of sterility left the earth's surface.

The Ras Shamra texts found on the Dead Sea divide the Weather God into two gods; whereas among the Hittites it was the retreat of Telipinu that left the earth sterile, in Ugarit another character caused the earth's devastation. Similarly, the dismemberment necessary to restore the earth's fertility was displaced onto another god. A similar displacement took place in Anatolia itself, among the Hurrians, for whom it was the Weather God's father who was emasculated. In this tale, the Weather God was born when the god Kumarbi castrated the all-father, Anu, by biting his testicles off. Told he'd become pregnant by swallowing the semen, however, he spit the testicles out again. The earth received the falling testicles and gave birth to the Weather God. This story, traveling to Greece with the Phoenicians, became that of Uranus and his son Kronos.

The Weather God, in these myths, is a dying-and-reviving deity similar to others beloved of goddesses in the eastern Mediterranean. Whether the name used was Tammuz, Dumuzi or Adonis, the story was the same: The god disappeared, the goddess sought him, and the earth was sterile until he returned. In ritual, devotees mourned the god's death, then exulted at his resurrection. In Syria, the boy-god Adonis was honored with the spring planting of potsherd "gardens"—herb seeds in broken pots—named after him. The plants flourished immediately, but just as quickly died, to great lamentation. Given that the dead were buried in pots, these potsherd gardens seem a clear plea for rebirth, of death's hold broken.

The cult had a wide following: in Alexandria the festival of Adonis was celebrated by the wedding of two statues, followed by violent sorrow over Adonis's death. In Hierapolis, red was hung all through the city during the festival; women cut their hair and wept inconsolably. Afterwards, to great rejoicing, Adonis was declared alive. In Syria, Adonis, after making love to Aphrodite, was gored to death by a wild boar—likely the equivalent of castration, considering where a boar might plunge its tusks; Heradotus says Atys was killed in the same way.

Tammuz, another Vanished God, died after the goddess Ishtar made love to him; thereafter she turned every lover into a eunuch immediately. Clearly no man could enjoy a mortal woman after making love with his goddess; castration would certainly assure that. And there is evidence of castration rituals dedicated to Tammuz; men chosen by the goddess thus pledged complete fidelity.

These maimed gods, Joseph Campbell contended, represent the moon; and indeed, Tammuz was so described. It should then follow that the goddess-lover in this cosmic pair is the sun.

In these myths, castration can be seen as a plea for rebirth: The sun monthly dismembers the moon, but he returns whole a few weeks later. In the same way, a man's offering his testicles to the goddess recreates the marred body of the moon god and thus assures her recognition of the worshiper's quest. Why else would a man, in the prime of his sexual life, risk death to castrate himself with a crude implement? But if he could become, by a single knife stroke, a surrogate brother-lover to the sun, would that not be worth the pain and loss? For would not the sun restore her brother—and grant the human worshiper immortality?

But if part is to stand for whole, and the quest is rebirth, why not cut off the tip of the little finger? Why the testicles? Why not a less vital portion of flesh? And was rebirth really the quest? There is no evidence for the rebirth of Attis; for Adonis, the evidence is only tenuous; and the goddess actually came for her lover Dumuzi to kill him. But, after the god's death, fertility is restored to the land; people prosper and live happily. The castrated god, then, sacrifices his male portion for a greater good, just as the Christian god offers his life for human salvation. The *gallus*, becoming half a man, is more than a man; he is a liminal being, not male nor female, neither truly human nor yet divine. For some, clearly, the sacrifice was worth the pain and loss.[9]

Simple individual rebirth therefore does not seem to have been the intent of the rituals. Rather, the aim was transformation: of the man into a *gallus*, of the sterile earth into a flowering one. Similarly, the amputation of a breast—which may have occurred in ritual, but certainly occurred in myth—would transform the woman. Breast-tearing, as Flugel points out, is the female corrollary to castration. Although, unlike a castrate, the breastless woman can bear children and suffers no hormonal changes, she alters her most obvious secondary sex characteristic. Like the castrate, she becomes liminal, the more so because she has destroyed the body's symmetry. She has become an artificially constructed being, not simply woman, certainly not man.

Becoming one-breasted, too, a woman becomes like the sun. We need only look overhead to see that the solar globe cannot represent two breasts. A single orb hangs there, nursing us with its light. This vision of the sun as a breast is one that appears most obviously in the sun-sister stories but occurs as well in lands like the Baltic, where the sun is depicted as a vessel full of milk—a food which, like meat, is created by bodily transformation. When the arctic sun-maiden demands that her brother eat her breast, she articulates what all mothers know: that she makes food of herself. Tearing off the breast changes her into her brother's mother; it also transforms the milk source into meat. Similarly, the *archigalli* makes himself a steer, a source of meat, for his goddess. Bloody and unsettling as these myths are, they bear the spiritual knowledge that some must sacrifice that others may eat and live.

The Greek Amazon, then, brought forth into historic times the image of a liminal woman, her single breast recalling the sun-mother's sacrifice to nurture us. But how was this image conveyed to the Greeks, who had no knowledge of the buried city of Catal Huyuk with its sacred breasts? The image was conveyed through yet another tribal people of the area. On the Greeks' northern borders lived, not the tribe of fierce women warriors the Greeks feared, but a nation best known today for its breathtaking golden jewelry. Here was the land of the Thracians, worshipers of the sun-breast. The breast was the most important solar image in Thrace. Early gold work showed the solar orb with breasts; similarly, women's breasts were sculpted with radiating lines like solar rays. Later, Thracians carved the sun with many breasts, a form recalling Ephesian Artemis hung with breasts or testicles. More than a hundred Thracian breast sculptures have been found in a solar temple on the mountain peaks above Hlyabvo, placed so that they would catch the first rays of the morning sun.

The Thracian religion has not been comprehensively studied, but we know it centered on sacred groves where orgies were held in honor of the goddess and her son-lover. One of the names of this goddess was Bendis; this word, meaning "to tie," is said to indicate her oversight over matrimony, an assumption that directly counters her bounds-breaking orgiastic rituals. What, then, did Bendis tie? The goddess was depicted holding a twig, which was said to grant passage to the underworld. We have seen this twig already, as an emblem of the heavenly sky-rope in Australia; it also appears as part of the Tree of Life. Tying or binding to a tree is a motif that informs one of Attis's most important myths, in which the Thracian god Dionysus tied the genitals of the sacred hermaphrodite Agdistis to a tree so they would be torn off.

This remote connection through Agdistis is not the only link between Dionysus and Cybele. In both Greece and Rome, Dionysus was honored in Thracian-style orgies similar to those of Cybele's. Called both a man and a woman, he was a liminal being, like the *galli*. He was presented women's attire by the goddess at a place called Cybla; his mother may in fact have been Cybele herself, for although her name is recorded as Semele, the Thracian *b* and *m* often replaced each other. Like Attis, Dionysus ended his days in torment after being castrated by Titans. Finally, although currently described as the god of wine, Dionysus may originally have been the god of honey-based mead, for he is depicted in early art wearing a neckpiece of honeycombs or crowned with a swarm of bees; he is said to have originated beekeeping. The god is therefore connected in many ways to the queen-bee goddess of castrates.

The Dionysian religion descended from Thrace into Greece in early historic times. Women especially were drawn to the rites, celebrated on mountaintops and often including the dismemberment of animals in frenzied abandon. The slit-eyed maenad, wearing across her shoulders the lion's pelt she tore from the living animal, her head thrown back in ecstasy, appears throughout Greek art. But her religion was persecuted and oppressed by the emergent patriarchy. She may have struck back—in an especially appropriate way, if we find historic truths in the myths of Pentheus, who was dismembered by his own mother when he spied upon the women's secret rituals, and Orpheus, who was beheaded by maenads as he sang his paeans to Apollo. It is also possible, however, that dismemberment has been wrongly interpreted by those who view it as a horrific punishment. A myth from Phrygia suggests that Dionysian dismemberment was a sacred act that could lead to rebirth. This is the myth of Medea.

In distorted form, the myth became a familiar topic for Greek tragedians. Originally a goddess of fire and the sun, Medea was transformed into a witch-princess who collaborated with the argonaut Jason. This hero had to fight "monsters" that recall ancient goddess-linked animals of the area. First he had to subdue fire-breathing bulls; then he fought a serpent to win a fleece hung upon a tree; the bulls, serpent and hung fleece are clear survivals of the Hittite myths of Telipinu. Then, escaping on his ship, the Argo, Jason turned to Medea to save himself and his crew from pursuers who would reclaim the Golden Fleece.

And how did Medea save them? She decapitated her brother, then dismembered his body and threw him—piece by bloody piece—into the water so that, stopping to collect portions of prince, her pursuers were unable to capture the fleeing Argo. She and her hero were then married in the very cave where the infant Dionysus (another dismemberment victim) had been nursed as a child. The story goes on to Greece where a ruined Jason is killed by a piece of the rotted Argo falling on his head, but the later events are less obviously connected with Thracian and Phrygian religious traditions.

Dismemberment, in this interpretation, was a powerful prayer for re-memberment. That Medea could have re-membered her brother is clear from a later incident in her myth. Visiting the king Pelias, Medea convinced his daughters to give the old man a new life. Easy, she told them: Cut him up into pieces, put him in a pot, and he'll pop out good as new. Even better, she said, he'll be restored by the experience. To prove how easily it was done, she cut up an old ram and boiled it; it leaped out as a newborn, frisky lamb. The princesses set to work dismembering their father—not, one would imagine, without the king's loud objections—but Medea somehow forgot to show them how exactly the trick was performed, and the old man's parts stewed sadly in front of his children.

The fact that it is her brother whom Medea dismembers may be important in interpreting the myth; an incest theme may hide here. Indeed, the later religion of the area, discernible through the folktales and folkways of Georgia (formerly Colchis), involved ritual incest as one of its basic elements. Indeed, sibling incest had an official status within Georgian mountain society: "Brother-husband" and "sister-wife" were the names given to young lovers doomed never to marry. In myth, too, it was said that incest was established by Tamar, a sun goddess who rode, like Medea, on a serpent with a golden saddle, bit and bridle. In addition, worship services to the lightning divinity, K'op'ala, required mock incest to take place between couples who called themselves by sibling titles.

Sexuality, especially taboo sexuality, is part of the Medea myth. The name of this goddess, usually translated as "wisdom," also means "genitals," and seems to pun on the connection between them. This myth tells us, indeed, that there is a deep wisdom in sexuality; it tells us that there is potential rebirth in what seems to be the bloodiest of deaths; like myths of North America and Australia, it tells us that there is a way to experience rebirth that is behind and beyond the visible pathways on the earth, a way unspeakably dangerous and taboo, but available to those with sufficient courage or desperation to take it.[10]

Medea's myth thus points again towards the bloody rituals of self-mutilation that we encountered in Asia as on other continents. Like the Christian communion, these rituals connect eating with salvation; unlike the later rites, however, they connect sex with both. For the wisdom of the genitals was not simply the astonishing recreation of life from itself. The wisdom was that life feeds upon life in order to survive. Reproduction demands death, for death creates food: Without sap of plants, blood of animals, the sexual being will not live to continue the species. Similarly, without light, the sun-mother's sap and blood, her people could not live. And without death, they could not travel with her beneath the earth to a new rising.

The connection of sex to mother's milk, of eating to both life and dying, was sufficient mystery for most people. But what of the bold ones, those who sought even deeper wisdom? For them, there was a secret path. It allowed them to join Mother Sun without dying, to move with her through the sky as they moved through the fields and woodlands of earth, to offer fertility to the world while pleading for rebirth. The gate to their pathway was so terrifying that few risked it. But some who did found the secret: that at the earth's center was a tree, one that allowed movement in all directions simultaneously. It was the way up and the way down at the same time, the path to the dreamtime, the way to rememberment. The Amazon and the *archigallus* both achieved a wondrous feat: They each made of the human body a road to the sun, created a living image of the ascent to the radiant sun-mother above and the descent to the hidden underworld traveler. These liminal beings bore a message emblazoned where all could see: that death is a door through which we must pass in order to be reborn, that we can travel the sun's dark journey into night knowing that a new dawn shimmers at its end.

Epilogue

WHEN THE GODDESS SMILES, SHE BARES HER TEETH

We have looked at reflections of the sun goddess in her myths, as though looking at the sun in a mirror. And now it is time to look directly into the sun's face.

What do we see when we stare straight at the goddess? As our eyes adjust to her light, we distinguish a round bright face, a face like a metal disc. Around it, hair flies in all directions like a halo. But this is no static corona: No, the flames twist and turn, like snakes.

Does she look familiar?

Doesn't she look like Medusa?

The mortal Gorgon, decapitated by the hero Perseus, is a familiar figure of Greek mythology—sufficiently so that most accept unquestioningly the standard definition of her as a Hellenic bogey, a cursed human transformed into an inhuman monster. Few simply look at Medusa and ask, what does she look like?

Let us consider this simple answer: She looks like the sun.

We have shown that the sun goddess was found in many parts of the world, in forms ranging from the mirror goddess to the heavenly spinster to the incestuous Amazon. And, despite Apollo's primacy, the Greek pantheon, too, included the solar feminine. To locate the sun goddess there, all we need to do is what Perseus could not: to look, to simply look, at the visage of the goddess.

The philosopher Helene Cixous dared to look upon the Gorgon's face, dared to gaze into those apotropaic eyes, to look upon that terrifying visage that indicates the point at which we must stop and seek no further. And Cixous did not find petrifying this confrontation with the face at the edge of received knowledge. Rather, Medusa is to the philosopher an antidote to the paralysis of patriarchal thought. Cixous emerges from her encounter with the Gorgon not only unscathed but empowered. Medusa, she reports, is "not deadly. She's beautiful, and she's laughing."[1]

Medusa is a fitting emblem of our search for whatever our culture wishes to keep hidden, whatever images of female power the culture finds too threatening to permit. Wherever her grimacing countenance appears, we should proceed most fearlessly, for Medusa hides the treasures. These include those hidden images of divine femininity heretofore suppressed by dualistic thinking.

One of these—a most powerful one—is the image of the sun goddess.

Medusa, that snake-haired petrifier who warns us against forbidden knowledge, holds in her very image the revolutionary idea of female solarity. The Gorgon is a sun image *par excellence*. Her visage—a circle surrounded by rays—is eminently solar. Even more importantly, her myth includes numerous images of solar femininity. Like the Japanese Amaterasu, she is associated with mirrors, the mirrors that appear on the costumes of Siberian shamans, where they are connected with the inner eye of visions. The power of Medusa's eye turns viewers to stone, as does that of the Scandinavian Sunnu. Medusa's hair is coiled with serpents; the snake, especially when seated on the head, is associated with Egyptian Hathor, feted with ritual mirrors. Medusa is the child of incest between brother and sister; she suffers dismemberment but gives birth at the moment of her death. Medusa is a veritable lexicon of female sun images.

How did these images join to form the unforgettable figure of the Gorgon? To understand, we must look at the accretion of details that finally forms the Medusa myth of classical times. In that oft-told tale, the mirror-wielding hero Perseus, instructed and equipped by Athene, decapitates snake-haired Medusa, who in dying gives birth to the winged horse Pegasus. This story, so familiar as to seem more ancient, is in fact the result of almost a millennium of literary and artistic creation, in which solar symbols were incorporated into a primal goddess myth.

Medusa was originally a cosmic goddess whose domain included the sun. Such a goddess held sway in Mycenean times, or even earlier. For Medusa is pre-Olympian; her worship predated the arrival of the Hellenes in the peninsulas and islands of Greece. Most of her myth, as we now have it, dates from approximately the eighth to seventh centuries B.C.E. Her image probably traveled to Greece from its original homeland, although the land of ultimate genesis is subject to argument. Some argue Medusa to be African in origin, possibly Egyptian; she was known in Sais as "mother of all the gods, whom she bore before childbirth existed." Others contend she originated in Assyria, with the story of the hero Gilgamesh dismembering the mother-goddess Humbaba; yet others locate the original in the same area, but place it as far back as the twenty-first century B.C.E. on the evidence of Sumero-Akkadian cylinder seals that show heroes beheading solar-maned demons. Some data connects Medusa with Crete, other with Anatolia. All these are areas where the sun goddess was acknowledged.[2]

Wherever Medusa's land of origin, she was a goddess of some import. Her name is from the same root as that of Medea, a word meaning "to know" or perhaps "to measure," suggesting her rulership over mind and time. But after the Hellenes gained power in her land, Medusa lost her earlier preeminence. Her fierce image was known in sculpture, but myths including her were scanty. Homer, in the ninth century B.C.E., knew of both Perseus and the Gorgon—he did not know her personal name—but recognized no connection between them. In fact, he barely recognized Perseus's existence at all; the lad was merely named among a passel of other heroes. Certainly Homer didn't mention of his summons by Athene to kill Medusa, nor of his use of the magical mirror in doing so.

Of the Gorgon, Homer knew more: He knew enough to fear her eyes. Whether she was thought to petrify people with her glance, or merely to undo them with terror, is unclear from the *Iliad,* in which her eyes are compared to those of the war god Ares as "destroying men." Homer called her visage, which appears on Agamemnon's shield, "shaggy-haired," but made no mention of snakes about the head.

Homer also indicates that the Gorgon's head appears alone, with no body beneath it. Whether this indicates that the Gorgon was envisioned only as a bodiless head, or whether we are to presume a beheading, is unclear. In Homer's time—actually, from as early as the archaic period—the Gorgon appeared in plastic art, too, only as a gorgoneion, or bodiless head. This image, Karl Kerenyi shows, brings together three motifs: the severed head; the winged disc or disc-faced divinity; and the mask. Of these, the first two are widely acknowledged solar symbols, suggesting that at her genesis Medusa was already connected with the sun.

Olympian Medusa, demoted into a mortal paramour of the sea god Poseidon, emerges in Hesiod, in the eighth century B.C.E. At this time she is one of three Gorgons; we hear of Perseus's heroic feat and of the birth of the giant Chrysaor and the winged horse Pegasus from Medusa's neck. The mirror, Athene's antagonism, the snaky hair, even the petrifying eye are absent, and it is clear that the Persean connection had been but recently forged.[3]

Egyptian influences, if they exist, would have occurred between the eighth and the seventh centuries B.C.E., when the Greeks made contact with Egypt; certainly the inscriptions to Medusa at Sais, near the beacon called by the Greeks "the Watchtower of Perseus," suggest that she was known there and that a connection to Perseus was recognized. In plastic art, we find the gorgoneion surmounted by snakes, like those indicating the solar Hathor of Egypt. The snakes appear on the shoulders, near the temples, or on the foreheads of the Gorgons—those on the foreheads especially recalling Hathor's uraeus serpent; they do not yet appear as hair.

By 580 B.C.E., the complete Gorgon—the Gorgon with female body as well as gorgoneion head—appeared at the Temple of Artemis in Corcyra. In a running swastika pose, she had wings on both her sandals and her shoulders. Her tongue protruded; her eyes stared ferociously; snakes danced near her forehead. Her human and equine offspring, Chrysaor and Pegasus, were tucked under her arms. No mirror, however in the picture, and the snakes had not yet migrated to the hair.

The beheading, when finally pictured in art and literature, was a bloody struggle that pitted Perseus against the full force of the Gorgon's strength and fury. Kraters were painted with gruesome scenes of winged bodies falling lifeless before flashing swords, and of infuriated, bereaved Gorgon sisters pursuing the hero-murderer. But in the fifth century B.C.E., an alternative version developed in which the Gorgon was killed while she and her sisters slept. Visual art developed away from the terrifying Medusa towards the beautiful one—asleep, with a calm face, only her snaky hair showing her terrible nature. Funtwangler has charted two developments of this image: the peacefully beautiful Medusa, from the end of the fifth century B.C.E., and the pathetically beautiful Medusa, from the third century B.C.E. In these, the only vestige of the ancient monster goddess was the writhing snakes that formed her hair.

It was apparently about the fifth century B.C.E. that the mirror-shield was added to the story—doubtless by a writer or storyteller rather than by an artist, for the mirror-shield appeared in legend before being visually depicted. There were no known visual representations of the Persean mirror until a full hundred years later. An inventive artist, attempting to add a solar mirror in the form of a shield, would quickly have discovered that distortion from a convex mirror would threaten Perseus's aim; and an artist might also have found it difficult to convey exactly how Perseus was holding the shield in order to use it as a mirror while simultaneously effecting a beheading. When, in the fourth century B.C.E., mirrors finally appeared in Persean art, the scene shown was not the murder itself, but the hero examining the reflection of the amputated head in a shield-mirror, apparently to protect himself against the still-active evil rays of Medusa's eyes.

It seems clear, then, that a poet, not a painter, added the mirror detail to the murder scene. Pherecydes of Athens, Euripides and Lycophron have all been named as likely candidates. The exact date, however, remains unclear, with the earliest datable literary reference occurring not until the first century B.C.E., in Ovid, who refers to the Medusan mirror as "polished bronze...the shield (Perseus) wore on his left arm." Ovid is also recognized for adding the detail about Medusa's snaky hair, as well as the information that Athene was behind the murderous plot on the Gorgon's life. Even so, the story as we know it was not utterly complete, for the evil glance of the Gorgon was as yet simply fearsome, not petrifying. Not until the second century A.D. does Apollodorus describe Medusa's petrifying stare; soon including this detail became *de rigeur*. Thus the entire myth took the better part of a millennium to construct.[4]

In the early part of the common era, Medusa lost her mythic power as new religions arose. But the Gorgon's image re-emerged from time to time over nearly two thousand years, as that of a boogey-woman associated with female sexuality. An early bestiary tells how to capture a Gorgon: Wait until she has her head underground, then rape her from behind while cutting off her head. Later, European medieval theorists continued to see Medusa as female sexual energy; to them, Perseus's mirror represented the reasoning powers of the mind, encouraging separation of head from body. Dante put Medusa in Hell as a warning of what will happen if we succumb to sexuality.

The Renaissance had little use for Medusa except as an architectural motif, a decorative (and possibly apotropaic) device for lintels. But the Enlightenment brought Medusa's image back in full force. Painters relished the visual force of the snake-haired beauty, an image at once both seductive and revolting. Among the British Victorians, the connection of Medusa to sexuality was extended to a deliberate conflation of sexuality with danger of death; Medusa became a vision of sexuality's depredations, especially of syphilitic infection resulting from sex with prostitutes. *Fin-de-siecle* poets glamorized Medusa as a symbol of death as much as of sexuality.

Only a few years later, Freud—fascinated by Medusa—proclaimed the Gorgon to be simply "the terrible symbol of the female genital region." Her image, he explained, evolved from the primal encounter of the child with his mother's genitals. He—for the child must, in this interpretation, be male, considering what follows—naturally sees this hairy patch as a severed head surrounded by pubic-hair snakes, rather than as the more obvious inverted triangle found throughout ancient art to represent the female vulva. While it is unclear under what circumstances, and from what perspective, the child could encounter this fearsome image, Freud believed the result to be spontaneous and inexorable: phallic petrification, which leads, spontaneously and inexorably, to fear of castration. "To decapitate=to castrate," Freud carefully explained. The child then projects this primal fear onto the mother, imagining the gorgonian vulva sliced off. And *voila!* the vision of Medusa.

Snakes are, in such interpretations, always seen as amputated phalluses. What *were* they doing, then, up around Medusa's head? Both position and gender are wrong. Sandor Ferenczi has a neat Freudian explanation for the swarm of writhing penises around the terrifying vulva-face: "Representation by the opposite" means that the mother has been castrated, the presence of the snakes proving it. The mother's lack of a penis is thus best demonstrated by a superfluity of them.

Today's feminists might apply Occam's razor rather than Perseus's sword to such theories. Feminists tend to see Medusa as a trope of female disempowerment at the hands of the patriarchy. Annis Pratt, for instance, interprets Medusa as primarily a "riddance" story, one in which "the beautiful and powerful women of the pre-Hellenic religions are made to seem horrific and then raped, decapitated, or destroyed." Many contemporary feminist poets and artists have adopted Medusa as an alter-image, and an empowering one. Artist Helen Kelebesadel finds Medusa an image of "the definitions of our Euro- and andro-centric culture…those things in myself that have paralyzed me." To many modern women, Medusa is the face of women's rage. May Sarton, a poet who identifies fiercely with Medusa, agrees; she calls the Gorgon's face "my face/…That frozen rage…what I must explore."[6]

Medusa is all these things and more; she is a rich symbol of female possibility. But one primary identity of Medusa is that of sun goddess. Although infrequently mentioned among scholars today, Medusa's solar nature has long been recognized. A. Frothingham, in 1897, noted that Medusa was usually shown with Apollo on early coins; that she alternated with him in temple pediments, appearing in the same place in the zodiac he occupied; that she was the favored mythic image for lamp handles. This led him to a simple conclusion: Medusa embodied "the productive and destructive forces of the sun and the atmosphere"; she was "an emblem of the sun-disk." E. R. Goodenough later pointed out how often mosaics were said by one observer to represent Apollo or Helios, by the next Medusa.[7]

Indeed, the snaky rays flying out from Medusa's circular face make her an obvious sun image. But, however obvious, her solar identity may seem, it has been disguised. For the myths told of her, violent and sexual as they are, have not meshed with the Apollonian vision of the sun as emblem of disdainful reason. Yet, when we compare her to other sun-goddess mythologies, the images become clearly solar. We will here examine Medusa's snaky hair, the mirror used by Perseus in his attack on her, and the winged white horse that is her offspring—all of them images of the sun found in cultures with which the Greeks had contact.

Although the serpent hairdo was, as we've seen, a late accretion to Medusa's image, today it is thought the distinguishing mark of the Gorgon. The solar suggestion, once introduced, became more obvious over time. Whereas snakes originally appeared only on the shoulders, by Pindar's time the serpents formed a nimbus around the Gorgon's entire head; in an archaic vase from Corneto, the disconnected writhing serpents are clearly not hair but sun's rays. These serpents recall the Egyptian uraeus, formed from the sun goddess Hathor when she was stripped of her solar vehicle and banished to the heads of the Pharoah. Since Medusa's snaky hair did not appear before Greek contact with Egypt, Hathor's asp may have suggested the Medusan hairdo.

Instead—or in addition—to an Egyptian genesis, Medusa's hairstyle may have had Cretan origins.[8] By the time of Ovid, Medusa's coronet of snakes was not hers by birth, but something bestowed upon her by Athene, supposedly as punishment for having illicit intercourse with her lover, Poseidon, in Athene's temple. A beautiful woman, Medusa was instantly transformed by Athene's curse: Snakes appeared in place of the unfortunate woman's hair.

And what, we may ask, gave Athene such power over snakes? The goddess of spinning had her own reptilian nature, embodied in the snake that coiled up next to her in a huge sculpture in her major temple, the Parthenon. Not only that: Athene was also said to have had a snake for a child—something of an embarrassment for a virgin goddess. This connection of goddess with serpent goes back to the oldest strata of Athene's multilayered identity, perhaps even as far back as Mycenae and Crete.

Athene's connections with the Gorgon go well beyond the snake image. Euripedes cuts out the mythical middleman and has Athene kill Medusa directly, and coins of Alexander the Great show Athene with a snake on her helmet; in some cases, the goddess is called by the Gorgon's own name, gorgo. The Athenian city goddess is herself a mirror of Medusa, born from Zeus's head as Pegasus is born from Medusa's. And, after Medusa's beheading, it is Athene who wears her image forever on her cloak as an aegis—or, tellingly, buries the head in the Athenian Agora.

If, as many argue, Athene had a Cretan origin, Medusa's link with the virgin spinstress creates an even firmer argument that Medusa was originally a sun goddess. Lucy Goodison has recently, and most cogently, argued that the Bronze Age Cretan solar divinity was female, rather than male, as has so often been assumed. This Cretan religious tradition linked snakes and the sun, unlike the later Hellenic opposition between them, found in the killing of the prophetic snake at Delphi by the newly solar Apollo. It is an intriguing possibility that Medusa was originally an aspect of Athene—or vice versa. Dual sun goddesses, one representing the fierce blazing sun while the other embodies the pacific, nurturing solar force, appear in other cultures. In some, like that of the Lithuanians and Letts, there is a strong hint that an older sun goddess is dispatched at winter solstice by her younger self or daughter. Such a conflict between sun goddesses could form a backdrop to the Persean legend as we know it. The Perseus cult at Mycenae may be important in this regard.

The Medusan snake-locks are found in another context, one that provides perplexing but intriguing possibilities. In Sri Lankan ecstatic cults, Gananath Obeyesekere found, priestesses with long, matted locks are convinced these locks are shaped like cobras. The locks are sometimes the gift of Kali, who had a hundred such snaky curls on her head. Obeyesekere interviewed a number of priestesses who claimed that matted, snaky locks suddenly appeared as they became aware of their gifts in trance and possession. Some, like the priestess Manci, use the locks for blessing and magic.

The connection of hair to snakes may be an archetypal one, for there are common superstitions about hair turning into snakes. Obeyesekere himself associates the snake-hair with the Tantric *kundalini* serpent, seeing the locks as representing repressed, transmuted sexuality. Like Freud, however, he interprets the sexuality embodied as masculine; he inclines towards interpreting the locks as more penises indifferent to location or gender. In support of this idea, he found that, despite the fact that the locks are in fact only matted hair, both the priestess and her observers described them as "tender fleshy growths" and believed that they would bleed if cut off. Such a belief is not, however, incompatible with a vision of the hair as snakes, rather than as misplaced penises. And snakes are a common symbol of female divinity.[9]

Although the link between the Gorgon's hair and the snaky locks of Sri Lankan ecstatic mystics might seem distant, another characteristic links Medusa to the black Kali of India. It is the protruding tongue, which we find in even the most ancient Gorgon figures and, as well, in

Kali's portraits. Sri Lankan mystics sometimes cut their tongues in order to more closely identify with the goddess Kali. The tongue offers a complex of interpretive possibilities, including food, sex and speech; it evokes multiple symbolic possibilities each time it appears.

Kali's first literary appearance is in 400 C.E. in the Devi Mahatmya, which tells the story of her birth from the goddess Durga's head—a motif which cannot help but recall both Athene's birth and Medusa's birth-giving. Kali was—and still is—worshiped in the form of a dancing goddess who wears severed heads around her waist or neck and whose lolling red tongue protrudes threateningly. Such an image could easily have derived from gorgoneions carried into India by Alexander the Great; conversely, the two images, the threatening Gorgon and Black Kali, may share the same original source. Although questions of cultural diffusion are notoriously difficult to argue, these eerily similar images suggest that much is yet to be learned about connections between and among ancient cultures.[10]

Medusa's solar mirror, too, hints at cultural transmittal in the ancient world. The mirror may, of course, simply be an obvious archetypal solar image that emerged in various cultures. Certainly more than one culture may have intuited the connection of a shining surface with the sun. Solar mirrors appear in Japan and Egypt, as well as among the Natchez and Incas in North and South America, respectively. But there is also the strong likelihood that Medusa's mirror connects her with other sun goddesses of the ancient Mediterranean, especially the Hittite Wurusemu, who was worshiped with solar mirrors. Syro-Hittite mirror goddesses are depicted on reliefs and seal cylinders; these frequently show the goddess holding a sun disc as well as a mirror.

To gaze into a mirror is to become aware of the power of sight and the reflective power of light. Many mirror goddesses, including Egypt's Hathor, are therefore eye goddesses; often the sun is seen as an eye in the sky. This solar eye occurs continually in the Medusa legend. Perseus is given a cap of invisibility by Athene, to protect him from being seen as he goes about his murderous deed. Once he arrives at Medusa's home, he finds the goddess and her sister Gorgons guarded by the three Graiai sisters, crones notable for having a single removable eye among them, which Perseus snatches to disable them. These Graiai are doubles of the Gorgons, for whereas the former had one eye among them, the latter had one sister with "a stony eye." And, as Tobin Siebers has pointed out, Perseus captured the vision of both pairs of sisters: Because of the common equation of eye and head, his theft of Medusa's head is equivalent to his theft of the Graiai's eye. Of course, Perseus also shut off Medusa's sight through death, thus truly stealing her vision.

Medusa is often cited as a personification of the evil eye, "the spiteful stare incarnate," the containment of malice in the form of an eye. Because of her association with eyes, she could remedy eye ailments; words used of the gorgoneion in Greek, Siebers says, "refer both to the evil eye and to its countercharms." Medusa's name alone could cure eye ailments, for one merely said, "I kill the Gorgon's face," and any foreign objects caught in the eye disappeared.

But it was not for curing that Medusa's eyes are best known: It is for killing. A mere glance from the Gorgon would turn the viewer to stone, as with her gaze the Scandinavian sun goddess Sunnu, made boulders out of dwarfs. This connection of sun, stone and eye is yet another solar motif in the Medusa myth. The petrification may be inspired simply by the fact that humans cannot look straight at the sun's disk without risking blindness. If so, however, one could save oneself from Medusa by simply averting the head or gazing elsewhere. And, indeed, in early art Perseus—not yet equipped with the solar mirror-shield—simply turns his head away before striking the mortal blow.

But, in other versions of the myth, it is not gazing upon Medusa that causes petrification; it is being gazed at by her. The myth of the Medusa gaze is thus related to other evil eye myths, in which glances function like poisoned darts. The fact that, in the classical story, Perseus needed a shield to divert the eye-rays suggests that the invisibility conferred upon him by the *kune*, Hades's vanishing hat, did not necessarily protect him from Medusa's eyes. As Hazel Barnes points out, it was important that Perseus not meet Medusa's eye; the eye contact would freeze him forever. And, as Edward Phinney notes, there is not a single representation of Perseus looking into Medusa's eyes—even after plastic art began to show her sleeping, with safely closed eyes.[11]

In sculpture, too, we find another connection between Medusa and other sun goddesses, but this one is more difficult to trace than the snake, the mirror and the eye. It is the horse Pegasus, the magical white steed who leaps from the neck of the goddess as her head is severed from her body. This horse figure is more intimately connected to Medusa than is generally recognized, perhaps because references to it slowly dropped away as other images—especially the snake and the mirror—were added.

But the horse was there at the beginning of Medusa's mythic life. In the earliest sculptures in which Perseus appears, he does not attack the snake-haired Gorgon of later times. Instead, as on the archaic Boeotian vase discussed by A. Frothingham, Perseus kills a Gorgon who looks very much like an ordinary woman—except that her hindquarters are those of a horse. In addition, we may look to the four carved gems from the sixth century B.C.E., described by John Boardman, which show a horse-bodied but Gorgon-haired creature. Medusa is, by these images, connected with another horse-goddess, who was the mate of Poseidon: Demeter.

Demeter is best known today as a corn-goddess who mourned the loss of her raped daughter Persephone. But many aspects of Demeter's myth suggest a submerged sun goddess: Persephone's name, which means "she who shines for all"; the wintery sterility of the earth during the goddess's grieving period; the return of fertility with the passing of Demeter's angry grief. And there are other, less obvious connections between Demeter and sun-goddess mythologies from other cultures. There is, for instance, the odd incident of Baubo's erotic jesting, which caused the grieving Demeter to smile and bring life back to the earth; the same story is told of solar Hathor in Egypt as well of Amaterasu-omi-Kami in Japan; and the Cherokee sun goddess Unelanuhi is brought back through expressive, erotic dancing.

It may have been this solar Demeter whom Pausinias observed as a horse-headed statue worshiped in a cave. Most remarkable about this statue, in terms of the Medusa-Demeter link, was the fact that images of snakes and other animals grew from its head. Demeter reputedly gained her horse shape because she was raped by Poseidon, the Olympian god of the seas; she then bore the first horse, as well as a daughter "whose name they are not wont to divulge to the uninitiated." The same tale is told of Medusa, who mated with Poseidon in Athene's temple; her offspring, the winged horse Pegasus and the hero Chrysaor, parallel those of Demeter.[12]

And here we have, perhaps, a hint at the origin of the dismemberment motif in the Medusa story. The severing of the head of Medusa, often interpreted as disempowering the primal goddess, may have had an original, and quite different, meaning. As we've seen, the gorgoneion existed before the image of the full-bodied Medusa. The gorgoneion may well have been, as Thalia Feldman argues, an archetypal image of fear. An experiment conducted at Xerkes Laboratory of Primate Biology shows that monkeys, exposed to a number of stimuli, invariably respond with intense fright to a severed head; a live person, sitting with body covered so as to give the impression of being only a severed head, elicited no such reaction.

And so the image of the gorgoneion may have spawned Medusa's myth. How, after all, did Medusa's head get separated from her body?

And why? Cutting off the head is, after all, not necessary to blind a monster; Odysseus poked a sharpened, burning log into the eye of the Cyclops, and that sufficed to permit the humans' escape. But decapitation is vital in the Medusa story. In no version of the story does Perseus kill, or blind, the Gorgon in any other way.

In the shamanic religions of Asia, those called to the craft must suffer a violent initiation that includes a visionary dismemberment, and especially decapitation, before being reborn in a new shamanic body. Interestingly, the emblem of Medusa's mate, Poseidon, is a trident, said to symbolize the sea; the same triple-pointed staff is found in Siberia and Korea to represent the Tree of Heaven, the connecting link between the three levels of the shamanic world. In Siberia, among the Buryat, a shaman's body was said to be made of "a mass of snakes," and pelts called snakes were hung from the shoulders of the shaman's costume. Among the Altaic people, ribbons attached to the shaman's cloaks were referred to as snakes, and among the Yakut similar ribbons were called hair. An ambiguous Siberian artifact is especially relevant here: It shows a sun-faced being, apparently a shaman, with snakes leaping towards, or from, the head. We should also note the chant "My serpent—my ancestor," which among the Evenki accompanies a sun-wise circling dance.

Once initiated, there was a way for the shaman to predict events that had not yet occurred, or to see things happening beyond the horizon. She used a mirror, one that brought the energy of the sun goddess to earth and that must be worn on the shaman's clothing at all times. This mirror is of such vital importance that shamanic rituals simply could not take place without it.[13]

And what connection does this ancient Siberian religion have to the Greek legend of Medusa? Freud may have been on the trail when he assumed that castration was invented to reinforce the incest taboo. He himself linked the goddess's decapitation with castration, though he said nothing about her incestuous conception. If, like Oedipus, Medusa is a distant relative of an ancient arctic sun goddess, we can find traces as well in those other polar stories in which the sun goddess cuts off her own breast when her incestuous relation to her brother is discovered. It is possible that, in Medusa, we have a vestige of an ancient circumpolar figure whose religion we now call shamanism.

The mirror of the shaman was called "the white horse of the shaman"—apparently it was a winged horse, for the shaman was said to fly upon the mirror. The horse sacrificed in shamanic rituals was virtually always white, believed to be the color most pleasing to heaven.

Therefore, Pegasus, sired by a god who carried the Tree of Heaven and leaping from the neck of his dismembered mother, may be a shamanic emblem of great antiquity. Traces of shamanism have been found in other Greek myths, although not previously in the Medusa tale, so that it is not impossible that this ancient goddess brought into Olympian times motifs of earlier millennia whose meanings were altered to fit the new religious ideals.

Rather than being a bleeding image of female disempowerment, Medusa may be read as an icon of rebirth, of mystic power, of initiatory prowess, of woman's sanctity. She may be one of the most ancient European symbols of women's spiritual abilities. As a female sun, she is certainly an empowering image of feminine potential. Where once the Gorgon warned us away from her treasures, now—her new body gliding on heaven's wings—Medusa calls for us to follow her.

Sources

NOTES TO CHAPTERS

Introduction

1   See Jessica Benjamin, *The Bonds of Love: Psychoanalysis, Feminism and the Problem of Domination* (New York: Pantheon Books, 1989), p.147; Camille Paglia, *Sexual Personnae: Art and Decadence from Nefertiti to Emily Dickinson* (New York: Vintage Books, 1991), chapter 1.

2   Monica Sjoo and Barbara Mor, *Great Cosmic Mother* (San Francisco: Harper and Row, 1986), p.25ff. Anne Baring and Jules Cashford, *The Myth of the Goddess: Evolution of an Image* (London: Viking Arkana, 1992), p.284.

3   For information on Apollo, see Homer, *The Iliad*; Yves Bonnefoy, *Mythologies* (Chicago: University of Chicago Press, 1991), p.462; ed. James Hastings, *Encyclopedia of Religion and Ethics* (New York: Charles Scribner's Sons, 1924), vol.I, p.23; Lewis Richard Farnell, *The Cults of the Greek States* (Chicago: Agean Press, 1961), vol.I, pp.316, 57; E. R. Dodds, *The Greeks and the Irrational* (Berkeley: University of California Press, 1968), p.152; William Tyler Olcott, *Sun Lore of All Ages* (New York: G. P. Putnam's Sons, 1914), p.199.

4   Roman material from Gaston Halsberghe, *The Cult of Sol Invictus* (Leiden: E. J. Brill, 1972), pp.28, 36; Franz Cumont, *Astrology and Religion Among the Greeks and Romans* (New York: Putnam's, 1912; Dover Publications, 1960), p.74; Frederick Williams, *Callimachus Hymn to Apollo: A Commentary* (Oxford: Clarenden Press, 1978), p.1ff; Jacquetta Hawkes, *Man and the Sun* (London: Crescent Press, 1962), p.195; Irach Taraporewala, "Mitraism," in *Forgotten Religions* ed. Vergilius Ferm (New York: Philosohical Library, 1950).

5   Paula Gunn Allen, *The Sacred Hoop: Recovering the Feminine in American Indian Traditions* (Boston: Beacon Press, 1986), p.19ff.

6   On the evolution of solar mythology, see Burton Feldman and Robert Richardson, *The Rise of Modern Mythology, 1680-1860* (Bloomington: Indiana University Press, 1975), pp.241, 279, 480; Andrew Lang, "Max Mueller," *Contemporary Review*, vol.78 (1900) p.785.

7   See Richard Dorson, "The Eclipse of Solar Mythology" in *The Study of Folklore* ed. Alan Dundes (Englewood Cliffs, N.J.: Prentice-Hall, 1965), p.82; Donald Ward, "Solar Mythology and Baltic Folksongs" in *Folklore International*, ed. D. K. Wilgus and Carol Sommer (Hatboro, Penn.: Folklore Associates, 1967), p.233; Stith Thompson, *The Folktale* (New York: Dryden Press. 1946), p.371; Miranda Green, *The Sun Gods of Ancient Europe* (Somerset: Hippocrene Books, 1991), p.12; Janet McCrichard, *Eclipse of the Sun* (Glastonbury: Gothic Image, 1990); Lucy Goodison,

Women, Death and the Sun (London: London Archeological Institute, 1989); Lucy Goodison, *Moving Heaven and Earth: Sexuality, Spirituality and Social Change* (San Francisco: Harper Collins, 1992); Rosalind Miles, *Women's History of the World* (Topsfield, Mass.: Salem House Publishing, 1989), p.45; Victoria Joan Moessner, "The Sun and Moon Were Man and Wife: Gender Interference in Translation" (Paper delivered to the American Association of Teachers of German, Berlin, 1986), p.5; Claude Levi-Strauss, "The Sex of the Heavenly Bodies," in *Structuralism: A Reader* ed. Michael Lane (London: Jonathan Cape, 1970) pp.330-332.

8   Carl Jung, *Essays on a Science of Mythology* (New York: Harper and Row, 1963), p.22.

Chapter One

1   Japanese myths are retold from Post Wheeler, trans., *The Sacred Scriptures of the Japanese* (New York: H. Schuman, 1952); and F. Hadland Davis, *Myths and Legends: Japan* (Boston: David Nickerson & Co., N.D.), p.195.

2   The one apparent exception is Incan Peru, where a mirror was said to represent a male sun divinity; even there, however, pre-Incan tribes held the sun goddess sacred and conveyed some of their beliefs to their conquerors.

3   Information on Japanese mirror cults and ritual is found in Charlotte Salway, "Japanese Monographs VI: The Use of the Mirror," *Asia Review*, 8: pp.402-8; Umehara Sueji, "Ancient Mirrors and Their Relationship to Early Japanese Culture," in *Acta Asiatica: Bulletin of the Institute of Eastern Culture*, vol.4 (Tokyo: The Toho Gakkai, 1963), p.72; Benjamin Goldberg, *The Mirror and Man* (Charlottesville: University Press of Virginia, 1985); Doris Roger, "The Divine Mirror of Japan," *Asia*, October: 1936, pp.650-57; Doris Roger, "Japanese Metal Mirrors: One of Nippon's Lost Arts," *Connoisseur*, vol.100, August 1937: pp.65-8.

4   From Donald Phillipi, *Norito: A New Translation of the Ancient Japanese Ritual Prayers* (Tokyo: Institute of Japanese Culture and Classics, 1959); Information on the shrine itself is available in an English-language pamphlet, *Guide to Jingu, Grand Shrine at Ise*, at the shrine.

5   Translations from Stuart D. B. Picken, *Shinto: Japan's Spiritual Roots* (New York: Kodansha International, 1980).

6   Some excellent sources on Shinto philosophy are J. W. T. Mason, *The Meaning of Shinto* (Port Washington, N.Y.: Kennikat Press, 1967); Jean Herbert, *Shinto: At the Fountainhead of Japan* (New York: Stern and Day, 1967). Other information is available in *New Larousse Encyclopedia of Mythology*, ed. Felix Quirand (New York: Hamlyn Publishing Group 1968). Michael Czaja, *Gods of Myth and Stone: Phallicism in Japanese Folk Religion* (New York: Weatherhill, 1974). Misahahu Anesaki, *Myths of All Races*, Japanese Mythology, vol.22 (Boston: Marshall Jones for the Archeological Institute of America, 1928); Misahahu Anesaki, *History of Japanese Religions* (Rutland, Vt.: Charles Tuttle Company, 1964); Horace Grant Underwood, *Religions of East Asia* (New York: Macmillan Company, 1910).

7   Carmen Blacker, *The Catalpa Bow: A Study of Shamanistic Practices in Japan* (London: George Allen & Unwin, 1975), p.34.

8   J. Edward Kidder, Jr., *Ancient Japan* (New York: John Day Company, 1965).

9   See Neil Munro, *Ainu: Creed and Cult* (New York: Columbia University Press, 1967); Basel Hall Chamberlain, *Aino Folktales* (London: Folklore Society XXII, 1888); and John Batchelor, *The Ainu of Japan* (London: The Religious Tract Society, 1892).

10 Yves Bonnefoy. *Mythologies* (Chicago: University of Chicago Press, 1991).

11 Denise Carmody, *Women and World Religions* (Nashville, Tenn.: The Parthenon Press, 1979); Felicia Gressitt Bock, *Engi-Shiki: Procedures of the Engi Era.* vols.I-V. Tokyo: Sophia University, N.D.).

12 Nahum Stiskin, *The Looking-Glass God* (New York: Weatherhill, 1971).

13 More information about Shinto rituals, especially as they involve the Hirohito family, is found in U. A. Casal, *The Five Sacred Festivals of Ancient Japan* (Rutland, Vt.: Charles E. Tuttle Company, 1967); Juliet Piggot, *Japanese Mythology* (London: Paul Hamlyn, 1969); and Harry Anderson, "Japan's Sacred Rice God," *Newsweek*, October 17, 1988: p.48.

14 Larry Gooding, *Shintoism in the Modern World* (Unpublished dissertation, University of Oregon, Department of Sociology, 1976), p.22.

15 Information on shamanism in Japan is best found in Carmen Blacker's *The Catalpa Bow*. Other sources are Mircea Eliade, *No Souvenirs: Journal, 1957-1969*. Trans. Fred H. Johnson, Jr. (San Francisco: Harper and Row, 1977); *Shamanism: Archaic Techniques of Ecstacy*, trans. Willard Trask (New York: Pantheon Books, Bollingen Series, vol.76, 1964); Ichiro Hori, *Folk Religion in Japan: Continuity and Change*. ed. Joseph Kitajawa and Alan Miller (Chicago: University of Chicago Press, 1968); Douglas G. Haring, "Chinese and Japanese Influences." in *Ryukyuan Culture and Society* ed. Smith, Allen H. (Honolulu: University of Hawaii Press, 1964); Kamata Hisako, "Daughters of the Gods: Shaman Priestesses in Japan and Okinawa." in *Folk Cultures of Japan and East Asia* (Tokyo: Sophia University Press, 1966).

Chapter Two

1   Information on Korean shamanism is relatively difficult to find in English. The following sources describe kuts: Yang Lee Yung, *Korean Shamanistic Rituals* (New York: Mouton Publishers, 1981), pp.30, 85, 124, 27-124; Laurel Kendall, *Shamans, Housewives and Other Restless Spirits* (Honolulu: University of Hawaii Press, 1986) pp.28-35; Huhn Halla Pa, *Kut* (New Jersey: Hollym International, 1983), pp.13-21; Alan Carter Covell, *Ecstacy: Shamanism in Korea* (Elizabeth, N.J.: Hollym International, 1983), pp.63, 102.

2   For the social history of Korean religion, see Charles Allen Clark, *Religions of Old Korea* (Seoul: Christian Literature Society of Korea, 1961), pp.174-77; Neil Munro, *Prehis-*

toric Japan (New York: Johnson Reprint Service, 1911), p.430; In-Hok Choi, *A Type-Index of Korean Folktales* (Seoul: Myong Ji University, 1979), p.6.

3   The place of women in Korean religion is discussed in Donam Hahn Wakefield, "Religious and Cultural Wellsprings of Korean Women," *Korea Journal*, May 1980: p.7; Tai-Dong Lee, "Princess Pari," *Korea Journal*, June 1978: p.5; Yoongsook Kim Harvey, *Six Korean Women: The Socialization of Shamans* (Saint Paul: West Publishing Company, 1979), p.11. See also Yung, p.5-7, 153; Kendall, *Shamans, Housewives and Other Restless Spirits*, p.94-101; Covell, *Ecstasy*, p.105.

4   Horace Grant Underwood, *The Religions of Eastern Asia* (New York: Macmillan Company, 1910), p.104.

5   The Tale of Grand-Aunt Tiger and its variants can be found in Zong In-Sob, *Folk Tales from Korea* (New York: Grove Press, 1953), p.7; Kim Yol-gyn, *Korean Folk Tales*, Korean Culture Series 7. (Seoul: International Cultural Foundation, 1979), p.29; Kathleen Seros, *Sun and Moon* (Elizabeth, N.J.: Hollym International, 1982), p.8; Wolfram Eberhard, *Studies in Taiwanese Folktales*. Asian Folklore and Social Life Monographs. vol.I. (Taipei: Orient Cultural Service, 1971), p.14.

6   Sources of information on aboriginal Korean religion are H. Hulbert, *The History of Korea* (Seoul: Methodist Publishing House, 1905), p.22; Tae-Hung Ha Ilyon, Tr., *Samyuk Yusa, Legends and History of the Three Kingdoms of Ancient Korea* (Seoul: Yonsei University Press, 1972), p.18; Mircea Eliade, *Shamanism: Archaic Techniques of Ecstasy*, trans. Willard Trask (New York: Pantheon Books, Bollingen Series, vol.76, 1964), pp.344, 449.

7   On Chinese mythology, see Donald McKenzie, *Myths of China and Japan* (London: The Gresham Publishing Company. N.D.), p.149; David C. Graham,*The Tribal Songs of the Ch'uan Mioa*. vol.102, Asian Folklore and Social Life Monographs, 1978. p.11; Sukie Colgrave, *The Spirit of the Valley: The Masculine and Feminine in Human Consciousness* (Los Angeles: J. P. Tarcher, 1979), p.42; Wolfram Eberhard, *Studies in Chinese Folklore and Related Essays* (Bloomington, Indiana: University Research Center for the Language Sciences, 1970), p.68; Kirchen Johnson, *Folksongs and Children's Songs from Peiping II*, Asian Folklore and Social Life Monographs. vol.17 (Taiwan: Orient Cultural Service, 1971), p.380.

8   For mirror superstitions see Sir James George Frazer, *The Golden Bough* (London: Macmillan, 1890; abridged edition (New York: Macmillan Company, 1959), p.332; Benjamin Goldberg, *The Mirror and Man* (Charlottesville: University Press of Virginia, 1985), p.4. Also Eliade, *Shamanism: Archaic Techniques of Ecstasy*, p.424.

9   Indian mythology is from Henry Whitehead, *The Village Gods of South India* (Calcutta: Association Press, 1916), p.23; Verrier Elwin, *Myths of the North East Frontier of India* (Shilloh: Northeast Frontier Agency, 1958), pp.1, 42.

10 Siberian shamanism and women's roles therein are discussed in V. Dioszegi and M. Hoppal, *Shamanism in Siberia* (Budapest: Akedemai Kiado, 1978), p.360, 436; Misahahu Anesaki, *Myths of All Races*. vol.22: Japanese Mythology. (Boston: Marshall Jones for the Archeological Institute of America, 1928. p.419; C. Fillingham

Coxwell, *Siberian and Other Folk-Tales* (London: The C. W. Daniel Company, N.D.), p.988; ed. V. Dioszegi, *Popular Beliefs and Folklore Traditions in Siberia* (Bloomington: Indiana University Press, 1968), pp.141, 424; O. Nohodil, "Mother Cult in Siberia," in Dioszgei, *Popular Beliefs*, pp.461, 491. Also Eliade, *Shamanism: Archaic Techniques of Ecstasy*, pp.69, 41, 321, 151-4, 498.

11 Goldberg, *Mirror and Man*, pp.4-10.

Chapter 3

1 See Benjamin Goldberg, *The Mirror and Man* (Charlottesville: University of Virginia Press, 1985), pp.25-26.

2 Sources of information on Egyptian mirror ritual are C. J. Bleeker, *Hathor and Thoth: Two Key Figures in the Ancient Egyptian Religion* (Leiden: E. J. Brill, 1973), p.22; G. Benedict, *Mirrors* (Cairo: CG, 1907), p.118; and Hickman, BIE, 37, 1956, pp.151-90.

3 Tina Troy, *Patterns of Queenship in Ancient Egyptian Myth and History* (Sweden: Uppsala University, 1986).

4 More information on Hathor, see Bleeker, pp.26, 65; ed. Hathor and Thoth, *New Larousse Encyclopedia of Mythology* (New York: Hamlyn Publishing Group, 1968), p.41; Rosalie David, *Cult of the Sun* (London, J. M. Dent and Sons, 1980), p.33; G. A. Wainwright, *The Sky-Religion in Egypt* (Westport, Conn.: Greenwood Publications, 1938), p.94; W. Max Mueller, *Myths of All Races*, Egyptian Mythology, vol.12 (New York: Cooper Union, 1964) p.88; W. I. Thompson, *The Time Falling Bodies Take to Light* (New York: St. Martins Press, 1987) p.232; Donald McKenzie, *Egyptian Myth and Legend* (London: Gresham Publishing Company n.d. xlviii). See also Troy, *Patterns of Queenship*, p.21-22; R. T. Rendle Clark, *Myth and Symbol in Ancient Egypt* (New York: Grove Press, 1960), p.219; Lawrence Parmley Brown, "The Cosmic Eyes," in *Open Court*, vol.33 (Chicago: Open Court 1981), p.688; O. S. G. Crawford, *The Eye Goddess* (Chicago: Delphi Press, 1991).

5 William Tyler Olcott, *Sun Lore of All Ages* (New York: G. P. Putnam's Sons, 1914), p.259.

6 Additional material on Egyptian goddesses is from Clark, *Myth and Symbol*, p.219; Mueller, Myths of All Races, p.29; Bleeker, *Hathor and Thoth*, p.29; McKenzie, *Egyptian Myth*, p.xxxviii; Olcott, *Sun Love*, p.60; M. Lichtheim, *Ancient Egyptian Literature: A Book of Readings*. vol.2: The New Kingdom (Berkeley: University of California Press, 1976), pp.197-98; Jaroslav Cerny, *Ancient Egyptian Religions* (London: Hutchinsons University Library, 1962), p.48; Lawrence Durdin-Robertson, *The Goddess of Chaldea, Syria, and Egypt*. (Ireland: Cesera Publications, 1976), p.27; E.A. Wallis Budge, *The Gods of the Egyptians*, vol.I. (New York: Dover Publications, 1969), p.448; Herodotus, *The Histories of Herodotus of Helicarnassus*, trans. Henry Carter (New York: Heritage Press, 1959), p.115.

7 Shirley Ardener, "A Note on Gender Iconography: The Vagina." in *The Cultural*

Construction of Sexuality, ed. Pat Caplan (London: Tavistock Publications, 1987), p.13ff.

8   For additional material on the Egyptian cat cult see David, *Cult of the Sun*, p.8. The rushing of cats back into a flaming house, often described as apocryphal and unlikely to occur, in fact occurred in Indiana in 1989, when a home for lost cats caught afire and many of its denizens indeed flung themself into the flames.

9   John Anthony West. *The Travelers' Key to Ancient Egypt* (New York: Alfred Knopf, 1985), p.394ff. See also Bleeker, *Hathor and Thoth*, pp.55, 66.

10 Miriam Robbins Dexter, "Proto-Indo-European Sun Maidens and Gods of the Moon," *Mankind Quarterly*.

11 See E. A. Wallis Budge, trans., *The Egyptian Book of the Dead* (facsimile edition, New York: Dover Publications, 1967), pp.230, 242; see also Bleeker, *Hathor and Thoth*, p.30.

Chapter 4

1   Sources of information of Bath include J. H. Croon, "The Cult of Sul-Minerva at Bath," *Antiquity* 27 (1953) p.81; Henry William Freeman, *The Thermal Waters of Bath* (London: Hamilton, Adams and Company, 1888), p.9-15; Miranda Green, *A Corpus of Religious Material from the Civilian Areas of Roman Britain* (London: British Archaeological Reports, 1976), p.26.

2   For information on the Celt's "Cult of Sul-Minerva," background see Croon, p.83; John Arnett MacCulloch,*Celtic Mythology*. in *Myths of All Races* (New York: Cooper Square Publishers, 1964.),p.11; and McCullough, *The Religion of the Ancient Celts* (London: Constable, 1911), pp.41, 68.

3   For Bridget, see Mary Murray Delany, *Of Irish Ways* (New York: Barnes and Noble, 1973), p.149; Henri Hubert, *The Greatness and Decline of the Celts* (London: Keagan Paul, Trench Brubner and Company, 1934), p.189; ed. Witley Stokes, *Three Middle Irish Homilies*, (Calcutta: privately printed, 1877), pp.53-65; Alice Curtayne, *Saint Brigid of Ireland* (London: Browne and Nolan, 1933), p.60; J. A. Knowles, *St. Brigid, Patroness of Ireland* (Dublin: Browne and Nolan, N.D.), p.158-62; Mary Condren, *The Serpent and the Goddess. Women, Religion and Power in Celtic Ireland* (San Francisco: Harper & Row, 1989), p.66; Michael Dames, *Mythic Ireland* (London: Thames and Hudson, 1992), p.68; A. Carmichael, *Carmina Gadelica*. vol.1-5, (Edinburgh: Oliver and Boyd1938-1941), p.310; E. Estyn Evans, *Irish Folk Ways* (New York: Devin-Adair, 1957), p.268.

4   Well lore is from Patrick Logan, *The Holy Wells of Ireland* (Gerrards Cross, England: Colin Smythe, 1980), p.67; Louis Spence, *Minor Traditions of British Mythology* (New York: Benjamin Blom, 1972), p.38; "County Clare Folklore Myths," *Folklore*, vol.24, 1913. (London: Sedgewick, Jackson, Ltd., 1913), p.96; Tom Hannon, personal communication, December, 1985; A. R.Wright, *British Calendar Customs*. vol. I. (Lon-

don: Glaisher, 1936), p.96; Kevin Danaher, *The Year in Ireland*, (Cork: Mercier Press, 1972), p.74; Donald MacKenzie, *Scottish Folklore and Folk Life: Studies in Race, Culture and Tradition* (London: Blackie and Sons, Ltd., 1935), p.279; Maire MacNeill, *The Festival of Lughnasa*. vols. 1 and 2 (Oxford: Oxford University Press, 1985), p.286; Sue Elizabeth Stampe, "Holy Wells of County Sligo." (unpublished masters' thesis, Indiana University, 1966) p.167; James Bonwick, *Irish Druids and Old Irish Religions* (London: Griffith, Farran & Company, 1894), p.241.

5   Miranda Green, *The Sun Gods of Ancient Europe* (Somerset: Hippocrene Books, 1991), p.38.

6   For more on the connection between Bridget and wells, see Logan, *Holy Wells of Ireland*, p.53; MacKenzie, *Scottish Folklore*, p.13; Donal O'Cathasaigh, "The Cult of Brigid: A Study of Pagan-Christian Syncretism in Ireland." in *Mother Worship*, ed. James J. Preston (Chapel Hill: University of North Carolina Press, 1982), p.76.

7   For more information on Aine, Grian, and the Cailleach, see Dames, *Mythical Ireland*, p.64; MacKenzie, *Scottish Folklore*, pp.13, 37, 131-37; T. P. O'Rahilly, *Early Irish History and Mythology* (Dublin: Dublin Institute for Advanced Studies, 1957. p.285; Sean O'hEochaidh. *Fairy Legends of Donegal*, trans. Maire MacNeill (Dublin: Comhairle Bhealoideas Eireann, 1977) pp.37, 315-317; Jean Markale,*Women of the Celts*. trans. Henry Hygind Harich (Rochester, Vt.: Inner Traditions, 1986), p.78; Charles J. Billson, *County Clare Folklore*. vol.I: Leicester, Rutland (London: David Nutt, 1895), p.8; Eleanor Hull, "Legends and Traditions of the Cailleach Bheara." in *Folklore* 39, (1927) pp.22-54; Robert Chambers, *Popular Rhymes of Scotland* (Edinburgh: W. & R. Chambers, N.D.) p.34.

8   Katharine Briggs, *An Encyclopedia of Fairies* (New York: Pantheon Books, 1976), p.24; Robert Graves,*The White Goddess* (New York: Farrar, Strauss, Giroux, 1966), p.221; also Spence, *Minor Traditions of British Mythology*, p.94, MacKenzie, p.177.

9   Cailleach material in this section is from MacKenzie, *Mythic Ireland*, p.138, 142-45, 168, 188; Spence, *Minor Traditions of British Mythology*, p.102; P. Marion McNeill, *The Silver Bough, vol. II: A Calender of Scottish National Festivals, Candlemas to Harvest Home* (Glasgow: William Maclennan, 1959), pp.21, 526; J. G. Campbell, *Popular Tales of the West Highlands*. (Edinburgh: Edmonston and Douglas, 1862), pp.150, 373; John G. MacKay, *More West Highland Tales*. vol.2. (Edinburgh: Oliver and Byrd, 1960), p.379; A. A. MacGregor, *The Peat-Fire*. (Scotland: The Moray Press. p.170); Mrs. M. MacLeod Banks, *British Calender Customs*, vol.II: Scotland (London: William Glaisher, 1939), p.153.

10 Maire MacNeill, *The Festival of Lughnasa*, p.526.

11 Campbell, *Popular Tales*, p.150.

12 Information on Newgrange is garnered from these sources: Tom p.Ray, "Newgrange." *Nature*, January 26, 1989: p.22; George T. Flom, "Sun Symbols of the Tomb-Sculptures at Loughcrew, Ireland," *American Anthropologist*, New Series, April-June, 1924: p.158.

13 Flom, *Sun Symbols*, p.142; Sean O'Riordain and Glyn Daniel, *New Grange and the Bend of the Boyne*, Ancient Peoples and Places Series (London: Thames and Hudson, 1964), p.16; Jon Patrick, "Midwinter Sunrise at Newgrange." *Nature*, 1974: pp.517-19; Miranda Green, 1991, p.27; George Terence Meaden, *The Goddess of the Stones: The Language of the Megaliths* (London: Souvenir Press, 1991), p.120.

14 Brennan, Martin. *The Boyne Valley Vision* (Portlaoise, Ireland: Dolmen Press, 1980), p.39.

Chapter 5

Introductory songs are from Adrian Patterson, trans. *Old Lithuanian Songs* (Lithuania: Pribacis Kaunas, n.d.), p.82; Algiris Landsbergis and Clark Mills,*The Green Linden: Selected Lithuanian Folksongs* (New York: Voyages Press 1964), p.35.

1 Lithuanian folktales in this section are found in Alexksi Rubulis, *Baltic Literature: A Survey of Finnish, Estonian, Latvian and Lithuanian Literatures* (Notre Dame, Indiana: University of Notre Dame Press, 1970); Stevas Zobarskas, *Lithuanian Folk Tales* (Brooklyn, N.Y.: Gerald Rickard, 1958); Theodor Vernalekan, *In the Land of Marvels: Folk-Tales from Austria and Bohemia* (London: Swan Sonnenschein and Company, 1889); Vytautas Beliajus, *Evening Song (Vakarine Daina)* (Los Angeles: privately printed, 1954).

2 The Lithuanian solar legend here related is available in total nowhere in English. It has been reconstructed from dainas published in Michel Jonval, *Les Chansons Mythologiques Lettones.* (Paris: Librarie Picart); Jonas Balys, *Lithuanian Narrative Folksongs.* A Treasury of Lithuanian Folklore IV, n.d.; Uriah Katzenelenbogen, *The Daina: An Anthology of Lithuanian and Latvian Folksongs* (Chicago: Latvian News Publishing Company, 1935); James Hastings, ed., *Encyclopedia of Religion and Ethics* (New York: Charles Scribner's Sons, 1924); Algirdas Landsbergis and Clark Mills, *The Green Oak: Selected Lithuanian Poetry* (New York: Voyages Press, 1964); Jan Machal, *Mythology of All Races*, vol. III: (Celtic, Slavic, Baltic) (New York: Cooper Square Publishers, 1964); Lena Neuland, *Motif-Index of Latvian Folktales and Legends* (Helsinki: Academeia Scientarium Finnica, 1981; Donald Ward, "Solar Mythology and Baltic Folksongs." in *Folklore International,* ed. D. K.Wilgus and Carol Sommer (Hatboro, Penn.: Folklore Associates, 1967; Martin Lings, "Old Lithuanian Songs," in *The Sword of Gnosis* (Baltimore: Penguin Books, 1974).

3 Information on Baltic folkways is from Marija Gimbutas, *The Balts,* Ancient People and Places Series (New York: Frederick A. Praeger, 1966); Janis Andrups and Vitauts Kalve. *Latvian Literature: Essays* (Stockholm: M. Goppers, 1954); Eso Benjamins, *Dearest Goddess* (Virginia: Current Nine Publications, 1985; Elena Bradunas, "If You Kill a Snake, the Sun Will Cry," *Lituanis,* vol.21, 1975); George Williamson, *The Book of Amber* (London: Ernest Benn, 1932), p.31ff.

4 For information on Baltic prehistory and the amber trade, see Patty Rice, *Amber, The Golden Gem of the Ages* (New York: Van Nostrand Reinhold Company, 1974); C. Scott Littleton, *The New Comparative Mythology* (Berkeley: University of California

Press, 1973; Monica Sjoo and Barbara Mor, *Great Cosmic Mother* (San Francisco: Harper and Row, 1984).

5   These comments are based on Gimbuta's earlier work and her specialized studies of the Balts. In recent years Gimbutas has been a strong proponent of the theory that the Indo-Europeans originated in the Kurgan area. She views the sun goddess as a survivor of Old European culture whose image punctures through the dark shroud of Indo-European patriarchy.

6   Information on spinning, and on the goddess as spinner, is from Eric Neumann, trans. Ralph Mannheim, *The Great Mother: An Analysis of the Archetype* (New York: Pantheon Books, 1955); Betty Hochman, The Story of Spinning (privately printed, 1980); W. E. Morton, *An Introduction to the Study of Spinning* (London: Longmans Green and Company, 1957).

Chapter Six

1   Information on mazes and attendent games can be found in Jeff Saward, "Amazing Turf at Saffron Walden," *Essex Countryside*, April, 1982: p.35; Ernst Krause (pseudonym "Carus Sterne"), "The Northern Origin of the Story of Troy," *Open Court*, August, 1918: p.449-ff. and "Labyrinths and the Pitcher of Tragliatella." *Open Court*, August, 1989: p.449.

Eithne Wilkins, *The Rose-Garden Game: A Tradition of Beads and Flowers* (New York: Herder and Herder, 1969), p.102.

2   For Scandinavian mythology of the sun goddess see Hilda Ellis Davidson, *Scandinavian Mythology* (New York: Hamlyn, 1969); Jan Machal, *Mythology of All Races*, vol. II: Celtic and Slavic (New York: Cooper Square Publishers, 1964), p.198; H.E. Davidson, and Pete Geller, *Chariot of the Sun and Other Rites and Symbols of the Northern Bronze Age* (New York: Frederick A. Praeger, 1969) p.38; Maria Leach, ed., *Dictionary of Folklore, Mythology and Legend* (New York: Funk and Wagnalls, 1949) p.1008; Karl Blind, "A Prehistoric Sun Chariot in Denmark," *Westminster Review*, 1903; Yves Bonnefoy, *Mythologies* (Chicago: University of Chicago Press, 1991), p.231; and Miranda Green, *The Sun Gods of Ancient Europe* (Somerset, England: Hippocrene Books, 1991.), p.44.

3   Additional information on sun goddesses and their connections to earlier and later Scandinavian culture can be found in Herbert Kuhn, *The Rock Pictures of Europe* trans. Alan Houghton Brodrick (London: Sedgewick and Jackson, 1956), p.168; Einar Haugen, "The Mythical Structure of the Ancient Scandinavians: Some Thoughts on Reading Dumezil," in *Structuralism: A Reader*, ed. Michael Lane (London: Jonathan Cape, 1970), p.172; Kevin Crossley-Holland, *The Norse Myths* (New York: Pantheon Books, 1980), p.xxxiii.

4   Information on the Eddas and the vision of the sun goddess contained therein can be found in Brian Branson, *Gods of the North* (New York: Thames and Hudson, 1964); William Tyler Olcott, *Myths of the Sun* (New York: Capricorn Books, 1967), (Origi-

nally published as *Sun Lore of All Ages*) (New York: G. P. Putnams, 1914); Patricia Terry, trans., *Poems of the Vikings: The Elder Edda* (Indianapolis and New York: Bobbs-Merrill Company, 1969); Snorri Sturluson, *The Prose Edda*, trans. Arthur Gilchrist Brodeur (New York: American-Scandinavian Foundation, 1929).

5   The primary source for information on German visions of the sun goddess is Jakob Grimm, *Teutonic Mythology*, trans. James Steven Stallybrass (London: George Bell and Sons, 1883). See especially pp.704-50 and 1500-10.

6   Max Mueller, "Solar Myths," *The Nineteenth Century* (London: H. S. King, vol. XVII: December, 1885), pp.900-22, p.916.

7   Alfhild's story is found in Victor Rydberg, *Teutonic Mythology* (New York; Norroema Society, l907), p.167.(

8   For more on dwarfs and the sun, see P. Berg, *Swedish Fairy Tales* New York: Walter Scott Publishing Company, 1907) p.82; Lotte Motz, "Trolls and Aesir," *Indogermanische Forschulgen*, 89 (1984), pp.179-95; Jacqueline Simpson, *Scandinavian Folktales* (New York: Penguin Books, 1988), p.165.

9   Frigg and Freya's mythology is found in M. Oldfield Howey, *The Cat in the Mysteries of Religion and Magic* (New York: Arthur Redmond Company, 1955), pp.58-60; Hilda Roderick Ellis, (Davidson), *The Road to Hel: A Study of the Conception of the Dead in Old Norse Literature* (New York: Greenwood Press, 1968), p.69; H.A. Guerber, *Myths of Northern Lands* (Detroit: Singing Tree Press, 1970, New York: American Book Club., 1895), p.147; Eric Okenstierna, *The Norsemen*, trans. Catherine Hutter (Greenwich, Conn.: New York Graphic Society, 1965), p.206; and Benjamin Thorpe, *North German Traditions* (London: Edward Lenley, 1852) p.32.

10   Folklore on the German sun is found in these sources, in addition to the Grimm Brothers, Thrope and Okenstiema, *Folktales of Germany*, ed. Kurt Ranke, Baumann Lotte, trans. (Chicago: The University of Chicago Press, 1966), p.157; Victorian Joan Moessner, "Gender Conflict in Translation: The Sun and Moon Were Man and Wife" (Paper delivered to the American Association of Teachers of German Annual Conference, Berlin, 1986), p.3; Philip Stephan Barto, *Tannhauser and the Mountain of Venus* (New York: Oxford University Press, 1916), p.37; Walter K. Kelly, *Curiosities of Indo-European Tradition and Folklore* (London: Chapman and Hall, 1863), p.96.

11   Some sources of information on the Lucia variant of the Scandinavian sun goddess, as well as egg rituals, can be located in Shirley Toulson, *The Winter Solstice* (London: Jill Newman and Hobhouse, 1981) p.62; Martha Ross, "Lucia Day," *Pennsylvania Folklife*, Winter 1984-85: p.82; and Janet and Colin Bord, *The Secret Country* (New York: Walker and Company, 1977) p.93.

12   Sources of information on Slavic and Russian goddesses, especially sun goddesses, are very difficult of access; some excellent and available works are Miriam Robbins Dexter, *Whence the Goddesses: A Sourcebook* (New York: Teachers College Press, 1991) p.66; Joanna Hubbs, *Mother Russia: The Feminine Myth in Russian Culture* (Bloomington: Indiana University Press, 1988); Elodie Lawton Mijatowic, *Serbian Folklore* (New York: B. Blon, 1968) p.59; Felix J. Oinas and Stephen Scudakoff, trans., *The*

Study of Russian Folklore (Paris: Mouton, 1975), p.114.

13 For more information on Hungarian goddesses, see Geza Roheim, *Hungarian and Vogul Mythology* (Seattle: University of Washington Press, 1954); Teckla Domitor, *Hungarian Folk Beliefs* (Bloomington: Indiana University Press, 1982); Mary Kelly, *Goddesses and Their Offspring* (New York: Binghamton, 1990).

14 The Saami are discussed in Rafael Karsten, *The Religion of the Sameks* (Leiden: E. J. Brill, 1955); Ornulv Vorren and Ernst Manker, *Lapp Life and Custom*, K. McFarlane, trans. (London: Oxford University Press, 1962), p.96.

15 Elias Lonnrot, *The Old Kalevala and Certain Antecedents*, prose translations with forward and appendices by Francis Peabody Magou, Jr. (Cambridge, Mass.: Harvard University Press, 1969).

Chapter 7

1 Evidences of bias in ethnographic accounts can be expecially found in E.W. Gifford, *Culture Element Distributions XII: Apache-Pueblo* (Berkeley: University of California Press, Anthropological Records. 4:1, 1940) pp.61-65. An in-depth exploration of the reasons for such bias are found in Jordan Paper, "The Post-Contact Origin of an American Indian High God: The Suppression of Feminine Spirituality," *American Indian Quarterly*, Fall 1983: p.3.

2 General information on Native Americans of California can be found in John Terrel Upton, *American Indian Almanac* (New York: World Publishing Company, 1971; A.L. Kroeber, *Religion of the Indians of California*. Berkeley: University of California Press, 1907; Kroeber, A.L.*Handbook of the Indians of California*. Washington, D.C.: Smithsonian Institution, 1925; Cartiere, Richard. "Prehistoric Structure Could be Oldest in North America." *Anchorage Daily News*, April 29, 1986, A7; M.A. Whipple, and R.F. Heizer, *The California Indians: A Sourcebook*. (Berkeley and Los Angeles: University of California Press, 1971) p.18; Stith Thompson, *Tales of the North American Indians* (Bloomington: Indiana University Press, 1966).

3 Spinning and basketry are covered in Kroeber, *Handbook of the Indians of California*, p.263; James Rawls, *Indians of California, the Changing Image* (Norman, Oklahoma: The University of Oklahoma Press, 1984); M.L. Ryder, "The Origin of Spinning," *Antiquity*, 1922: pp.293-94.

4 For information on menstrual rites see Kroeber, *Religion of the Indians of California* 1907, p.324; and Whipple and Heizer, *The California Indians*, pp.44-49.

5 Maidu myths and rituals are from Kroeber, *Religion of the Indians of California*, p.351; Elaine Goodale Eastman, *Indian Legends Retold* (Boston: Little, Brown and Company, 1929) p.31. Richard Simpson, *Ooti, A Maidu Legacy* (Millrae, CA: Celestial Arts); Roland Dixon, *Maidu Texts*, Publications of the American Ethnological Society, Vol. IV. Leyden, Kingdom of the Netherlands: E. J. Brill, 1912. p.175; Edward Gifford, and Gwendolyn Block, *A California Indian Night's Entertainment* (Glendale, CA:

Arthur Clark Co, 1930) p.158; Don. M. Chase, *People of the Valley, The Concow Maidu* (Sebastopol, CA: Privately printed, n.d.).

6   Comparison are to be found in Bosi, *The Lapps* (London: Thames and Hudson, 1960.), p.150; and Mary Haas, *Tunica Texts* (Berkeley: University of California Press, 1950), p.532; Melville Jacobs, *The Content and Style of Oral Literature: Clackimas Chinook Myths and Tales* (Chicago: University of Chicago Press, 1959) p.167; Jaime De Agulo and L. S. Freeman, "Miwok and Pomo Myths," *Journal of American Folklore* 41 (1928) pp.232-90, 323.

7   An excellent description of frogs, from a female point of view, is found in Irene Elia, *The Female Animal* (New York: Henry Holt, 1988), p.83ff.

8   Information on shamanism in northern California is from Kroeber 1907, pp.327-333.

9   The Nisenan are described in Leon L. Loofbourow, *The Creator and The Coyote* (Sebastopol, CA: privately printed, n.d).; A.L. Kroeber, "The Valley Nisenan" in *Publications in American Anthropology and Ethnology* (Los Angeles: University of California, Los Angeles, 1929) vol. 244, p.286; Ralph Beals, "*Ethnology of the Nisenan,*" *University of California Publications in Archeology and Ethnology* 3, no.6: pp.379-80.

10 The myths of the Miwok are contained in Istet Woiche, *An-nik-a-del* (Boston: Stratford Company, 1928); See also Eugene Conrotto, *Miwok Means People* (Fresno: Valley Publications, 1973); Gifford and Block, 154 ff.; C. Hart Merriman, *The Dawn of the World* (Cleveland: Arthur Clarke Company, 1910).

11 The comparative mythological information on spiders is from Marta Weigle, *Spiders and Spinsters* (Albuquerque: University of New Mexico Press, 1985), pp.3-19; A. Metraux, 1946. *Myths of the Toba and Pilaga Indians of the Gran Chaco* (Philadelphia: American Folklife Society, 1946) p.113; Judy Grahn, *The Queen of Wands* (Trumansburg, N.Y.: Crossing Press, 1982), p.109.

12 Information on the natural history of spiders is from John Henry Comstock, *The Spider Book* (New York: Doubleday, Page and Company, 1912), p.214.

Chapter 8

1   Basic information about the Southeastern Complex is from Charles Hudson, *Elements of Southeastern Religion* (Leiden: E. J. Brill, 1984); Jordan Paper, "The Post-Contact Origin of an American Indian High God: The Suppression of Feminine Spirituality." *American Indian Quarterly*, Fall, 1983; William Fenton, "Cherokee and Iroquois Connections Revisited," *Journal of Cherokee Studies* Fall 3, No. 4, 1979: pp.239-49.

2   Information on the Iroquois and other northern relatives of the Cherokee is from Stith Thompson, *Tales of the North American Indians* (Bloomington: Indiana University Press, 1966) p.14ff; Harriet Maxwell Converse, *Myths and Legends of the New York Iroquois* (Port Washington, N.Y.: Ira J. Friedman, 1962), p.34; Claude Levi-Strauss, "The Sex of the Heavenly Bodies," in *Structuralism: A Reader*, Michael Lane, ed. London: Jonathan Cape, 1970; Elizabeth Tooker, "An Ethnology of the Huron Indi-

ans, 1615-1649," (Washington, D.C.: U.S. Government Printing Office, Bureau of American Ethnology, Bull. 190, 1964), p.147; M.W. Stirling "Concepts of the Sun Among American Indians, " Smithsonian Institution, Annual Report (Washington, D.C.: U.S. Government Printing Office: 1946), p.395; Thomas McElwain, "Mythological Tales and the Allegheny Seneca," *ActaUniversitatis Stochholmiensis*, 1978; Paula Gunn Allen, *The Sacred Hoop: Recovering the Feminine in American Indian Traditions* (Boston: Beacon Press, 1986); Anthony Wallace, *The Death and Rebirth of the Seneca* (NY: Vintage Books, 1972); Martha Champion Randle, "Iroquois Women, Then and Now," in *Culture*, (Washington, D.C.: U.S. Government Printing Office, Bureau of American Ethnology, Bull. 149, 1951)

3 Cherokee mythological material is derived from the following sources: Dhyani Ywahho, *Voices of Our Ancestors* (San Francisco: Shambala, 1987), p.1ff; Payne Manuscripts, Ayers Collection, Newberry Library, Chicago. vol.120; Emma and James Kirkpatrick, *Walk in your Soul* (Dallas: Southern Methodist University Press, 1965); Uguwiyuak, *Journey to Sunrise: Myths and Legends of the Cherokee* (Clearmore, OK: Egi Press, 1977); John Davis, "Some Cherokee Stories," *Annals of Archaeology and Anthropology*. vol.3 (1910) pp.26-459; Daniel Buttrick, *Antiquities of the Cherokee Indians* (Unita: Indian Chiefs Publishing, 1884); Alan A MacFarland, *American Indian Legends* (New York: Heritage Press, 1968).

4 Cherokee cultural material is from the following sources: Raymond Fogelson, "The Cherokee Ballgame Cycle: An Ethnographer's View. " *Ethnomusicology* 15 (1971) pp.327-38; D. H. Cochran, "The Sacred Fire of the Cherokees," *Southern Indian Studies* 5 (October, 1953), pp.21-26; D. H. Cochran, "Cherokee Sun and Fire Observances," *Southern Indian Studies* 5 (October, 1953), pp.33-38; Thomas MacDowell Nelson Lewis and Madeline Kneberg, *Tribes that Slumber* (Knoxville: University of Tennessee Press, 1958); Charles Fairbanks and John Goff, "Cherokee and Creek Indians," *Ethnographic Report on Royce Area 79* (New York: Garland Publication, 1947).

5 Information on the Yucchi myths and culture are from F.G. Speck, "Ethnology of the Yucchi Indians"in *Anthropological Publications of the University of Pennsylvania Museum*, vol.1: 1909-11, p.55; Albert Gatschet, "Yucchi Mythic Stories," *American Anthropologist*, vol. VI (July 1893) 280ff; John Swanton, "Myths of the Southeastern Indians," (Washington, D.C.: U.S. Government Printing Office, Bureau of American Ethnology, Bull. 8)

6 The Tunica and other smaller nations' myths are included in John Upton Terrell, *American Indian Almanac* (New York: World Publishing, 1971); Mary Haas, "The Solar Deity of the Tunica," in *Papers of the Michigan Academy of Science, Arts and Letters* (Ann Arbor: 1942) pp.531-35; Faye Touff, and W. Bradley Twitty, *Sacred Chichimacha Indian Beliefs* (Pomono Beach, FL: Twitty and Twitty, 1971); Duane King, and Laura, "The Mythico-religious Origin of the Cherokee,"*Appalachian Journal* 4 (Summer 1975).

7 Snake lore is derived from the following sources: K. P. Aravaanan, *The Serpent Cult* (Madras, India: Ainthinai Pathipagam, 1988); Balaji Mundkur, *The Cult of the Serpent* (Albany: State University of New York, 1983).

8   For background on the Uktena and the Southeastern Death Cult, see Hudson, *Elements of Southeastern Religion*, pp.145-167; Uguwlyuak, *Journey to Sunrise*, pp.6-7; Antonio Waring, *The Waring Papers*, p.64; Cyrus Thomas, *The Problem of the Ohio Mounds* (Washington, D.C.: U.S. Government Printing Office, 1889), p.33.

9   Information on the Natchez is from E. L. Berthoud, *A Sketch of the Natchez Indians* (Golden: 1886); Edna Kenton, ed., *The Jesuit Relations and Allied Documents* (New York: Vanguard Press, 1954).

10 For more on chaos and the Great Serpent Mound, see *Mystic Places* (Alexandria, VA: Time-Life Books, n.d.) p.123; and James Gleick, *Chaos: Making a New Science* (New York: Viking, 1987), p.22.

Chapter 9

1   Versions of the Inuit sun goddess myth are from Yves Bonnefoy, *Mythologies* (Chicago: University of Chicago Press, 1991), p.1149; William Thalbitzer, *Legendes et chantes esquimaux en Groenland* (Paris: Librarie Ernest Leraux, 1929), pp.154-56; Edward Moffat Weyer, *The Eskimos, Their Environment and Folkways* (New Haven: Yale University Press, 1932), p.383; Jean Malhaurie, *The Last Kings of Thule*, trans. Adrienne Foulke (New York: E. P. Dutton, 1976), p.241; Dorothy Jean Ray, *Aleut and Eskimo Masks: Tradition and Innovation in South Alaska* (Seattle: University of Washington Press, 1981), p.22; Knud Rasmussen, *Intellectual Culture of the Hudson Bay Eskimos* (Copenhagen: Gyldendalske Boghandel Nordisk Forlag, 1930), pp.77-81; J. L. Giddings, *Kobuk River People* (Fairbanks: University of Alaska Department of Anthropology and Geography, 1961), pp.65-66; Johannes Rink, *Tales and Traditions of the Eskimo* (London: W. Blackwood and Sons, 1875), pp.236-37; John W. Chapman, *Ten'a Texts and Tales*. vol.6 (Leiden: E. J. Brill, 1914), p.21-22; Stith Thompson, *Tales of the North American Indians* (Bloomington: Indiana University Press, 1966) pp.4-5.

2   See Hole in Jesse Jennings, ed. *Ancient South Americans* (San Francisco: W.H.Freeman and Sons, 1983), p.11.

3   Isma'il Raji and Al Farugi, *Historical Atlas of the Religions of the World* (New York: Macmillan and Company, 1974) p.51.

4   Information on the moon-man and attendent rituals from Giddings, p.I.4; Rasmussen, p.79-123; Weyer, *The Eskimos*,p.382-3; Nelson in William W. Fitzhue and Susan A. Kaplan, *Inua: Spirit World of the Bering Sea Eskimo* (Washington, D.C.: Smithsonian Institution, 1982), p.192.

5   Material on shamanism from Bonnefoy, p.1102; Mircea Eliade, *Shamanism: Archaic Techniques of Ecstasy*, Bollingen Series, vol.76, trans. Willard Trask (New Jersey: Princeton University Press, 1964) p.288-89; Jean Blodgett, *The Coming and Going of the Shaman: Eskimo Shamanism and Art* (Winnipeg: Winnepeg Art Gallery, 1978), p.48-61; Ann Brodzky et. al., *Stones, Bones and Skin: Ritual and Shamanic Art* (Toronto: Society for Art Publications, 1977), p.8; and Marta Weigle, *Spiders and*

Spinsters: Women and Mythology (Albuquerque: University of New Mexico Press, 1982), p.24-25.

6   Material on Sedna and on incest from Rink, *Tales and Traditions*, p.40-41; Wally Herbert, *Eskimos* (New York: Collin Publishing, 1976), p.36; Sally Falk Moore, "Descent and Symbolic Filiation." *American Anthropologist*, vol.66, no.6 (December 1964) pp.1308-20. p.1313; Wendy Doniger O'Flaherty, *Hindu Myths: A Sourcebook Translated from the Sanskrit* (New York: Penguin Books, 1980), p.33.

7   Sources for North and South American variants of the Inuit myth are Jett in Jennings, p.229-45; John Upton Terrell, *American Indian Almanac* (New York: World Publishing 1971), p.133; David Kinsley, *The Goddesses' Mirror.: Visions of the Divine from East and West* (Albany: State University of New York Press, 1989), p.75; John Bierhorst, *The Mythology of South America* (New York: William Morrow and Company, 1988), pp.17-20, 33, 50; Rafael Karsten, *The Toba Indians of the Bolivian Gran Chaco* (Oosterhout, The Netherlands: Anthropological Publications, 1967), Acta Academiae Aboensis, Humaniora IV. p.19; Metraux 19-21; Coriat. *Religion and Medicine.* p.201; eds. David Browman and Ronald Schwarz, *Spirits, Shamans and Stars: Perspectives from South America* (New York: Mouton Publishers, 1979), p.245.

8   Sources for Indian and Sri Lankan relatives of the Inuit story are Rafy, Mrs. *Folk Tales of the Khasis* (London: Macmillan and Company, 1920) p.90; Bachataki, S.N. *Tribal Tales of the Assam Hills* (Assam: Gauhati, 1974) p.149; I. M. Simon, *Khasi and Jaintia Tales and Beliefs* (Delhi: Gauhali University Department of Tribal Cultural and Folklore Research, 1966), p.32-3; *Folktales of Nagaland* (Kohima, N.D.: Naga Institute of Culture, N.D.), p.57; Verrier Elwin, *Folktales of Mahokoshal* (Oxford: Oxford University Press, 1944), p.374; Verrier Elwin, *Tribal Myths of Orissa* (Oxford: Oxford University Press, 1954), p.53; Mira Pakrasi, *Folk-Tales of Assam* (Delhi: Sterling Publishers, Ltd. 1969), p.67-69; David Dean Shulman, *Tamil Temple Myths* (N.J.: Princeton University Press 1980), p.254—259; Gananath Obeyesekere, *The Cult of the Goddess Pattini* (Chicago: University of Chicago Press, 1984), p.18; Verrier Elwin, *Myths of the North East Frontier of India* (Shillong: North East Frontier Agency, 1958), p.3; Michael Dames, *The Silbury Treasure: The Great Goddess Rediscovered* (Glastonbury: Gothic Image Press 1982).

Chapter 10

1   The Djanggawul story is previously published in Ronald Berndt, *Djanggawul: An Aboriginal Religious Cult of North-Eastern Arnhem Land* (London: Routledge and Kegan Paul, 1952); Ronald M. Berndt, and Catherine M. Berndt, *The World of the First Australians* (Chicago: University of Chicago Press, 1969), p.711; Louis A. Allen, *Time Before Morning: Art and Myth of the Australian Aborigines* (New York: Thomas Y. Crowell Company, 1975), p.44ff; Mircea Eliade, *Australian Religions: An Introduction* (Ithaca: Cornell University Press, 1973), p.169.

2   For basics on Australian religion and for the history of Australian/anthropologist rela-
    tions, look to Max Charlesworth et.al. *Religion in Ancient Australia* (Queensland:
    University of Queensland Press, 1984), p.9; C.Berndt in Dahlberg, Frances, ed.
    Woman the Gatherer (New Haven: Yale University Press, 1981), p.153; Patricia Pany-
    ity Waterman, A *Tale-Type Index of Australian Aboriginal Oral Narratives* (Helsinki:
    Academia Scientiarium Fennica, 1987), p.28; Elkin in Kaberry, Phyllis. *Aboriginal
    Woman: Sacred and Profane* (London: George Routledge and Sons, 1939), p.xxix;
    Berndt in Gale, Fay, ed.*Women's Role in Aboriginal Society*. Canberra: AustralianIn-
    stitute of Aboriginal Studies, 1974. p.66; Tiffany, Sharon W. and Kathleen J. Adams.
    The Wild Woman: An Inquiry into the Anthropology of an Idea (Cambridge, UA :
    Schenbman Publishing Co, 1985), p.25.

3   Sources for Australian women's roles and rituals is from Berndt and Berndt, p.159; Eli-
    ade, p.116, 169; Betty Hiatt Meehan, "Woman the Gatherer," in *Women's Role in
    Aboriginal Society*, ed. Fay Gale (Canberra: Australian Institute of Aboriginal Studies,
    1970), p.2-7; Baldwin Spencer and F.J. Gillen, *The Native Tribes of Central Australia*
    (London: Macmillan and Co. 1899), p.134; Diane Bell, "Women's Business is Hard
    Work: Central Australian Aboriginal Women's Love Rituals" in *Signs*, Winter 1981:
    pp.314-37; Ronald Berndt, *Kunapipi* (New York: International Universities Press,
    1951) p.8; Sthrethow, *Aranda Traditions*, p.94.

4   Sources of information on Australian cosmology and solar myths are C. Berndt, p.99;
    Wilber S. Chaseling, *Yulegor: Nomads of Arnhem Land* (London: The Epworth Press,
    1957), pp.132-48; Aldo Massola, *Bunjil's Cave: Myths, Legends and Superstitions of
    the Aborigines of South-East Australia* (1968) p.16; Spencer and Gillem, *The Native
    Tribes of Central Australia*; N. B.,Oosterhout (The Netherland: Anthropological
    Publications, 1969), p.623; Alfred William Howitt, "Legends of the Dieri and Kin-
    dred Tribes of Central Australia," *Journal of the Anthropological Institute of Great
    Britain and Ireland*, 34:100, p.428; Michael Sims, "Tiwi Cosmology." in *Australian
    Aboriginal Concepts*, ed. L. R. Hiatt (Canberra: Australian Institute of Aboriginal
    Studies, New Jersey; Humanities Press, 1978), p.164.

5   Australian women's connections with the land are discussed in Kaberry, *Aboriginal
    Women*, p.192; Diane Bell, *Daughers of the Dreaming* (Melbourne: McPheeGrib-
    ble/George Allen & Unwin, 1983), pp.21-2; Hans Mol, *The Firm and the Formless:
    Identity in Aboriginal Australia* (Waterloo, Ont.: Wilfrid Laurier University Press,
    1982), p.6.

6   The myth of Yhi is from W. Ramsay Smith, *Myths and Legends of the Australian Abo-
    riginals* (Sydney: George G. Harrap & Company New York: Johnson Reprint Service,
    1970) p.23; and A.W. Reed, *Myths and Legends of Australia* (New York: Tapplinger
    Publishing Company, 1973), p.15.

7   Australian solar myths appear in Spencer and Gillem, *The Native Tribes of Central
    Australia*, p.561; Eliade, *Australian Religions*, p.116; Smith, *Myths and Legends*, p.49;
    Massola, *Bunjil's Cave*, p.99.

8   Myths related to incest and the subincised penis are from Herbert Basedow, *The Aus-
    tralian Aborigine* (Adelaide: F. W. Preece and Sons, n.d.), p.265; Waterman, A *Tale-*

Type Index of Australian Aboriginal Oral Narratives, p.34-35; Mol, *The Firm and the Formless*, p.27; Eliade, *Australian Religions*, p.333.

9   Information on Australian shamanism is from Eliade, p.130-36; Howitt,"Legends of the Dieri" p.51; Balaji Mundkur, *The Cult of the Serpent* (Albany: State University of New York Press, 1983), p.58; Chaseling, p.163.

10 Details on connection between women, fire and trees in Australia are from Judith Wright, "Landscape and Dreaming," *Daedalus*, Winter 1985: p.29; E.O. James, *Primitive Belief and Ritual* (London: Methuen and Company, Ltd. 1917), p.181; Peter Lucich, *Children's Songs from the Worora* (Canberra: Australian Aboriginal Studies #18, Australian Institute of Aboriginal Studies, 1969), p.37; Spencer and Gillen 1899, p.181; Spencer and Gillen 1969, p.181; Basedow, p.265.

11 Connections between snake, woman and sun are from Bradzky 93; Lucich, p.37; M. Oldfield Howey, *The Encircled Serpent* (New York: Arthur Richmond Co, 1955.), p.275; Berndt and Berndt, p.213; Berndt 1951, p.22; Chris Knight, "Menstrual Synchrony and the Australian Rainbow Serpent," in *Blood Magic: The Anthropolology of Menstruation*, eds. Thomas Buckley and Alma Gottleib (Berkeley: University of California Press, 1988), p.242; Berndt 1952, p.25; Knight, p.232; Mol, p.62; Emile Durkheim, *The Elementary Forms of Religious Life* (New York: The Free Press, 1915.), p.24; Berndt, *Kunapipi*, pp.17, 51.

12 Subincision and its symbolism is discussed in Geza Roheim, *The Eternal Ones of the Dream* (New York: International University Press, 1969), p.34; Berndt and Berndt, p.213; Ashley Montague, "The Origin of Subincision in Australia," *Oceania* 7 (1937-38), pp.193-207; Rita Gross, "Tribal Religions: Aboriginal Australia," in *Women in World Religions*, ed. Arvind Sharma (Albany: State University of New York Press, 1987), p.49; Knight, p.33, 248; Charles P. Montford and Ainslie Roberts, *The Dreamtime Book* (Englewood Cliffs, N.J.: Prentice-Hall, 1973).

Chapter 11

1   Information on Cybelline rites is gleaned from E.O. James, *The Cult of the Mother Goddess* (New York: Frederick Praeger, 1959), p.191; Grant Showerman, *The Great Mother of the Gods* (Madison: University of Wisconsin, 1901) p.222; Axel W. Persson, *The Religion of Greece in Prehistoric Times* (Berkeley: University of California Press, 1942), p.106; Maarten J. Vermaseren, *Cybele and Attis: The Myth and the Cult* (London: Thames and Hudson, 1977), p.96.

2   Anatolia and ancient Anatolian goddesses are covered in Margarete Bieber, *The Statue of Cybele in the J. Paul Getty Museum* (California: J. Paul Getty Museum 1968); Showerman, *The Great Mother of the Gods*, p.231; Barnett in *The Aegean and the Ancient Near East*, ed. Saul Weinberg (Locust Valley, New York: J.J. Augustin, 1956) p.22; James Macqueen, *The Hittites and Their Contemporaries in Asia Minor* (Boulder, CO: Westview Press, 1975), p.12.

3   For parallelism of penis and breast, see Shirley Ardener, "A Note on Gender Iconog-

raphy: the Vagina." in *The Cultural Construction of Sexuality*, ed. Pat Caplan (New York: Tavistock Publications, 1987), p.135; Eichinger Ferro-Luzzi in Ardener, p.135.

4 The goddess of the Amazons is discussed in Persson, p.90l; James, p.151; Burkert, p.130.; Vermaseren, p.13; Walter Burkert, *Structure and History in Greek Mythology and Ritual* (Berkeley: University of Callifornia Press, 1979), p.130; William Blake Tyrell, *Amazons: A Study in Athenian Mythmaking* (Baltimore: Johns Hopkins Press, 1984), p.86; Florence Bennett, *Religious Cults Associated with Amazons* (New York: AMS Press, 1967), p.36.

5 For details on the continuity of material in Anatolia, see James Mellaart, *The Goddess from Anatolia*, vol.2: Catal Huyuk and Anatolian Kilims (Adenau: Eskenazi, 1989), pp.22-35.

6 Sources for the goddess in Anatolia are: Jan A. Todd, *Catal Huyuk in Persepective* (Menlo Park, CA: Cumming Publishing, 1976); Mellaart 1989, pp.3-24; James Mellaart, *Catal Huyuk: A Neolithic Town in Anatolia* (New York: McGraw Hill, 1967.) p.721; Emily Vermuele, *Greece in the Bronze Age* (Chicago: University of Chicago Press, 1972), p.53; W. I. Thompson, *The Time Falling Bodies Take to Light*, pp.127-138; Hamit Zubeyr Kosay, "Disques Solaires mis au jour aux fouilles D'Alaca-Hoyuk," *Annual of the British School at Athens* 37 (1986-87) pp.160-5.

7 Information on the sun goddess of Arinna and the Hittites who served here is from James Macqueen, "Hattian Mythology and Hittite Monarchy," *Anatolian Studies* 9(1959):pp.118-126, 171-88; Yves Bonnefoy, *Mythologies* (Chicago: University of Chicago Press, 1991), p.216; Theodore Garstang, *Thespis: Ritual, Myth and Drama in the Ancient Near East* (New York: Anchor Books, Doubleday and Company, 1961), pp.112-14; Bennett, p.223; Kurt Bittel, *Hattusha: The Capital of the Hittites* (New York: Oxford University Press, 1970), p.182; Ekrem Akulgal, *The Art of the Hittites* (New York: Harry N. Abrams, Inc, n.d.) p.78; O.R. Gurney, *Some Aspects of Hittite Religion* (Oxford: Oxford University Press, 1977), pp.11-18, 59; Vermuele, p.292; Hans Gustav Guterbock, "Hittite Religion," in *Forgotten Religions*, ed. Vergilius Ferm (New York: The Philosohical Library, 1950), p.90; O. R. Gurney, *The Hittites* (New York: Penguin Books, 1952), pp.66, 152, 479; Lehmann 271; James, p.125; Hans Gustav Guterbock, "Hittite Myth," in *Mythology of the Ancient World*, S.N. Kramer (Chicago: Quadrangle Books, 1961), p.144.

8 The bee-goddess material is from James, p.151, Barnett 218, Bennett, p.37; Mellaart 1989, p.24; Hilda M. Ransome, *The Sacred Bee in Ancient Times and Folklore* (Boston: Houghton Mifflin Company, 1937), pp.107-10; Barnett, "Ancient Oriental Influences on Archaic Greece," in *The Aegean and the Ancient Near East*, ed. Saul Weinberg (Locust Valley, New York: J.J. Augustine, 1956), p.224.

9 The Weather-God, Attis, Tammuz and their relatives is from Bennett, p.221; James, pp.61-129; Persson, p.115; Burkert, p.108; Marendra Nath Bhattacharyya, *The Indian Mother Goddess* (India: Manobar, 1977), p.91; Joseph Campbell, *Oriental Mythology*, p.391; Langdon 62; Burkert, p.101.

10 Information on Amazonian goddesses, especially those of Thrace and Georgia, can be

found in Gananath Obeyesekere, *The Cult of the Goddess Pattini* (Chicago: University of Chicago Press, 1984) p.479; Alexander Fol and Ivan Marazov, *Thrace and the Thracians* (New York: Saint Martin's Press, 1977), pp.21-26; Bennett, p.37; Ransome, p.102; Marianne Nichols, *Man, Myth and Monument* (New York: William Morrow, 1975),p.244; Robert E. Bell, *Women of Classical Mythology: A Biographical Dictionary* (Santa Barbara, Calif.: ABC-Clio, 1991), p.294; Bonnefoy, pp.310-13.

Epilogue

1 Helene Cixous, "The Laugh of the Medusa," trans. Keith Cohen and Paula Cohen.,*Signs* 1 (Summer 1976) pp.875-93.

2 Background on the ancient Medusa is from Thalia Feldman, "Gorgo and the Origins of Fear," *Arion* (Autumn 1965) pp.484-93; Susan R. Bowers, "Medusa and the Female Gaze," *NWSA Journal* 2, no.2 (Spring 1990) p.220; Clark Hopkins, "Assyrian Elements in the Perseus-Gorgon Story," *American Journal of Archeology* 38 (1934), p.345; Edward Phinney, "Perseus's Battle with the Gorgons," *Transactions and Proceedings of the American Philological Association* (1971): p.446.

3 The ancient Greek Medusa is from Hazel Barnes, *The Meddling Gods* (Lincoln: University of Nebraska Press, 1974), pp.3-6; William Blake Tyrell, *Amazons: A Study in Athenian Mythmaking* (Baltimore: The Johns Hopkins Press, 1984), p.106; Feldman, pp.486-87; Homer, *The Iliad*, trans. Richard Lattimore (Chicago: University of Chicago Press, 1951) p.349; Karl Kerenyi, *Athene: Virgin and Mother in Greek Religion*, trans. Murray Stein (Switzerland: Spring Publications, 1978), pp.62-7; Hesiod, *Theogony*, in *Hesiod*, trans. Richard Lattimore (Ann Arbor: University of Michigan Press, 1959), p.139.

4 Information on later portrayals of Medusa information is from Rhys Carpenter, *Folk Tale, Fiction and Saga in the Homeric Epics* (Berkeley: University of California Press, 1946), pp.92-96; Feldman, p.485; Phinney, pp.452-458; Ovid, *The Metamorphosis*, trans. Horace Gregory (New York: New American Library, 1958), pp.134, 460; Apollodorus, *The Library* vol.1, trans. Sir James George Frazer (Cambridge, Mass.: Harvard University Press, 1959), p.161.

5 Post-Hellenic, pre-feminist interpretations of Medusa are from W. R. Halliday, *Indo-European Folk-Tales and Greek Legend* (Cambridge: University Press, 1933), p.22; Silvia Huot, "The Medusa Interpolation in the *Romance of the Rose*: Mythographic Program and Ovidian Intertext," *Speculum* 62 (October 1987): pp. 815-77; John Freccero, "Dante's Medusa: Allegory and Autobiography," in *By Things Seen: Reference and Recognition in Medieval Thought*, ed. David Jeffrey (Ottawa: University of Ottawa Press, 1979), p.39; Bram Dykstra, *Idols of Perversity* (New York: Oxford University Press, 1986), pp.209, 309; Bowers, pp.224-25; Sigmund Freud, "Medusa's Head," vol.5, *Collected Papers*, ed. James Strachey (New York: Basic Books, 1950), pp.105-6; Marija Gimbutas, *The Language of the Goddess* (San Francisco: Harper and Row, 1989), p.237; Sandor Ferenczi, *Further Contributions to the Theory and Technique of Psycho-Analysis* (New York: Boni and Liveright, 1927), p.360.

6   Feminist interpretations of Medusa include those of Annis Pratt, 'Aunt Jennifer's Tigers': "Notes Towards a Preliterary History of Women's Archetypes." *Feminist Studies* 4, February 1978. p.168; Helen Klebesadel, "Medusa Faced," *Woman of Power* 15: p.58; Emily Erwin Culpepper,"Ancient Gorgons." *Woman of Power* 3: p.22; May Sarton, *Selected Poems* (New York: W. W. Norton, 1978), p.160.

7   Solar references in Medusa were noted by A. Frothingham, "Medusa, Apollo and the Great Mother," *American Journal of Archaeology: The Journal of the Archeological Institute of America* (New York: Macmillan Co., 1897), pp.349-77; and E. R. Goodenough, *Jewish Symbols in the Greco-Roman Period* vol.7: *Pagan Symbols in Judaism* (Pantheon Books 1958), p.224.

8   Athena's Cretan connections are documented in Miriam Robbins Dexter, Whence the Goddesses, p.22.

9   Sources on connections between Medusa and snakes, hair, Athena, Crete and Sri Lankan connections are Frothingham, p.270; Pettrazoni in Howe, Thalia Phillies. "The Origin and Function of the Gorgon-Head," *American Journal of Archeology* 58, no.5 (July 1956) pp.209-21; Pausanias. *Description of Greece* (vols. 1-5). trans. W. H. S. Jones (Cambridge, Mass.: Harvard University Press, 1965); Attica xxiv 5-8; Kerenyi, p.17; Tobin Siebers, *The Mirror of Medusa* (Berkeley: University of California Press, 1983) pp.14-16; Marina Warner, *Monuments and Maidens* (London: Weidenfeld and Nicholson, 1985), p.114; Robert E. Bell, *Women of Classical Mythology: A Biographical Dictionary* (Santa Barbara, CA: ABC-CLIO, 1991), p.212; Lucy Goodison, *Women, Death and the Sun: Symbolism of Regeneration in Early Aegean Religion* (London: University of London Institute of Classical Studies, Bulletin Supplement 53; 1989), p.176; Michel Jonval, *Les Chansons Mythologiques Lettones* (Paris: Librarie Picart) p.52; Martin P. Nilsson, *The Mycenaean Origin of Greek Mythology* (Berkeley: University of California Press, 1932), p.41; Gananath Obeyesekere, *Medusa's Hair: An Essay on Personal Symbols and Religious Experience* (Chicago: The University of Chicago Press, 1981), pp.7-33, 35-37, 158; Charles Berg, *The Unconscious Significance of Hair* (London: George Allen & Unwin 1951), p.33; Gimbutas, p.121.

10   Information on Medusa's connections to Kali is from Ajit Mookerjee, *Kali: The Feminine Force* (New York: Destiny Books, 1988), p.61.

11   Sources of information on the eye and mirror in Medusa's legend are Axel Persson, *The Religion of Greece in Prehistoric Times* (Berkeley: The University of California Press, 1942), p.44; Joseph Fontenrose, *Python: A Study of Delphic Myth and its Origins* (Berkeley: University of California Press, 1959), p.285; Siebers, pp.3-12; Barnes, pp.7-13; Lotte Motz, "Trolls and Aesir," *Indogermanische Forschungen* 89 (1984) pp.179-95; Clark Hopkins, "The Sunny Side of the Greek Gorgon," *Berytus Archeological Studies* XIV (1961-62): pp.26-35, 30; Phinney, pp.447-50.

12   Sources on Medusa's horse, and the goddess's connections to Demeter, are Frothingham, p.373; John Boardman, *Archaic Greek Gems: Schools and Artists in the Sixth Century B.C.* (London: Thames and Hudson, 1968), p.27-28; Pausinias, Arcadia xlii, 1-4, xxv 4-8; Walter Burkert, *Structure and History in Greek Mythology and Ritual* (Berkeley: University of California Press, 1979), p.125; John Pollard, *Seers, Shrines*

and Sirens (London: George Allen & Unwin, 1965), p.75; Feldman, p.489.

13 Connections between Medusa and shamanism are derived from Carmen Blacker, *The Catalpa Bow*: p.24; Mircea Eliade, *Shamanism: Archaic Techniques of Ecstacy*, trans. Willard Trask (New Jersey: Princeton University Press. Bollingen Series,vol.76, 1964), pp.68, 150-54; Balaji Mundkur, *The Cult of the Serpent: An Interdisciplinary Survey of its Manifestations and Origins* (Albany: State University of New York Press, 1983), p.77; Bruno Bettelheim, *Symbolic Wounds: Puberty Rites and the Envious Male* (London: Thames and Hudson, 1955), p.154; Michael Czajo, *Gods of Myth and Stone: Phallicism in Japanese Folk Religion* (New York: Weatherhill, 1947), p.187; E. A. S. Butterworth, *The Tree at the Navel of the Earth* (Berlin: Walter De Gruter and Company, 1970), p.10.

THE CROSSING PRESS

publishes a full selection of books
of interest to women.
For a free catalog, please call toll-free,
800-777-1048.